Interwar Itineraries

Interwar Itineraries

Authenticity in Anglophone
and French Travel Writing

EMILY O. WITTMAN

Amherst
College
Press

The complete manuscript of this work was subjected to a partly closed ("single-blind")
review process. For more information, visit https://acpress.amherst.edu/peerreview/.

Published in the United States of America by
Amherst College Press

DOI: http://doi.org/10.3998/mpub.12404656

ISBN 978-1-943208-30-2 (paper)
ISBN 978-1-943208-31-9 (OA)

CONTENTS

ACKNOWLEDGMENTS

Writing this book has been a fantastic journey. I have had the good luck to join forces with so many learned and generous people over the course of writing this book and they have afforded me indispensable feedback and much support: Abraham Smith, Martón Dornbach, Maria DiBattista, Eve O. Wagner, Lisa Sewell, John Harvey, Alexandra Sterlin, Yolanda Manora, David Deutsch, Joe Hornsby, Bill Ulmer, Albert and Ruth Pionke, David Bellos, Suzanne Nash, Jean Jamin, Nico Israel (sine qua non), Lior Levy, Noah Wittman, Ornela Vorpsi, Yann Apperry, George Thompson, Joshua Wittman, Nadeem Haj, Louise Paige, Omnia El Shakry, Heather Cass White, Hank Lazer, Michael Martone, and the late André Green. Special thanks are due to Sweet Dog for his eternal support, enthusiasm for the project, constant peaceful presence, and for his ability to make me laugh in the face of almost every situation. I thank the two brilliant reviewers of this book—it is a better book for their astute commentary and crucial suggestions. I thank my superb and talented editor Hannah Brooks-Motl for deftly guiding this book through many stages and also offering excellent suggestions, incisive feedback, and enthusiasm. It has been a pleasure working with Amherst College Press and I am thrilled to publish inclusively. I dedicate this book to my parents, Sally and Donald Wittman.

Introduction:
The Questers and "*That* Way of Traveling"

> We were all trained in *that* way of travelling. We were all as
> scrupulous about visiting the Barrio Chino in Barcelona,
> the closed quarter in Hamburg, or simply the working-class
> neighborhoods of Trastevere, as the Germans used to be
> twenty years earlier about checking through print collec-
> tions, Baedeker in hand. We too had our Baedekers, but they
> weren't visible And that fag-end of an evening I once spent in
> a Naples brothel where some sailors had taken me—that was
> still grand tourism.[1]
>
> —Jean-Paul Sartre,
> War Diaries: Notebooks from a Phony War, 1939–1940

Stationed in Alsace in 1939 and 1940, during the so-called phony war [*drôle
de guerre*] that preceded Nazi Germany's invasion of France, Sartre contemplates the structure of adventurous and gritty travel, pitting it against
the seemingly mundane practice of tourism, but ultimately locating an in-
delible link between the two. As he describes it, even his attempts to break
through the rigid strictures and plots of tourism by traveling off the beaten
path and transgressing the cultural norms of his era were destined to fail
because the impulse that guided them was already inherent to the practice
of tourism. There is no real difference between tourist and traveler on the
existential level; his transgression was merely convention. Sartre's belated
response to the cliché is already a cliché. Yet, in his careful self-analysis,
he identifies the logic that he is now wise to, the logic that assigns value
to travel abroad when it provides a "true" and "profound" experience of
self, other, and place. As he casts it in the epiphanic passage, his attempts
to find fresh adventures and discover unseen vistas were themselves the

result of a problematic equation between veritableness and genuineness on the one hand, and purity and aesthetic recompense on the other. In the terms of this book, Sartre had been a quester for authenticity.

I argue that, as a quester for authenticity, Sartre can be placed in a group portrait of contemporaries from a number of traditions who go abroad with fundamental questions in mind—both new, era-specific ones and age-old ones—in search of experiences that will function as a key to unlock a seemingly inauthentic present, but are also "harassed [by] questions that must have been known to the caveman," as Emil Cioran put it.[2] Indeed, Sartre's meditations on the "phony war" and his desire for experiences that he imagines as unique, raw, and unadulterated by commercialism, echo the dying cry of a group of traveling writers from a broad array of traditions. In this book, I identify questers for authenticity among interwar-era travel writers and writers of travel fiction from Anglophone and French traditions. I argue that authenticity becomes both a forceful yet problematic desideratum and a regulatory idea for them as they travel and write about travel. Further, I establish that their searches illuminate our present era as well, telling us much about privilege, gender, and race inter alia, as well as the philosophical concept of authenticity and its many valences.

What follows is an analysis of such questers, including, among others, Graham Greene, André Gide, Michel Leiris, Ernest Hemingway, Isak Dinesen, and Beryl Markham. At the same time, I bring in writers who mock the concept of authenticity, including Peter Fleming and the protofascists Louis-Ferdinand Céline and Evelyn Waugh. I include them precisely because they are not indifferent to the notion of authenticity; indeed, these writers, who mock the concept or write against the grain, have much to tell us about the structure and nature of quests for authenticity in travel narratives from this period, both their hazards as well as their elements of good and bad faith. I simultaneously register the similarity of the questers and anti-questers, as well as their instructive fractures and points of departure.

The title of this book refers to what I argue is the guiding logic that threads these diverse works from a wide range of traditions and two languages, the belief that the goal of authenticity can be attained through carefully curated travel abroad, often in non-European or non-North American places. Questers believe that geographical displacement, particularly when accompanied by ordeals and frustrations, can lead to wisdom and unique insight. Inevitably, questers also arrogate to themselves the role of cultural translator. I look at the questers' defining ethos, registering solemn but often subtly ludic approaches to their representations of the challenges of travel. In the chapters that follow, authenticity constitutes the blade of the chef's knife, whereas language is the paring knife with which I slice out crucial microstories and engagements.

Interwar Itineraries began as a comparative study between Hemingway's *Death in the Afternoon* (1932) and *Green Hills of Africa* (1935), Graham Greene's *Journey Without Maps* (1936), and Leiris's *Phantom Africa* (1934), all of them the fruit of very different kinds of travel: the Spanish bullfight and the East African safari for Hemingway, the trek across Liberia for Greene, and, for Leiris, the Mission Dakar-Djibouti, a large-scale French state-sponsored ethnographic group project that lasted eighteen months and whose participants crossed the African continent from West to East. For many years now, a number of scholars of travel literature (see, for example, Kai Mikkonen and Robert Burden) have productively considered both fictional and nonfictional work, a move that illuminates conventions but also crucial dissentions. When we mix genres, just as we mix national-linguistic traditions, we enlarge the conversation, thereby deepening our understanding of each writer's project and commitments. I borrow a warrant from Mikkonen, who makes a forceful argument for cross-genre studies when dealing with literature about travel during the interwar period in particular, arguing that the genres are entwined, describing a confluence of "travel writing, autobiographical narrative and journal keeping, and fiction (in particular the novel)."[3] I engage this warrant throughout the book.

I found provocative thematic and ideological overlap between the works of the post-analysis Englishman, the self-doubting and retiring Frenchman, and the brash and braggadocious American who made spectacles out of the very kind of masculinity the former two lamented. Both *Journey Without Maps* and *Phantom Africa* attend, *sans le savoir*, to the norms of masculinity that Hemingway tests and teases in *Death in the Afternoon*. Each of these books, I argue, reflects a search for very specific kinds of questions about authenticity, and a desire to make exact what can only be inexact, whether a nascent social science, a self-study, or else an exhaustive body of knowledge about the Spanish bullfight.

In 1939, Leiris reviewed the 1938 French translation of *Death in the Afternoon* for the storied French journal *La Nouvelle Revue française*. It appears at first blush curious that such an introverted and fastidious writer would write so fondly about a book that is a decidedly unsubtle and even violent one-man show. But then, just as much as *Death in the Afternoon* is crowded with self-recognition, so is *Phantom Africa*, in which Leiris, presciently, turns the ethnographic lens back on himself.

This filigree of considerations demonstrates that there are productive ways to bring together these four works of the same period, but from very different traditions and languages. Reading broadly in French and Anglophone travel literature and travel fiction from the interwar period, I found more questers. In addition to Greene, a number of English travel writers are questers and anti-questers, including, among others, D. H. Lawrence, Evelyn Waugh (as noted above), and George Orwell. I borrow Helen Carr's term "traveling writers" to refer to these and other writers who are writers foremost and travel writers and travel fiction writers second. The English traveling writers whom I look at are young men in their twenties and thirties, the majority of whom came from privileged backgrounds, and benefitted from elite educations. Their gleefully adventurous tone is worth reflecting upon with Leiris in mind. But, like Leiris, all of them, including the refuseniks, are concerned with the authenticity of indigenous peoples as well as their encounters with them. All of them assert their own cultural authority and permit themselves wide latitude as cultural translators.

At the end of the Mission Dakar-Djibouti, Leiris, in *Phantom Africa*, rewrites the plot of Joseph Conrad's novel *Victory* (1915), setting it in colonial Africa as opposed to the Southeast Asian island where Conrad's protagonist lives in isolation with his daughter. I saw how Leiris's adaptation of *Victory* opens an investigation into the multiple valences and pressures of a normative notion of virility. Aware that André Gide, also a traveling writer, had translated Conrad's *Typhoon* (1918), I turned to Conrad's French reception more widely and located his afterlife in French travel literature of the interwar period. It became immediately clear that, for Conrad's early consecrators and rewriters, Conrad was a powerful source that they could draw on to adjudicate questions about authenticity, travel, and masculinity. As I surveyed relevant reviews, translations, letters, journal entries, and criticism that dealt with his work, the contours of a French Conrad appeared before my eyes like a face developing on a Polaroid. Again and again, Conrad stands as an emblem of authenticity and virility. He is a writer of the prewar world, and a bard of now-obsolete masculine adventures both at sea and on land; he inspires feelings of belatedness among his fellow writers.

Conrad's consecrators and rewriters were particularly invested in the fact that his early writing was travel themed and narrated stories of adventure *abroad*, typically in rarely visited places, often, with the exception of the narrator or protagonist, free of European people, and with relatively few amenities. Translated into French, these were double traveling texts influenced, as Yves Hervouet and Paul Kirschner have argued, by nineteenth-century French literature, before returning to France in translation.[4]

With *Heart of Darkness* so often an intertext, three of the six chapters in this book deal with travel literature about sub-Saharan Africa. By using the designation "sub-Saharan Africa," I am in no way ignoring the specificity of any particular countries or regions, and particular countries and regions will certainly be named and honored, but I refer to this region in a more generalized way to capture and investigate the way in which the writers themselves problematically generalized various regions in sub-Saharan Africa into "Africa," a concept larger than any unique place, the fruit of making totalizing statements about the specific. Greene, for instance, trekked through Liberia but wrote about Africa. Dinesen lived in East Africa and did the same. Leiris, who traveled the most extensively across the African continent, gives perhaps the most weighty nod to this whole tradition by titling his travelogue *Phantom Africa* [*L'Afrique fantôme*].

I maintain that the quest for authenticity in the works of both Beryl Markham and Isak Dinesen involves belief in an ontological state available only to those who live or have lived long periods in sub-Saharan Africa. Even more than Hemingway in Spain, I argue, theirs is the literature of possession and mastery, their books seemingly intended as books of record, and embraced as such by a grateful readership and by a grateful Hollywood, in the case of Markham and, later, Dinesen.

With regard to Graham Greene's *Journey Without Maps*, Hemingway's *Green Hills of Africa*, and Leiris's *Phantom Africa*, among others, I argue that writers problematically turn to sub-Saharan Africa for personal growth as well as an understanding of the people they encounter, moving from the solemn trek to the hunting safari to the self-shadowed ethnographic journey. I analyze the settler colonialism of Markham and Dinesen in part to remind us that we cannot excuse women from the colonial project or locate them outside the frame of antiblackness. Indeed, these three chapters offer a detailed analysis of the representation of sub-Saharan Africans from a number of places, and I alertly sketch the veins of anti-Blackness that run through this literature. This is also highly relevant to our time, as illustrated by the international Black Lives Matter movement, as well as the injustices and inequalities so starkly illustrated by the global Covid-19 pandemic. As Calvin L. Warren resolutely writes, it is "a world of antiblack brutality, a world in which black torture, dismemberment, fatality and fracturing are routinized and ritualized—a *global* sadistic pleasure principle."[5] One of the chief concerns of this book is to think through the twinned interwar-era pleasures of the fetishization of Africa as a backdrop for the discovery and self-fashioning of the Euro-American self, on the one hand, and the realities of Black death and systemic exploitation under colonialism, on the other. Ever-new theories and strategies are needed to combat both subtle and blatant forms of racism and bigotry while understanding their history and etiology. *Interwar Itineraries* joins that struggle.

Mixed in with antiblackness in this literature are other forms of racism, as well as homophobia and, arguably, transphobia (in *Death in the Afternoon*). In order to understand writers' views on authenticity, I often pause at uncomfortable places where derogatory terms are used, and cruel and offensive views articulated. I must warn readers that there are passages that may cause discomfort and other strong emotions. Why turn to such material? I turn to it to argue that racist and homophobic passages alert us to what is problematic about the very notion of authenticity, while also telling us much about racism and homophobia in general. I hope that this book will count, in its way, as a contribution to the dismantling of whiteness and, at many points, hegemonic masculinity. As I argue throughout the monograph, although they have lost their interwar specificity, the terms of these writers' quests are still with us; we still utter their vocabulary and must know more about their complex racism and homophobia; it is both of its time and of the present. In this way we may, as Mary Louise Pratt puts it, "decolonize knowledge, history, and human relations."[6]

Imbricated with this are, of course, questions about the politics of travel and travel writing overall. In their introduction to *The Cambridge History of Travel Writing* (2019), Nandini Das and Tim Youngs suggest that racism and murky ethics have not disappeared from Euro-American travel writing:

> [T]ravel writing, like travel itself, still depends largely upon the distinction between self and other. Often, that distinction continues to be made through the rehashing of crude stereotypes. Texts that empathize with the

other or that experiment with alternative points of view are few and consumed by a minority. We must be wary of assuming that most contemporary travel texts are more enlightened in their outlook [. . .]."[7]

The look at antiblackness and racism in travel writing thus remains extremely relevant. Like authenticity, travel is a problematic activity imbued with structural racism, and we will see that borne out in travel writing. Complicating the concept of authenticity and studying travel in quests of it, I investigate ideological implications, contribution to crimes, colonial or not, and geopolitical consequences.

Travel and subsequent travel literature both then and now, as Das and Youngs argue, is so often a gesture of ownership, of mastery, of biased knowledge. In an era of enforced mobility and transnational migration, travelers such as these benefitted from great privilege. All of the questers were financially solvent, if not wealthy, travelers; they were passport holders, and, gladly or not, benefitted from and participated in colonialism. They were inevitably allied with colonial power, infrastructure, and ideology, even the most anticolonial among them. Due to economic inequalities, they were able to live life in more lavish and advantaged stations while abroad. They traveled with carriers, cooks, servants, and local informants and guides. In what follows, I argue that the quest for authenticity is tied to these privileges and often makes little sense without them.

The larger cultural world at this time is of course important to consider. James Joyce's *Ulysses* and T. S. Eliot's *Waste Land* were published in 1922, a banner year for ambitious and innovative (in content as much as form) modernist literature. Over a decade later, Heidegger drafted his essay "The Origin of the Work of Art," which, among many other tendencies and commitments, valorizes outdoor rural activities, with particular attention to a Van Gogh painting of a pair of worn and dirty, and therefore noble, peasant shoes. Concern with alterity, albeit internal and European, brought the urban professor into an influential one-sided dialogue with men who work with their hands. In the same year, Hemingway published *The Sun Also Rises* (1926), bringing cultural savoir faire together with sexuality in a way that clashed formidably with the New Humanists and their allies, groups of idealist and culturally conservative thinkers whose strong disapprobation was telegraphed to the American public at large. It was during these years that Pablo Picasso, relevantly for our project, took his cue from cultures and eras deemed "primitive," covering his canvasses with visual nods to the single-line painting of earlier millennia. With the First World War in mind, Sigmund Freud widened his case studies to examine the fractures of culture at large in *Civilization and its Discontents* (1930), and the history of a people in *Moses and Monotheism* (1939).

As noted above, and as I will discuss in the conclusion, it was also during this period that Sartre worked out his conception of authenticity, one that he later presented in his mammoth 1943 treatise *Being and Nothingness*. While I do not concentrate at length on the works enumerated above, with the exceptions of *The Sun Also Rises* and Sartre, it is important to understand the context, and I alert readers to any notable overlap of style or content in these and other contemporaneous works. For instance, Graham Greene had just finished Freudian psychoanalysis when he went to Africa, registering his journey as a continuation of that practice, while also using many of its tools and vocabulary.

Few of the writers treated in *Interwar Itineraries* have been traditionally associated—with the exceptions of Robert Bryon (as Paul Fussell argues) and D. H. Lawrence—with the Anglo-American high modernist project. With the exceptions of Leiris, Céline, and Hemingway, most of the travel writing and travel fiction in this book is more experimental in subject matter than in form, even if writers such as Gide are experimental in their fiction. I argue that the questers form another tradition, coterminous in time, but very different in approach; they are oriented, for the most part, toward the past, and nostalgia is their primary mode, just as authenticity is their ultimate goal. Extreme experimentations with form, with a few exceptions, were, during the interwar years, more the domain of modernist writers such as James Joyce, H.D., T. S. Eliot, and Ezra Pound. While there is something to be said about each literary artifact's relation to that school, and others could argue that I might further attend to identifying more modernists among the group of writers I do look at, I prefer to limit that discussion, unless instructive, as it is outside the scope of my book. However, even as they differ in form and content, writers typically bring into their travel writing and travel fiction the elements for which they were praised and noted as authors of fiction and more. Waugh is humorous. Hemingway broods and parries. Even as Gide leaves behind the experimentation that characterizes much of his literary work, he remains cerebral and alert but also oriented towards sensation.

The writers under discussion emphatically insist on their difference from the reader. It is axiomatic that, in any instance, writers will be different in countless and inevitable ways from each reader, but it is the insistence on the fact that is worth noting. Indeed, these writers often stress the uniqueness of their accounts. Another way in which this interest in differentiation is played out is through what I refer to as "anticipatory nostalgia," building on and nuancing work by Ian Baucom and Patricia Rae who, respectively, have written about "proleptic nostalgia" and "proleptic elegy."

The words "proleptic" and "nostalgia" have been joined together in a variety of ways in several fields in the last decades. Ian Baucom's use of the term "proleptic nostalgia" (following John Ruskin), in a 1996 article, denotes a way of looking at ruins that "imagines the residue latent in hegemony" and "does not see the wholeness of the ruin, but a promise of the ruin in the whole."[8] In his 1999 book, *Out of Place: Englishness, Empire, and the Locations of Identity*, he further elaborates his theory of the concept:

> This proleptic nostalgia, in which the traveler anticipates the bitter pleasure of occupying the present only in memory and thus begins the work of forgetting or evacuating the present in order that it might later be remembered or imaginatively reoccupied, finds its most common moments in the practice of tourism [. . .].[9]

While my use of nostalgia is also anticipatory, it is also generative and characterized by plenitude rather than vacuity. Indeed, it does not entail an evacuation of the present, or a fetishistic reterritorialization of it through photographs and souvenirs. It functions instead as a strategy of differentiation when the questers deploy an elegiac mode to describe the present, one that signals, once again, the inaccessibility of the world described to the reader, who will never be anything but belated with respect to the writer.[10]

Anticipatory nostalgia further functions as a strategy of differentiation when these writers, relatedly, put great pressure on the obvious point that things will be different due to the time lapse between composition and publication. The present is in the past; readers are confronted with traveling writers already in mourning. In this, questers for authenticity must be differentiated from Rae's proleptic elegists, who, in 1930s Britain, in anticipation of a seemingly inevitable war, combine a "'looking forward' to sorrows not yet realized with a 'memory' of sorrows already experienced."[11] The questers do write in anticipation of sorrow; however, theirs is not the "consolatory writing" of Rae's proleptic elegiasts, but rather the agonistic writing of questers who create a future past in order to authenticate and intensify the present, distinguishing themselves both from other travelers and future readers.[12]

Germane and useful to my argument is Ali Behdad's use of the word "belated" as I used it above. In *Belated Travelers* (1994), Behdad uses the word as a thick description for a traveler's disappointment in the face of a much-anticipated foreign destination as well as the scholar's own necessary belatedness with respect to the material he navigates. All the while conscious of Behdad's focus on Orientalist nineteenth-century literature, I borrow but nuance the adjective and its usage, as it is a useful descriptor for the imbricated emotional state and response of the traveler of the interwar period as well. At the same time, I argue that it so often results in strategic anticipatory nostalgia that sets up the reader, and not the writer, as belated. I likewise show the writers reproducing, and augmenting, the enabling colonial discourses Behdad identifies in nineteenth-century travel writing.

An account replete with historical detail will follow, but how, at the starting point, and following the cultural indices noted above, to understand the interwar period? What facts about the period can assist this intervention? I have found it most important to think about three things in particular: the legacy of the war, the anxiety about another, and the relative ease and popularity of travel. Ships were powered by steam engines, not sails; cars and airplanes appeared on the scene with luxury ships and express trains. Traveling writers felt deeply ambivalent about these developments and the kind of travel they facilitated. As Orwell wrote in *The Road to Wigan Pier* (1937), such travel functioned as no less than "a kind of temporary death."[13] Historians and literary scholars of the interwar period tell us that it was a period of great anxiety. Vincent Sherry describes its "ready conventions of elegy."[14] The war was, for many of these writers, a kind of test that one had passed, and those who had not passed expressed guilt; a number of them, Greene perhaps most explicitly, also felt that they had missed an opportunity.

As noted above, my search is a bilingual one, and it is my hope that readers who may know one, but not all, of the writers I cover, will stroll across the library floor or scroll online to discover something worthwhile in another region of the world republic of letters. Much of the French work I discuss has been translated. However, I cite previously untranslated writing by, among many others, Gide, Céline, Valery Larbaud, Paul Valéry, and Leiris, all of them part of crucial current scholarly discussions; selections from this untranslated work appear for the first time in my translation. Many of them are noteworthy. For instance, excerpts from Gide's definitive statement on translation from a 1928 letter to André Thèrive, as well as excerpts from Gide's memorial essay on Conrad, what remains to us from the four-volume series that he envisioned but never executed. Also translated for this book are passages from a crucial Leiris paratext: his 1951 preface to *Phantom Africa*, in which he rereads his book from a critical perspective and reflects on the era overall. In addition to this, is a telling passage from a letter he wrote to the Picassos during the Mission Dakar-Djibouti, promising to "play Africa" with their son upon his return. I am excited to offer this material to English-language readers.

This book has benefitted from critical work from a variety of eras that explores the aesthetics, ethos, and politics of travel literature. At its critical inception are Edward Said, who renewed and legitimized the study of travel writing and travel fiction with his monumental *Orientalism* (1978), and Paul Fussell, whose classic *Abroad: British Literary Traveling Between the Wars* (1980) treats a small canon of English traveling writers of the interwar period. This canon comprises many of the writers I look at in the third chapter. *Orientalism* remains a classic and *Abroad* has not lost its appeal, but its approach has been beneficially reworked with the developments of the last three decades in particular, in terms of finding vocabularies with which to discuss race, class, privilege, colonialism, postcolonialism, and the politics of travel. Recent and contemporary studies of travel and travel fiction are oriented, for the most part, around these concerns.

In the last three decades in particular, following Dennis Porter's 1991 charge that "written accounts of foreign places and their peoples" have been too "belletristic" and "merit a more sustained" attention, new studies of travel literature have proliferated and travel literature as a genre has seen a rise in literary status, just as it is examined for its complicity with a variety of ideologies and practices.[15] Influential for this book in this regard is Barbara Korte's wide-ranging study, *English Travel Writing: From Pilgrimages to Postcolonial Exploration* (2000), in which she complicates—albeit with respect to a longer history of travel writing and not merely the interwar period—many of Fussell's theses and brings in postcolonial perspectives. Also, in many ways responding to Fussell, Bernard Schweizer's

Radicals on the Road: The Politics of English Travel Writing in the 1930s (2001) treats many of the same writers as *Abroad*, setting their work within the various cultural discourses and highly divergent political and ideological contexts of the 1930s. These studies have provided me with important angles of approach to questions of colonialism, neocolonialism, intercultural encounters, modernity, autobiography, and more, as have projects by literature scholars who theorize the project of European imperialism and the inequities of global capitalism.

With respect to scholarship on travel literature specific to the era under consideration, I find it helpful to keep an eye on discussions of modernism and travel writing or travel fiction in order to remember the specificity of the era and its shifting cultural, economic, and moral capital. Key for this project, a number of studies of travel writing and modernism were published in the last dozen years, including, among others, David G. Farley's *Modernist Travel Writing: Intellectuals Abroad* (2010), Alexandra Peat's *Travel and Modernist Literature: Sacred and Ethical Journeys* (2011), Stacy Burton's *Travel Narrative and the Ends of Modernity* (2013), Joyce E. Kelley's *Excursions into Modernism: Women Writers, Travel, and the Body* (2015), and Robert Burden's *Travel, Modernism, and Modernity* (2016). They show the way in which a study of travel literature can involve fruitful juxtapositions of erudite writing with popular or scientific writing and, in a number of cases, as I note above, fiction with nonfiction.

Burton devotes a chapter to the topic of authenticity, seeing it as a concern of the twentieth century more broadly. Although I clearly agree that authenticity was a chief concern for traveling writers of the interwar period, I complicate her thesis that modern (here she means Anglophone literature from the twentieth and the twenty-first centuries) travel writing questions "the presumption of narrative authority."[16] Although true for the majority of writers that she treats, I argue that this is not true for most of the particular works I look at in this study. As I have suggested above, rather than dispense with it, the writers seize narrative authority on their quests for authenticity; this is one of their chief characteristics. Indeed, in this book, narrative authority refers to what our writers granted themselves by way of their eagerly demonstrated "mastery" and "insider's view." The questers, by and large, positioned themselves as experts; in this way, questions about narrative authority are routed explicitly through experience, in particular experiences freighted with concerns about authenticity writ large—of self, of other, or of place.

I make use of seminal work in descriptive translation studies (by Susan Bassnett, Lawrence Venuti, and André Lefevere in particular) to further understand the dynamics of the writing addressed in this book. Although questions of translation undergird every chapter, particularly in the first and third chapters, I heed Lefevere's call for us to examine who translates and why and in what way; this call derives from his principle that translations, like other forms of rewriting, "reflect a certain ideology and a poetics and as such manipulate literature to function in a given society in a given way."[17]

Likewise, I am also in dialogue with scholars Michael Cronin (2000), Loredana Polezzi (2001), and Bassnett (2019) foremost among them, who have used tools from translation studies to analyze the practice of cultural translation (and vice versa) as Clifford Geertz and many since have defined it. They demonstrate the similarities between travel writer and translator, and the usefulness of seeing the former through the latter's terms. As Polezzi notes in her study of Italian travel writing translated into English, the question of audience is always at the forefront of literary translation and cultural translation: "Both are influenced [. . .] by the norms and expectations operating in the target culture [. . .], both actually belong, as texts and as processes to that system, and potentially tell us as much about it as about the source culture and 'text.'"[18] For this reason, she suggests, we should turn the lens back on the cultural translator and understand her vantage point as much as her depiction of alien cultures. Bassnett orients the relationship between literary translator and cultural translator around Pratt's concept of the "contact zone," which denotes a place where people "previously separated by geography and history are co-present, [. . .] often in highly asymmetrical relations of domination and subordination."[19] Bassnett likens the "creativity" of literary translators to the way in which the travel writer "negotiates between cultures":

> [B]oth translators and travel writers inhabit a contact zone where cultures converge. Moreover, just as translators exercise a high degree of individual creativity in their rewritings, so the travel writer negotiates between cultures, bringing to a target audience his or her subjective impressions of a journey undertaken. This role is akin to that of the translator, who is, above all, a mediator between cultures, a Janus-faced being who inhabits two different worlds and whose task is to bring those worlds into contact.[20]

Important in both cases, I argue, is the trust that the writer expects from the reader. Relatedly, Bassnett also points out that readers of travel literature, like readers of translations, are concerned with authenticity; none of them want to be fooled or misled. Indeed, there is an implicit pact between travelling writer and reader, the former promising an authentic account and the latter her faith in it.

To the extent that my work explores the representation of speech, it is also in conversation with both established and newer ethnographical work, as well as literary criticism dealing with multilingualism; I am grateful to Juliette Taylor-Batty for the concept of "translational style." My understanding of literary consecration, which I engage in the first chapter, is informed by and in dialogue with Pascale Casanova's study of the topic in *The World Republic of Letters* (English version: 2004). Although I do not concur with Casanova on every judgment and challenge her on many fronts, her work provides a welcome vocabulary for my discussion of Conrad's consecration in France.

Indeed, in the first chapter, "Apprenticeship: French Writers Read Conrad," I sketch, in part, what I think of, arguing for its rich hermeneutic opportunities, as a map of translation. In Part One, "The Traveling Text," I argue that Conrad, and his travel-themed work, functioned as both a model and a locus of anxiety for his early French consecrators, who saw his work as authentic and the last of its kind. This involves examining the way in which Conrad, himself an inheritor of nineteenth-century French fiction, served in his early writing both to hasten and support an emphatic valorization of authenticity among his fellow men of letters [*littérateurs*] across the channel. I maintain that André Gide and Paul Valéry, among other French writers, most of them affiliated with the prestigious literary journal, *La Nouvelle Revue française*, found in Conrad a recipe for traveling and writing about travel. Through the vagaries of translation and consecration, I argue, Conrad became a standard of authenticity to which these established writers, including Valery Larbaud, Pierre Mac Orlan, and Jacques Rivière, pitched their own experience, and in response to which they crafted their own narratives.

Although I avoid her stagist approach, I make use of Casanova's contention that centers of consecration (Paris, in this case) reward, with translations, introductions, and favorable reviews, foreign writing that reflects literary trends prevalent or otherwise privileged in the center. Her work assists me in accounting for Conrad's particular resonance for this community of consecrators, as well as their overwhelming preference for his early travel-themed works that featured masculine homosocial adventures and seafaring.

In the second part of the chapter, "Unknown and Prestigious Shores," I turn to Conradian afterlives in the travel writing of Leiris as well as the French journalist and man of letters Joseph Kessel, both of whom reveal complex discipleships of Conrad when accounting for their own masculine trials and quests for authenticity.

In the second chapter, "Exposing the Secret: Hemingway's Authentic Spain," I argue that the quest for authenticity combines with cultural translation in an emblematic manner in Ernest Hemingway's massive treatise on Spain and the Spanish bullfight, *Death in the Afternoon* (1932), as well as his novel *The Sun Also Rises* (1926), which is set, for the most part, in Spain. This look at Hemingway's opus and novel begins where the first chapter leaves off, as if the young writer had taken the French Conrad and made out of him a recipe for traveling and writing about travel. In addition to joining the elegiac collective nod to the nineteenth century, Hemingway, I argue, reproduces, whether as the "author," or as Jake Barnes, the same anxieties about a changing world, and expresses anticipatory nostalgia, a concept which I nuanced above, and on which I meditate at length in this chapter. In *Death in the Afternoon* in particular, anticipatory nostalgia allows Hemingway to distinguish his writing and, as part of the pattern of narrative choices examined above, put strategic pressure on the once inevitable gap between the time of writing and the time of publication. Indeed, I submit that this inevitable time lag in the publication process is one of the chief motifs in his treatise, one that he pairs with a marked hostility to his anticipated readership, expressed, in part, through his dogged emphasis on exclusive experiences, and his rebarbative narrative tone.

I examine Hemingway's use of Spanish and his depictions of Spanish customs, as well as his depictions of interactions with individual Spaniards. I analyze what happens to cultural translation when he casts hardship as a means to secure authenticity and authority. I draw particular attention to an overlooked account of Hemingway's outsized act of retaliatory violence against a Spaniard.

In the third chapter, "'Speaking Native': The Sound of Authenticity," I attend to English writers of the interwar period who both trumpeted and mocked the notion of authenticity. Examining a selection of sources by Robert Byron, Peter Fleming, Orwell, Lawrence, and Alec and Evelyn Waugh, I argue that much can be learned from an investigation into what is left untranslated, what is perceived as untranslatable, and what is simply made up. I study representations of the speech of indigenous peoples whom the writers encounter, identifying norms and considering ethical and epistemological questions. I argue that these representations, when scrutinized, provide insight into writers' overall literary treatment of indigenous peoples, and the way in which this treatment gets mapped by their quests for authenticity. The questers become translators; they translate language as much as culture, extending the Geertzian metaphor noted above. I analyze the ways in which translation is part of a relationship of domination, while relatedly arguing that the close relationship between translation and colonization is highly apparent in many of these writers' commitments to establishing cultural dominance and expertise and claiming authenticity. I maintain that these writers, like Conrad's French consecrators, and like Hemingway, commit to the notion of authenticity—which they locate, once again, in putatively purer and simpler cultures—even when the notion itself is robustly mocked by writers writing against the grain. I ultimately position this work squarely within both contemporaneous and current debates about the complicated ethics and epistemology of travel.

In the fourth, fifth, and sixth chapters, in the shadow of Conrad, and with the concepts of authenticity, authority, and translation in mind, I turn to writing about travel in many regions in sub-Saharan Africa. In the fourth chapter, "The Romance of Hardship: Questing in Sub-Saharan Africa," I cover a broad cross-section of the English (Evelyn Waugh), Anglophone (Markham, Dinesen), and French traditions (Céline, Gide, Leiris, Albert Londres, Paul Morand). I argue that a romance of hardship characterizes much of American, English, and French interwar-era writing about sub-Saharan Africa, a place of reputed difficulty for travelers and, for reasons that I explore in what follows, fascination during the interwar years. Relatedly, I analyze the ways in which these writers staged aesthetic contemplation and self-dramatization in sub-Saharan Africa during the high colonial period. In this and in the final two chapters, I trace and anatomize the violent fractures of antiblackness in these works.

In the fifth chapter, "Writing and Cultural Translation in Sub-Saharan Africa," while continuing to treat a broad transatlantic cross-section of work, including writers looked at in the fourth chapter, I argue that conventions determined what was included in the writing, resulting in what I argue is their strikingly dynamic yet congruent navigation between the personal and the universal, the anecdotal and the speculative. I maintain that there is an implicit "African plot," suggesting that it both supports and contradicts the apparent spontaneity of the narratives. This chapter thus once again engages debates about the ethics of travel and representation that are relevant for understanding our present. I draw particular attention to racial discourses and identify antiblackness in the way in which sub-Saharan Africans are represented in these interwar-era quests for authenticity.

In the sixth chapter, "The One-Man Show: Greene, Hemingway, Sub-Saharan Africa, and the End of the Interwar Period," I return to Hemingway, this time with his *Green Hills of Africa* (1935), which I compare with Graham Greene's *Journey Without Maps* (1936). Published only a year apart, these two works by writers with markedly different sensibilities—the post-analysis introvert and the testily encyclopedic and pedagogical expulsive—share remarkably foregrounded narrators and parallel versions of quests for authenticity as the Second World War draws unmistakably close. I demonstrate that a robust blend of autobiographical revelations, appropriative rhetoric, and cultural analysis characterizes both African travel narratives. I draw particular attention to each writer's strategies for managing the troubled epistemology of travel, one that leaves both men in positions of considerable power. I explore how Greene and Hemingway overshadow the combustible politics of interwar-era Liberia and East Africa with personal and aesthetic concerns. The mélange of cultural speculation, solemnity, and self-exposure orients both books towards an individual exceptionalism, but also towards a collective past in the face of collective disaster. "The Way to Africa," as Greene titles his first chapter, is, I argue, for both writers, routed through the self as much as the continent; I submit that the blend of solemnity, speculation, bragging, and self-revelation that sets both books apart ultimately unites them.

At this time, the group portrait is finished. *Interwar Itineraries* ends with a terminus: "Inward Travel Narratives of the War Years." In the terminus, I revisit the central claims of the previous five chapters, laying the groundwork for future scholarship with a brief study of the afterlives of the writers' ethos and commitments during the Second World War period. I designate as "inward travel narratives," works by Sartre, Virginia Woolf, and Gertrude Stein that, during an era of enforced nonmobility, turn the quest for authenticity inward, and stake out a path through the hinterlands of the self.

CHAPTER ONE

Apprenticeship: French Writers Read Conrad

> The one statement that can safely be advanced about travel-
> ing at sea is that it is not what it used to be. It is different now
> elementally. It is not so much a matter of changed propelling
> power; it is something more.[1]
>
> —Joseph Conrad, "Ocean Travel"

Part One: The Traveling Text

Each generation, informed by the predilections of its particular Zeitgeist,
selects its own favorites from a writer's body of work. It was the early period of Conrad's work that most attracted the coterie who established his
reception in France, guaranteeing his early, albeit limited, popularity in
that country. It was, in particular, the writers associated with the highly
influential literary journal *La Nouvelle Revue française* (henceforth *NRF*)
who made extraordinary attempts to acquaint Francophone audiences
with Conrad's writing during the interwar period.

Conrad's virile image in France was a group product on the part of
Conrad, his translators, and the writers and critics who introduced him to
the French public. Along with the assistance of several fellow intellectuals
and literary critics, the contributors and the directors of the *NRF* worked
together to shape the period's particular obsession with Conrad. French
writers as diverse in style as André Gide, Joseph Kessel, Pierre Mac Orlan,
and Michel Leiris participated in this process of creating a French Conrad,
one tied up with notions of authenticity. It is not important here to speculate if the English and Americans of the interwar period had a similar
reading of Conrad; what is important is rather to understand the way in
which a writer can be made to stand as an emblem for his literary succes-
sors, in this case, the literary coterie that consecrated Conrad during the

First World War through the middle of the interwar period. Conrad, read by French writers during these periods, was a formidable, intimidating, and inspiring precursor, ushering in ideals for what they cast as authenticity, ideals that are also articulated in many of the first publications to explicitly address the fashioning of masculinity in Conrad's early work.[2]

It is unfortunate that there is less material by French women to consult when turning to the early reception of Conrad. It is certainly to be hoped that anyone who finds such material would share it with scholars more widely. It would be fascinating and instructive to know, for instance, what French women of the interwar period thought of the model of masculinity on display in Conrad's early writing, a model that Conrad's male consecrators were so quick to celebrate. More generally, Conrad offered an unusual literary balm for male writers during this era of relative, albeit precarious, peace. He allowed them, as apparent in early literary responses to his work, to vicariously undertake adventures no longer possible in the postwar world, while, as noted above, also offering them a model of masculinity to engage with. Additionally, they culled a set of ideals from Conrad's writing, which they would, in turn, make use of to paint the present unfavorably and establish a clear sense of disappointing belatedness with respect to the prewar period. Overall, he offered them what might be described as a vocabulary to express, by means of comparisons, the perceived limitations of their own era, one that they deemed inauthentic. In many ways, the role of transportation in setting ideals is paramount; Conrad's French consecrators claimed both implicitly and explicitly that true adventures at sea were undertaken with sails, not powered by steam. After all, anyone who could afford the fare could take an eight-day ship transfer from Europe to the United States (the conceit of numerous contemporaneous Hollywood productions and romance novels). Indeed, the retraction of prolonged periods of travel at sea—periods seen as generative and geared toward both contemplation and action—due to naval innovations, is one of the principal lamentations of both Leiris and Gide.

The following account of Conrad's reception in France asks why his early writing in particular—writing perceived as partially, if not entirely, autobiographical—attracted the coterie associated with the *NRF*, many of whom identified a marked decline in his later work. This selective appreciation of Conrad means that these writers celebrated, almost exclusively, his novellas and novels narrating seafaring, writing that they did not hesitate to tie to his own years at sea, and whose basis in real events they often assumed. Their appreciation is discernable in French translations and critical commentary from 1910 onwards, as well as the commemorative issue of the *NRF* that appeared in December 1924, barely four months after Conrad's death. It is also discernable in interwar-evocations of Conrad found in personal diaries and ethnographic journals (I nod here to the claim, articulated most widely by James Clifford, that all ethnography is, in its essence, at least partially autobiographical).

Conrad's positive reception in France often outshone that of Anglophone writers living as expatriates in France. Niels Buch Leander addresses this in his scholarship:

> Why did the leading French literary review persist in a belated interest in Conrad's early modernism at a time when its editorial board probably should have moved on to the emerging generation of high modernist authors such as Scott Fitzgerald, Ernest Hemingway, Ezra Pound, Wyndham Lewis, and James Joyce, who all even resided in the French capital?[3]

Perhaps a response to Susan Bassnett's earlier call for scholars to study how and why some writing grows as cultural capital across cultural boundaries while other writing does not, Pascale Casanova's *The World Republic of Letters* (English edition: 2004) offers useful conceptual tools to help us understand Conrad's consecration and reception in France during an era of expatriate writers in Paris. Casanova revisits Pierre Bourdieu's concept of consecration to illustrate the ways in which literature is produced, circulated, and evaluated. Particularly germane to a study of Conrad's French reception, she details the way in which metropolitan literary centers controlled the translation and critical evaluation of writing from what she terms the "periphery."[4] In the history Casanova outlines, acceptance by Paris—which she argues is the principle center of consecration from the fifteenth through the first half of the twentieth century—was primarily limited to books that met the aesthetic criteria dominant at the time.[5] In her view, consecrated books have to reflect enough of their diverse origins to make them interesting and even fascinating, but they also, if only in part, must display adherence to current trends at the center.

Casanova does not, however, attend to the role of translation in the circulation of world letters; a robust discussion of translation is notably absent from her account. I thus build on part of her thesis as I undertake a fresh exploration of Conrad's literary appearance in France. Indeed, this chapter takes off from where Casanova left off, in the belief that the role of translation in Conrad's consecration has not been addressed. In this chapter, I demonstrate that we can gain important new perspectives if we do address it, insofar as so many elements, especially a particular modality of authenticity at this time, are tied up in it. Ever a site of contention, a look at translation can reveal much about the ways in which Conrad's work is negotiated by his French consecrators. I combine this with a fresh study of both his contemporaneous critical reception and his literary afterlife in France, overall identifying a crucial construction of masculine heroism, one that, as seen in the forthcoming chapters, haunts later writers.

Casanova lists Conrad as one of many writers from the "periphery" who adopted English to find a wider audience. Casanova, however, over- looks Conrad's claim in his autobiographical *A Personal Record* that he was "adopted by the genius of the language" when he first heard Eng- lish, and would not have written at all if he "had not written in English."[6] Furthermore, Yves Hervouet, while suggesting that Conrad "thought in French" and was influenced by nineteenth-century French literature, also claimed that, by the time Conrad started writing fiction, his Polish had deteriorated to the point that writing in his mother tongue was no longer an option.[7] In addition to that, Conrad once protested to Spiridion Kliszc- zewski that he "would lose [his] public" if he wrote about Poland, let alone in Polish.[8]

What did Conrad's critical reception mean to him and what did it mean for his French consecrators? Conrad had long desired that his writ- ing be translated into French. Until the publication of the English edition of *Chance* in January 1913, Conrad's English book sales had lagged. Dur- ing an unproductive period in his sixties, he turned his sights towards France. He sensed that translation would afford him greater recognition on the continent where he had spent his first twenty years, four of them in the coastal city of Marseilles (1874–78). Indeed, he had been looking for French translators since the beginning of his literary career. In 1894, a year before its publication in English, he unsuccessfully invited Margue- rite Poradowska, his French-speaking cousin by marriage, to undertake a collaborative translation of *Almayer's Folly* (1895).[9] In 1900, Poradowska translated "An Outpost of Progress," but it was never published.[10]

Conrad did indeed offer a welcome challenge to his French counter- parts, who, in their writing, express a complex admiration for his inimi- table life and letters, both models of authenticity. He appeared to anticipate

Jacques Rivière's 1913 call in the *NRF* for an infusion of English adventure novels capable of renewing French literature by example. In his seminal essay, "Le roman d'aventure" ["The Adventure Novel"], Rivière emphatically insists that French literature will profit from the translation of English literature: "It seems to me that the moment has come when French literature, which has already and so often been able to rejuvenate itself through its borrowing, is going to seize upon the foreign novel and melt it into its blood."[11] He hopes that French writers will find a new orientation, one far removed from the static products so often, in his view, characteristic of Symbolism. He submits that French writers' new tendencies should better represent the era's new concerns; whereas, in his view, Symbolist writers privilege the mind, writers should now turn to the wider range of subjects offered by life and action. He argues that the Symbolists deem life a vulgar topic. But contemporary French writers, he maintains, should turn to life for subject matter: "We are people for whom the novelty of living has been reborn."[12] Rivière's account of this rediscovered life is replete with images of youthful adventure. For Rivière, a kind of miraculous rejuvenation awaits French writers, whose subsequent writing will, in his view, restore something that was thought forever lost:

> Once more it is morning. Everything is beginning again; we have been mysteriously reborn; we no longer touch the world through our habits; our hands no longer slide along that smooth, worn surface of things about us without our even noticing them. A sharp, living, lively spirit has begun to burn in the midst of our being once more; in its light we approach objects; our new spirit encounters them, receives them, experiences them.[13]

A new relationship with objects, events, and people is proposed in Rivière's essay; he encourages contemporary writers to forge a new relationship with the world of real things that he argues is abandoned and disdained by Symbolist writers.

Rivière's encomia for this new literature supplements his rejection of what he sees as Symbolism's elitism, the elitism of writers who do not care for common men or popular pursuits: "[T]he slightest adventure seemed a dishonor to them; they thought they had been compromised if they happened to be involved in a street incident."[14] In his view, the novel that corresponds to the new mentality will privilege action over dreams and cerebration; it will include all kinds of materials, enlarging the scope of the genre and freeing it up stylistically. The new manner of novel proposed by Rivière is characterized by diversity and miscellany:

> Its atmosphere is multiplication, exaggeration, excess; it is obsessed by hugeness. Finally, it is a monster; it seems to be covered with excrescences— interminable tales interrupting the main story, confessions, pages from diaries, a statement of principles professed by one of the characters. It forms a kind of natural agglomerate, a mud pie whose elements stick together in some unknown fashion.[15]

Such novels, he maintains, make use of the variety of human experiences and are directed toward the future, not the past. He specifies that the designation "adventure" ["aventure"] refers to both form and content, and indicates that the novels will share an element of unexpectedness with regard to both plot and character. In his depiction of the future novel's heterogeneous style, he also anticipates English travel narratives of the interwar period and their debt to Conrad.

Anticipating Sartre's *What is Literature?* (1948) by over thirty years, Rivière's essay pits the adventure novel against Symbolist poetry more specifically, identifying the latter with stasis and opposing it to the progression that, he argues, will characterize the new adventure novel. The adventure novel, he maintains, is about existence itself; its narrative mode is more oriented toward experience than other kinds of novels:

> The emotion we must ask of the adventure novel is, contrary to that awakened by poetry, the emotion of awaiting something, of not yet knowing everything, of being led as close as possible to the edge of what does not yet exist. [. . .] When we read a novel of adventure, we give ourselves unreservedly to the movement of time and life; we agree to experience, in the very depths of our marrow, this obscure, indefatigable question which moves and torments all living beings."[16]

Rivière anticipates that foreign novels will cause a literary awakening that will, in turn, change French letters, rejuvenating them from without. A foreign writer who could renew the forms and subjects of the French novel, Conrad appears as a solution to what Rivière perceives as its state of crisis. Significantly, Rivière linked his call for a renewal of French literature to the overall project of the *NRF*. Putnam has documented André Gide's overwhelmingly positive response to Rivière's essay, an essay that meshed well with Gide's own robust interest in English literature.[17]

Conrad's early French translators, reviewers, and champions, including writers as diverse as Gide, Henri Ghéon, Jean Schlumberger, Joseph Kessel, Pierre Mac Orlan, Paul Valéry and Valery Larbaud, favor works that they can connect with his first career as a seaman. Their preference for Conrad's early writing, I will demonstrate, in large part, reflects their attraction to seemingly obsolete trials of manhood, particularly those associated with the sea. As seen above, for writers of these eras, Conrad's depictions of dangerous and life-defining experiences provided literary models of honor, masculinity, and authenticity. For many among the coterie, Conrad's first career justified and authenticated his writing. As André Chevrillon, scholar, traveling writer, and *immortel* of the Académie française noted after Conrad's death: "His paintings of the sea are those of an artistic genius but it is the experience of a professional seaman that he interprets."[18] In this view, Conrad's writing would not have been possible without his first vocation.

Conrad was consecrated in France prior to and after the First World War, yet his consecrators celebrated a heroism anchored in the nineteenth century, in merchant ships. Commenting on the phenomenon of literary reception writ large, André Lefevere posits that this kind of selective appreciation is an essential part of literary history, which "often projects the 'fray' of its own times back into the past, enlisting the support of those writers it canonizes for a certain ideology, a certain poetics or both."[19] Through their praise, commentaries, and translations, these French writers of the period encourage a reading of Conrad that conforms to their nostalgia for risky prewar-era adventures. This is nostalgia for something that none of the urban writers had themselves even experienced directly; it is a synthetic yet highly convincing nostalgia.

Relevantly for this project, Georges May has observed that the "most effective way of attracting the French public to a foreign writer has always proven to be the translation of his writing by an established French writer."[20] Conrad's success in France during the interwar period, however narrow its circumference, owes a great deal to the prestige of Gide and the other writers and critics associated with the *NRF*. Thomas Cazentre reports that Gide, after meeting Conrad, articulated a rather quixotic plan to have a literary informant in every country: "To this desire for discovery we can partially attribute the pains Gide took to find in each country a native literary correspondent who could advise and inform him."[21] Conrad's champions at the *NRF* function as what Pascale Casanova terms "foreign exchange brokers," that is, eminent writers and translators whose work involves "exporting from one territory to another texts whose literary value they determine by virtue of this very activity."[22] The French word *passeur*—often used to describe writers and literary critics who introduce and help foreign writers seeking recognition in the *passeur*'s own country—is relevant here, particularly with respect to Gide and Larbaud, and I explore this further in what follows. Casanova also explores other relevant forms of literary consecration, including the introduction of peripheral writers through "the canonizing effect of prefaces and introductions" contributed by writers at the center.[23] She also notes that when a peripheral writer benefits from the attention of "great translators," those translators themselves are often also beneficiaries of this success.[24] Instances of both are analyzed in what follows.

Indeed, this chapter takes it as a given that the tradition of invisibility and neglect for translators in the Anglo-American tradition, so thoroughly explored by Lawrence Venuti, did not hold for French letters. As this analysis of Conrad's reception will show, Casanova's thesis reiterates Lefevere's contention that a foreign writer's success in translation is never exclusively due to the intrinsic value of his writing. Drawing particular attention to the politics of rewriting writ large, he contends that the literary study of a text should include a study of its appearance, reception, and, wherever relevant, its adaptations and translations.[25] Conrad's early recognition in France must be attributed to the translators, reviewers, and scholars who translated, reviewed, and promoted his writing. In what follows, I identify these Conrad champions and demonstrate how they, as a group, fashion a stereotyped Conrad out of his early writing as well as his later works that also featured material that they believed was gathered from his life as a seaman. As I show, this French version of Conrad is, in their terms, authentic. He embodies and narrates the seemingly unrepeatable masculine adventures undertaken during the prewar period and, for this group of readers, he invokes a feeling of belatedness and a related sense of awe.

André Gide played a pioneering role in introducing Conrad to French readers, first by translating *Typhoon* in 1916, and then by overseeing the translation of his complete works for the Gallimard *NRF* publishing house. Conrad and Gide's relationship originated in Gide's visit to Conrad at Capel House in Kent in the company of Larbaud, among others. Their discussions on that occasion marked the beginning of a long personal and professional connection. In Kent, Gide became interested in aiding Conrad in his perennial attempts to have his work appear in French translation. In the years during and following the First World War, Conrad's work was then translated and presented to French readers with the mark of both writers' styles and temperaments.

Gide was not the first Frenchman to express interest in translating Conrad, and the details of his early translation are, for the most part, already known. Prior to Gide's visit, H. D. Davray, an accomplished translator of Kipling, Meredith, and Wells, and a committed advocate of English letters, had already promised Conrad that he would translate several of his novels. Davray, who contributed a *"Lettres anglaises"* column to the literary journal *Mercure de France*, had begun corresponding with Conrad in 1898. In 1902, Davray initially proposed translating two of Conrad's works, *Tales of Unrest* and *Typhoon*, and in 1908, Conrad signed a formal contract with him that would give him permission to translate all of his writing, with the exception of the *"Narcissus,"* which the French poet and translator Robert d'Humières had already begun translating.

Like Gide, Davray was interested in translating and promoting the work of foreign writers in France, and his translations appeared regularly in the *Mercure de France*. But Davray only completed translations of "Karain: A Memory" in 1906 and *The Secret Agent* in 1910 before apparently losing interest in what Conrad describes in a letter to D'Humières as the project of "creating me a readership."[26] D'Humière's heavily bowdlerized translation of the *"Narcissus"* was serialized in the Catholic literary journal *Le correspondant* in 1909 and published as a book by *Mercure de France* in 1910. A botched translation of *Typhoon* by Joseph de Smet appeared in 1911. At the time of Gide's visit, Conrad was tired of disappointments and pyrrhic victories.

Gide initially attempted to help Conrad by pressuring Davray to complete the promised translations. When this approach failed, Gide assumed responsibility for Conrad's translation into English, thereby continuing his role of, as Lefevere has put it more generally, "the twentieth-century translator trying to 'bring the original across' cultures."[27] In 1914, Gide proposed that Conrad break with Davray and offered to oversee both translations of his works and their eventual publication by the Éditions de *la Nouvelle Revue française* (known, since 1961, as Les Éditions Gallimard). Gide had long hoped to enlarge the scope of the *NRF* and its affiliated publications by introducing foreign authors in translation. Conrad would be the first foreign writer to have his collected works translated for the edition, a choice that testifies to Gide's exceptional interest as well as that of his fellow literary influencers. Gide initially hoped to contribute at least two translations of his own every year and was particularly interested in *Heart of Darkness*. However, his initial ambition quickly waned, and he began assembling other translators in 1915. In 1916, he finished his one and only translation of Conrad's work, the early novella *Typhoon*. In part, Gide wanted to lend prestige to the translation enterprise by translating *Typhoon* himself.

Gide charged himself with Conrad's reception in France. Yet the alliance between Gide and Conrad, which lasted until the latter's death in 1924, was often fraught. Gide had aligned himself with an author conversant in French and apprehensive about the foreign reception of his work. But his French consecrators were ready to continue the task of bringing him into French letters. In 1917, Gide writes cheerfully in his journal of "new translators who are offering themselves for Conrad."[28]

Gide had begun English lessons around the time he met Conrad. His journals document how he studied Conrad's novels with his English tutor. As he notes in his journal on November 12, 1912: "This morning at work at six o'clock. Spenser and Skeat, then Conrad. I write to my teacher to resume my lessons."[29] In a 1910 letter to Edmund Gosse, he confesses, with apparently no little chagrin, that his knowledge of the language is poor. Gide's interest in Conrad and the English language, in addition to his trip to England, was part of a broader interest in the English language and in English writers, an interest that, during these years in particular, assumes the nature of a vocation.

It is fruitful to consider why Gide immersed himself in Conrad's writing and intervened so energetically on his behalf. If Gide was learning English at least in part in order to read authors such as Conrad, he was also using Conrad to learn English. Like Rivière, Gide hoped that the lessons offered by the contemporary English adventure novel could revitalize both his writing and French literature in general. Even before his trip to England, Gide hoped to enlarge the scope of the *Nouvelle Revue française* by introducing foreign writers in translation, English ones in particular. Conrad fit neatly into the scheme of Gide's wider interests at the time. In 1911, the same year that he visited Conrad, Gide had begun *The Vatican Cellars*, which he conceived of as an adventure novel along English lines.

We should certainly contemplate the significance of Gide's imperfect command of English when exploring his translation of *Typhoon*, as well as his revisions of translations by other translators. For instance, in his study of Gide's reworking of Isabelle Rivière's translation of *Victory*, J. H. Stape argues that Conrad's style posed particular problems for Gide: "Often highly idiosyncratic and rhetorical, and even at times unidiomatic, it poses formidable difficulties even for the experienced translator, let alone for the neophyte."[30] It is clear from Gide's journal that the work is slow and exhausting; while translating *Typhoon*, he ponders the task: "Translation. However backbreaking it may be, this work amuses me. But how much time it takes! I count, on average, and when all is going well, an hour to half a page (of the Heinemann edition—I am speaking of *Typhoon*). I think the result will be very good; but who will be aware of it?. . .No matter."[31] Is Gide's loose theory of translation the result of his linguistic shortcomings? To what extent does it exacerbate the appropriative elements of his translation? In a 1928 letter to the writer André Thérive about the "thorny question of translation" ["épineuse question des traductions"], he notes that it is "a question upon which I have reflected much and for a long time."[32] Gide argues that translation is but one of many kinds of authorship. In his view, writers should translate works with which they feel a particular kinship, works that share the translating writer's dominant spirit. Relevantly, West has argued that Gide felt a particular affinity with *Typhoon*, one informed by his "desire to escape the anguish and heartbreak caused by the war."[33] Others, however, including Conrad translator and scholar Sylvère Monod, maintain that Gide's translation of *Typhoon* is a loose translation that bears neither thematic nor stylistic resemblance to Gide's own work: "[N]othing resembled less than *Typhoon* the kind of narrative that Gide had written or could even conceive of producing."[34] I fall in the middle, accepting West's assessment of the influence of the war as well as Gide's own explicit claims of affinity, while also agreeing with Monod, and others, that the stylistic gulf between Conrad and Gide appears insurmountable.

In his defense of translation in his letter to Thérive, Gide joins affinity and recognition; for him, the work of translation involves an affinity that is, in this case, the awakening of something already latent in the writer; further, literary influence, in this view, is not the result of utterly new ideas but rather the activation of dormant impulses. Accordingly, in Gide's view, instead of offering a word-for-word translation, a translator should attempt to capture the essence of a book:

I think that it's absurd to cling to the text too tightly; I repeat, it's not only the sense that needs to be rendered. It's crucial to translate phrases not words, to express—without losing anything—thought and emotion, just as if the author, without cost to his writing, had written directly in French, which can only be done by perpetual cheating, by incessant detours and often by straying far from simple literalness.[35]

Ultimately, he maintained, the translator should capture the flow of thought in the original. It is worth considering an example of translational choices that Gide made while translating *Typhoon* into French. Close to the end of the novella, he translates the following passage: "You couldn't tell one man's dollar from another's [. . .]"[36] into "'[p]eu importe que ce soit précisément son dollar à lui ou celui de l'autre; tous les dollars sont pareils."[37] Translated into English, Gide's added words would be, in my translation, "[i]t's not important if it is exactly his dollar or another's; all dollars are alike," additional commentary on dollars that has no basis in the source text.[38]

For Gide, who also translated Goethe, among many other notable writers, translation often served as a substitute for original writing during unproductive periods (here I put to the side the question of translation as, in itself, an original, and accept the traditional sense of "one's own writing"). In his journal, Gide reflects on the task of revising Isabelle Rivière's "médiocre" translation of Conrad's *Victory*, contrasting performing that task with the practice of translating *Typhoon*: [I]n that case, it is my own work, freely chosen, and I shall gladly sign it."[39] He also begrudges Rivière what he sees as her wearisome literal approach to translation, an approach that contrasts ill with his paraphrastic approach. Following an evening spent revising her translation, he complains of her work in his journal noting, in particular, her "childish theories about how *faithful* a translation must be."[40] For him, Rivière's theories led to a translational approach that engendered a product that was: "studded with errors, awkward expressions, cacophonies, ugly passages."[41] He laments the arduous process of revision which "ages me a fortnight."[42]

Although Gide admired both *Victory* and *Typhoon*, they were not among his favorite works by Conrad. He preferred *Heart of Darkness*, *Lord Jim*, and "Youth," all of which he had considered translating. However, following the publication of his translation of *Typhoon*, he parceled them off to other translators, ultimately participating in none of the translations that he had envisioned. Translating *Typhoon* was a difficult task for Gide with his limited English. With a deeper understanding of the difficulty involved in translating Conrad, Gide gave *Heart of Darkness* to fellow *NRF* translator Andre Ruyters. Gide's first experience translating Conrad was his last; his translation of *Typhoon* was his only contribution to the collection.

Ruyters gently criticized the version of *Typhoon* that appeared in the *Revue de Paris* in March 1918. Gide graciously accepted Ruyters's criticism, and reworked the novella for its volume publication, ultimately dedicating the translation to Ruyters himself. No doubt his decision to stop translating after this was at least partly motivated by a much harsher critique of his translation by René Rapin, a young Conrad scholar. Rapin studied the definitive edition of Gide's translation that appeared in 1923, making an exhaustive study of its errors and perceived infidelities, before doing his own translation. Conrad, however, approved of Gide's translation, which he felt remained true to the original, despite Gide's numerous mistakes.

As I have demonstrated, Gide took translation very seriously; he hoped to elevate its status, in Putnam's words, "to the rank of a noble art."[43] However, his preference for a paraphrastic approach over a literal or "word-for-word" approach led to conflicts with translators, as Putnam has also reported: "It was precisely this question of literal translation that pitted Gide against other translators of Conrad, Isabelle Rivière and André Ruyters in particular."[44] Again, Gide's criteria for translation were highly subjective, as he submits that the translator could meet them by satisfying the "sensibility" ["sensibilité"] of both writer and translator.[45]

Accepting Lefevere's argument that translation is one among many forms of rewriting, Gide's view of translation is both true and false; Gide is right to argue that the work is his own, but he avoids a larger question when he casts his ownership primarily in terms of aesthetic affinity. As Venuti has repeatedly demonstrated, translation targets the translator's mother language and culture, resulting in a translated traveling text inscribed with "domestic intelligibilities and interests."[46] Although Conrad offered a breath of fresh and doubly foreign literary air perfectly suited to renewing French literature, the theories that guided his translation by Gide and by others were appropriative and "densely motivated," to the extent that they allowed translators to claim partial authorship through claims of identification.[47]

Lefevere demonstrates the extent to which the ideological concerns of patrons and publishers influence the character of translations as well as the presentation of a translated writer.[48] Gide, as a translator, clearly occupied a high position within many notable literary institutions. Nevertheless, Gide's position in the world republic of letters, and his adoption of Conrad's cause, did not sustain Conrad's declaration in a 1916 letter to Gide that his "friendship" ["amitié"] was "[q]uite the greatest treasure I have won at the point of my pen."[49] Conrad's unmitigated gratitude did not outlive the following three years, due, principally, to the question of female translators. Gide initially gave *Victory* and *Typhoon* to women, the former to Isabelle Rivière, the latter to Marie-Thérèse Müller. Frederick R. Karl gives a detailed account of the "trying period of the translation of *Victory*."[50] In a 1924 letter to Gide, who had just assigned the translation of Conrad's "Youth" to Marthe Duproix, fellow Conrad translator G. Jean-Aubry writes that any woman, "whoever she is, is incapable, by nature, of understanding Conrad [. . .] Conrad is a fundamentally male author: when a woman translates him, she emasculates him."[51] In the same letter, Jean-Aubry maintains that this was Conrad's view as well: "Moreover, this was Conrad's feeling as well."[52] Jean-Aubry reproduces Conrad's own anxiety about masculinity; he does not want to lose in translation the very qualities he admired when reading him.

This concern about emasculating Conrad had its origins in a significant 1919 dispute between Gide and Conrad, the latter enraged by the former's choice of a woman translator for the novel *The Arrow of Gold*. With the *NRF* translation well underway, Conrad sent Gide a copy of *The Arrow of Gold* shortly upon its publication, suggesting that Jean-Aubry, his friend and future biographer, translate it.[53] Gide, however, had already given the task of translating the novel to Madeleine Octavie Maus. In a now lost letter, Conrad insists again that Gide take his novel away from Maus, arguing that the essential "virility" ["virilité"] of his writing could not be sacrificed without damaging the whole:

> If my writings have a pronounced character, it is their virility—of spirit, inclination, style. No one has denied me that. And you throw me to the women! In your letter, you say yourself that in the final reckoning, a translation is an interpretation. Very well, I want to be interpreted by masculine intelligences. It's perfectly natural.[54]

Conrad cleverly makes use of Gide's own philosophy of translation in his letter. Despite his declaration in a 1911 letter that "[w]omen as far as I have been able to judge have a grasp of and are interested in all the facts of life," Conrad here suggests that women are incapable of correctly interpreting and therefore translating *The Arrow of Gold*.[55]

Conrad's assertive response surprisingly anticipates contemporary theories of translation, most notably those of Venuti, who casts it as an interpretive act. However, if appropriation and disfigurement are inevitable in a translation, the choice of a translator is not. As seen above, Conrad's preference for a male translator appears to him "perfectly natural" ["tout naturel"], and he perceives Gide's decision as a personal betrayal. Conrad's letter invokes an implied code of masculine conduct, and ends with a plea for Gide to respond to his request with a yes or no—"as is proper between men."[56]

Conrad's incensed letter to Gide dates from November 1919. One month earlier he wrote another letter to Jean-Aubry, explaining the disagreement from his perspective: "I have just now had a letter from Gide in which he says that a woman has just got hold of *The Arrow* for translation. I am going to protest with all my might. He throws me as bait to a gaggle of women who have made a fuss (he says it himself). All this annoys me."[57] Jean-Aubry supported Conrad in the dispute; perhaps Gide's response to Conrad's letters—"Are you really so certain that a masculine translation would necessarily be superior to a female one?"—was interpreted by either Conrad or his preferred translator as a slight.[58] Surprisingly, earlier women translators performed their task without attendant commotion. For example, an earlier letter to Gide suggests that Conrad was satisfied with Gabrielle d'Harcourt's 1919 translation of his novella *The End of the Tether* (1902). Conrad also expressed admiration for Geneviève Seligman-Lui's 1919 translation of *Almayer's Folly*. But these specific instances of harmony run counter to the bumpy nature of Conrad's wartime and interwar-era translation into French, as overseen by Gide. Part of this logic, negotiated early in Conrad and Gide's relationship, characterized the relationship between Conrad, the writer, and Gide, the translator and overseer of other translations. Conrad's writings could not, in his own view, be detached from Conrad himself; fidelity to his work required fidelity to Conrad the man. Gide knew that Conrad was an unusual case in that he was alive, at least semi-fluent in French, and particularly concerned with the cali-

ber and fate of translations of his work, reviews of which he could read in
the French press. In like fashion, Gide's early intervention into Conrad's
French reception was merely the first step in what would result in a complex negotiation between Conrad and his patrons and translators as he
entered into French letters as both writer and embodiment of an ethos.

Jean-Aubry's translation of *The Arrow of Gold* was published in 1928,
four years after Conrad's death, by which time Jean-Aubry had long before
taken Gide's place as overseer of the Conrad translation project. It is unclear whether Gide's conflict with Conrad might have influenced his decision to hand over supervision of the entire Conrad project to Jean-Aubry in
1920. After their disagreement, Gide limited his own participation in the
NRF Conrad edition to reviewing translation manuscripts. The project was
successful nonetheless. Under the combined direction of Gide and Jean-
Aubry, the *NRF* published twenty-two translations of Conrad's works between 1919 and 1946, approximately half of them translated by Jean-Aubry.

Conrad knew the difficulties his work posed for translators and was
often generous with his support. He approved of several translations that
differed significantly from the original, including Gide's translation of *Typhoon*, and, not surprisingly, given the drama over *The Arrow of Gold*,
all of Jean-Aubry's translations. Gide's 1916 translation won Conrad's approval, although it included numerous vocabulary errors and inaccura-
cies. As Conrad wrote to his literary agent, J. B. Pinker, upon first reading
it, Gide's errors seemed inevitable and, therefore, acceptable:

> It's wonderfully done, in parts. In others utterly wrong. And the worst is
> that with all my knowledge of the two languages I can't do much either
> in the way of suggestion. I was not fully aware how thoroughly *English*
> the Typhoon is. I am immensely proud of this, of course. There are pas-
> sages that simply cannot be rendered into French—they depend so much
> for their meaning upon the very genius of the language in which they are
> written. Don't think I am getting a "swelled head." It's a fact.[59]

Here and elsewhere, Conrad insists that his writing works exclusively in
English; in a letter from 1916, he counsels Gide to translate his idiomatic
style "faithfully by seeking the equivalent idioms."[60] Describing himself as
"an English writer who lends himself so little to translation," he encourages translators to match him in spirit—as with the idioms—if not in exact
sense.[61] The latitude Conrad conferred Gide in his translation of *Typhoon*

underscores his preference for paraphrastic translation over literal translation. *Typhoon* was the first publication of the *NRF* Conrad edition and, true to the formula May outlined above, Gide's name gave Conrad's writing a boost in literary circles as well as with the general public. In his meditation on translation, *Sous l'invocation de Saint Jérôme* (1946) [*An Homage to Jerome: Patron Saint of Translators*], Larbaud remarks the value of translations by writers "highly placed in the judgment of literary people."[62] *Typhoon* indelibly connected Gide with Conrad and contributed to both writers' prestige in France.

Conrad was in dialogue with and befriended many of his translators, critics, and biographers, such as Richard Curle, Larbaud, Paul Valéry, Hugh Walpole, and, as seen above, Jean-Aubry. In addition to correcting translations, he sought to rectify misconceptions about himself. In particular, he wanted to see details about his seafaring past relegated to his biography rather than the stuff of literary criticism; he made this clear to Gide numerous times. A telling moment is when the latter commented favorably on an engraving of the sea at Conrad's home: "Don't bother yourself with that, he said, while leading me into the salon [. . .] Let's talk about literature."[63] This interest in Conrad's life was prevalent in England as well. He wrote as much to his friend, biographer, and critic Richard Curle on July 14, 1923, one year before his death:

> I was in hopes that on a general survey it could also be made an opportunity for me to get freed from that infernal tale of ships, and that obsession of my sea life which has about as much bearing on my literary existence, on my quality as a writer, as the enumeration of drawing-rooms which Thackeray frequented could have had on his gift as a great novelist. [64]

Conrad chides Curle in response to an article he had written earlier that year for the *Times Literary Supplement*. Curle's article emphasizes the role in Conrad's writing of his years at sea. Conrad did not want critics to understand his vision and style as the direct outcome of the seafaring life of his early adulthood. He was particularly concerned with his posthumous reputation; he wanted to be cast as a literary man of opinions, rather than as a writer who had sailed on ships. In this sense, the group-created French Conrad was at odds with the intentions and desires of the writer himself.

Conrad's initial limited appeal, in England as well as France, enhanced his allure for his more elite contemporaries. Curle, like many of Conrad's avid readers, saw Conrad's limited popularity as a mark of distinction. He appears to articulate a more general sentiment when he opines that this limited popularity is linked to recognition of his genius among the happy few. In his 1914 study of Conrad, he writes: "I do not mean, of course, that he will ever be popular. His work is not cast in that mold. But I mean that he will be genuinely revered."[65] Curle did not foresee widespread interest in Conrad. The same is true in France, where Conrad appeared during and between the wars as a writer's writer.

Conrad reluctantly but cannily published his only explicitly autobiographical work, *A Personal Record*, in 1912. By his own account, he published the book version of a serialized set of reminiscences—originally published in Ford Madox Ford's *English Review* between 1908 and 1909—in order to indulge his English readers and sell more books, as he wrote to Thomas Fisher Unwin a year before its publication: "I know that there are people who'll want to read it. My public. I also think that if published at a proper time as, for instance, in the months following the issue of a novel of mine it may secure a larger sale."[66] Earlier in that same letter, however, he also made it clear that—although he would revisit his seafaring years—his book would be "the work of an author, who, whatever his exact merit, has his place in English literature."[67] Conrad did not hesitate to make use of his renowned past, particularly in his self-professed capacity as a natural writer born into literature after eighteen years at sea. However, he always suggested that this past was of secondary or even tertiary interest.

Although he had always been an avid reader, of nineteenth-century French literature in particular, Conrad resisted the notion of influence. He also claimed that he had a near total lack of ambition during the two decades he spent at sea. Early in *A Personal Record* (1912), he describes a whimsical relationship with the written word:

> And I too had a pen rolling about somewhere—the seldom-used, the reluctantly-taken-up pen of a sailor ashore, the pen rugged with the dried ink of abandoned attempts, of answers delayed longer than decency permitted, of letters begun with infinite reluctance and put off suddenly till next day—till next week as likely as not![68]

This presentation of self is quite at odds with the extensive correspondence that survives Conrad's years at sea. It is echoed by those of his admirers who seek to emphasize his distance from other writers by noting that his powerful vocation resulted from a maritime past and what they saw as a related—and self-professed, as I argued above—lack of literary ambition.

In the half dozen years during which Gide worked on *Les Faux-Monnayeurs* [*The Counterfeiters*], his only lengthy novel, he oversaw the translation and publication of four Conrad works: *Under Western Eyes* (1920), *Victory* (1923), *Lord Jim* (1924), and *Heart of Darkness* (1924). *Heart of Darkness* was serialized in the *NRF*, starting with the commemorative edition in 1924 and continuing through 1925. Following Conrad's death and the publication of *The Counterfeiters* in 1925, Gide made an extended journey to French Equatorial Africa. This trip resulted in two published journals: *Travels in the Congo* (1927) and *Back from Chad* (1928). He dedicated these journals to the memory of Conrad, who had been in Africa in 1890, approximately thirty-five years before. Gide appeared to be on the trail of Conrad as he searched for the extreme experiences that might authenticate the account of his travels. *Travels in the Congo* and *Back from Chad* mark Gide's transition from novelist to engaged activist and fellow traveler. Indeed, Gide was instrumental in raising a debate about the egregious abuses of the concessionary companies; excerpts from his *Travels in the Congo* were read aloud at a session of the Chambres Députés on November 23, 1927, creating considerable controversy and marking a break between the aging writer's fiction writing and his activism. Gide cites *Heart of Darkness* numerous times in his journal, making use of Conrad's novella to lend historical context to his observations and reporting. For instance, he has recourse to *Heart of Darkness* when speculating on the very real problems of navigating Congo by boat: "[A]nd as for the boats themselves, since the Congo becomes navigable again only at a great distance from its mouth, it is necessary—it was long necessary at least (see *Heart of Darkness*)—to transport through the jungle, on human backs, the heavy dismantled parts of any boat whatever."[69] However much Conrad became a source of information to Gide during his activist years, Gide also still held Conrad in high literary esteem, and, while in Africa, champions him with much approbation, reflecting on *Typhoon*, the novella he had translated:

Conrad has been blamed in *Typhoon* for having shirked the climax of the storm. He seems to me, on the contrary, to have done admirably in cutting short his story just on the threshold of the horrible and in giving the reader's imagination full play, after having led him to a degree of dreadfulness that seemed unsurpassable.[70]

Despite this generous reflection, Gide's late-life writing about Conrad nevertheless mixes reservation with admiration. Reading *Under Western Eyes*, he notes his ambivalence: "One does not know which deserves more admiration: the amazing subject, the fitting together, the boldness of so difficult an undertaking, the patience in the development of the story, the reader would like to say to the author. And now let us rest a little bit."[71] Gide envisioned, but never began, a four-part study of Conrad that would no doubt have helped elucidate the influence that the latter had on his own work, as well as his diminishing appreciation of Conrad's postwar-era writing.[72] His journals indicate that he read this later work in a desultory fashion, often years after it was initially published. He openly preferred the earlier works which recounted the moral dilemmas and challenges experienced by young men at sea, particularly *Lord Jim*, which he mentions at length twice in his journal. He was particularly interested in Jim's struggle to regain honor after his, widely perceived as, cowardly jump from the *Patna* and her imperiled passengers. In February of 1930, he compares *Lord Jim* favorably with *Under Western Eyes*, noting that the notion of redemption after disgrace is at the core of both books:

> Much interested by the relationship I discover between *Under Western Eyes* and *Lord Jim*. (I regret not having spoken of this with Conrad.) That *irresponsible act* of the hero, to redeem which his whole life is subsequently engaged. For the thing that leads to the heaviest responsibility is just the *irresponsibilities* in a life. How can one efface that act? There is no more pathetic subject for a novel, nor one that has been more stifled in our literature by belief in Boileau's rule: that the hero must remain, from one end to the other of a drama or a novel, 'such as he was first seen to be.'[73]

By August 2nd of 1930, Gide had reflected further on this issue and came to the conclusion that such irresponsible acts were not necessarily redeemable:

> Noteworthy that the fatal *irresponsible* acts of Conrad's heroes (I am thinking particularly of *Lord Jim* and of *Under Western Eyes*) are involuntary and immediately stand seriously in the way of the one who commits them. A whole lifetime, afterward, is not enough to give them the lie and to efface their mark.[74]

For Gide, however, this does not take away from the books' value. Nor did it take away from the principal characters' heroism. Indeed, it was precisely this lasting mark of shame that permitted heroism by making it truly human. If Conrad's early writings were indeed works of apprenticeship, for Gide this was an existential apprenticeship. More was at stake in Gide's view than the mastery of a craft; for him, the significance of Conrad's early work was crystallized in his characters' search for a life code that would ease the confrontation between youthful aspiration and the challenges of adulthood.

Gide was critical of *Falk* (1903), *The Secret Agent* (1907), and *The Rescue* (1920). Gide read *The Secret Agent* before his trip to Africa in 1926 but was not able to finish it: "[U]nable to finish *The Secret Agent*."[75] He was disparaging of *Romance* (1903), *Nostromo* (1904), and *Chance* (1913), all three of which he read before the Second World War.[76] Although he read the more realistic novels that were anchored more explicitly into socio-historical contexts, he continued to favor the works about seafaring that transformed human adventures into existential quests.[77] Through the penumbra of a language that he never fully mastered, Gide found what he saw as formidable but inconsistent writing.

In some respects, Conrad exhausted the aging Gide; the accounts of various forms of extreme experience that Gide admired in Conrad's early work came to overwhelm him in his later years. Yet, as I will explore at length in the fourth and fifth chapters, Conrad's imprint is highly visible in both *Travels in the Congo* and *Back from Chad*, and not merely insofar as Gide sees his work as providing some kind of historical record. And, despite his later reservations, Gide succeeded in introducing Conrad to French readers by associating their names together. He was a central factor in determining how Conrad was read and received in France. His interventions into Conrad's translation into French and his open preference for his early work colored Conrad's reputation in France. His preferences are echoed in other writers' assessments of Conrad during the interwar period.

Overall, I argue that French writers of the interwar period situate Conrad between nineteenth-century aspirations and twentieth-century paradoxes. Although a unique and fresh writer, Conrad was also a writer of disjunction, of spoiled dreams, and seemingly noble but outmoded aspirations. They saw him as an authentic writer, his authenticity gained by the life he lived before he began writing. The majority of these writers discovered Conrad during or after the First World War, but his writing was rooted in the illusions and aspirations of the prewar period. Would it be possible to emulate Conrad in life or in letters? This is a question that Conrad's French readers confronted at that time, tainting, I argue, their reading with anxiety.

Coupled with anxiety about belatedness, French writers of the interwar period often also expressed a complimentary awareness of what they saw as Conrad's limitations as a writer, particularly with respect to the novels that did not deal with young men and the sea. Admiration and disillusion were, as I demonstrated with Gide, important elements of interwar-era French writers' encounter with Conrad's work; their writing mixes disenchantment and awe in a manner both unusual and provocative. As I will argue when turning to the *NRF* commemorative edition, critical responses to Conrad quite often mix praise with muted criticism and characterize his writing as endowed with a kind of flawed perfection. Such mixed praise is first articulated by Valery Larbaud and Pierre Mac Orlan, as I demonstrate in what follows. Both French writers identify flaws while also suggesting that such flaws, minor for the most part, contribute to Conrad's sublimity by providing a humble background for his talents. Flaws and failures serve the function of fashioning Conrad into a writer who will be appreciated by a select interpretive circle. Casanova distinguishes between literary centers, Paris, in this case, and literary peripheries. But the case of Conrad clearly demonstrates that there were equally important hierarchies and power struggles at work within the center itself. Several of Conrad's French admirers and translators make the case for Conrad as a writer's writer; the gains for general French readers are rarely mentioned. One could of course argue that such views offered consolation to Conrad's early champions and translators, who had only a modest initial response to their efforts.

Although conspicuously absent from the commemorative edition—likely due to an argument with editor Jacques Rivière about publishing James Joyce's *Ulysses* in the *NRF*—Larbaud mixes criticism and praise in a review of Conrad's 1914 novel *Chance*, which predates the commemorative edition by ten years.[78] In the first review of Conrad's work in France, Larbaud dismisses Conrad's plots as perfunctory nods to the demands of a large reading public. Larbaud, himself arguably a writer's writer, laments that there is not "in England, as there is here, a clear division between the larger public and the happy few."[79] He maintains that English writers—he also names H. G. Wells and Charles Dickens—must write in two different registers, one for "the discreet elite" ["la discrète élite"], and the other for the "general reader".[80] In this view, because Conrad has to write for the general reader, he tarnishes his work by means of a stylistic compromise. Larbaud explicitly rejects any equation between widespread popularity and greatness; for Larbaud, Conrad's limited appeal is due to the fact that, to put it simply, the chord he strikes is audible, in his account, only to those with a highly developed literary sensibility. If Conrad is a writer's writer, Larbaud is an elitist's elitist.

Larbaud sets Conrad apart from his contemporaries not by the complexity of his plots, for which he had won particular praise from early English reviewers, but by his use of an indirect narrator. Larbaud points to the indirect narrator as both the conscience of the novel and its distinctly modern element, arguing that the reader must read Conrad's writing through the optic of this conscience, and in spite of the "old rusty carcass of the plot."[81] What distinguishes Conrad from his contemporaries, in Larbaud's view, is the tragic element that governs his writing. Larbaud offers *NRF* readers the portrait of a writer whose work he sees as characterized by inconsistent genius, conjoining a frank assessment of Conrad's limitations with an unequivocal affirmation of talent: "Joseph Conrad and his oeuvre still await a thorough and detailed study that will introduce novels like *Nostromo* and *Chance* to numerous readers in France. We hope that such a study will be offered first to the readers of this journal."[82] For Larbaud, at least, the greatness of Conrad's writing outshines his stylistic shortcomings.

In part, we can see Larbaud's misgivings as rooted in Conrad's perceived failure to echo the more experimental style of writing popular among the literary elite at that time. In Larbaud's view, Conrad is an extraordinary writer but stylistically retrograde; I turn to Casanova's notion of literary temporality here, but with the understanding that Conrad, writing in English in England, was—contra Casanova—both a peripheral and a central writer. Despite his misgivings, Larbaud, informal agent and *passeur* of English, American, and Irish literature, is nevertheless quick to emphasize the role that the *NRF* might play in encouraging translations and publishing future studies of Conrad.

Pierre Mac Orlan reviewed Conrad's first published novel, *Almayer's Folly* (1895), for the *NRF* upon the work's translation into French in 1919.

In his review, he maintains that Conrad is one of just a few writers who had had extraordinary adventures and writes convincingly about them. In his initial invocation of Conrad as the author of *Almayer's Folly*, he telegraphs the doxa of his early French Conrad criticism: "Joseph Conrad, Englishman of Polish heritage and long-haul sailor, is at the top of this set of writers who were molded by a harsh and wild existence and whose literary genius was able to retain images of this past in order to create a harsh and wild book."[83] Conrad's work is singled out for the way in which it marshals the writer's past into writing capable of conveying "harsh" ["dure"] experiences.[84] In Mac Orlan's view, adventure is glimpsed at in *Almayer's Folly* but never realized; indeed, he suggests that an atmosphere of "anxiety" ["inquiétude"] dominates Conrad's first novel.[85] But this is as it should be, Mac Orlan opines; such novels are successful when they are disturbing.

Unlike Larbaud's review, Mac Orlan's mixed review of *Almayer's Folly* was published directly after the war and considers the implications of the war for reading Conrad. In Mac Orlan's view, Conrad's work is characterized by an appropriate tone for the generation rising in the postwar period, who will be able to appreciate novels whose scope has been radically enlarged, novels in which accounts of adventure have been reworked in heretofore-unseen ways, "offering characters an unlimited field of action."[86] Conrad offers a new way to write about modern experience, even if most of his work had been published before the war. Further, it is this interwar-era generation that is primed to appreciate and understand this work. Mac Orlan—who will further elaborate on Conrad's shortcomings in the commemorative edition that I turn to next— specifies that the work will be particularly relevant for those who have lived through the war and are thirsty for new forms of literature that will be adequate in scope for their experiences.

The group response of members of the *NRF* to Conrad's death in 1924 illustrates the influence and effects of the Gide/Conrad collaboration. The 1924 *NRF* commemorative issue "*Hommage à Joseph Conrad*," published four months after Conrad's death, offers the testimony of a large number of notable writers and critics (and those who were both). All of these were men, associated with the *NRF*, including both those who knew him, and those only familiar with his work. There are also translated contributions from the English writers John Galsworthy and Cunninghame Graham. In addition to several eulogies, the deluxe commemorative issue includes

photographs, letters written in French by Conrad, and the initial install-
ment of André Ruyter's serialized translation of *Heart of Darkness*.

The commemorative essays in the volume are divided into two sections: "*souvenirs*,"or remembrances, of Conrad the man, and "*l'œuvre*," essays that address Conrad's body of work. They are remarkably consonant,
again evoking the connections they perceive between Conrad's personal
history and his fiction. Nearly every contributor addresses Conrad's national heritage, questioning how it informs his writing, and alternately
identifying English, French, and Slavic elements. Contributors ponder his
cultural and linguistic background and consider why he chose to write
in English, his third language. Many contributors to the commemorative issue argue that Conrad's connection with France is aesthetic as well
as linguistic, and situate him in the French literary tradition. Relatedly,
contributors often comment on Conrad's mastery of French. "[N]ever a
faulty article, never a grammatical error," declares Jean-Aubry, who would
later correct Conrad's French writing while editing his French-language
letters for the 1929 *Les lettres françaises* compilation.[87] Contributors to
the commemorative edition also suggest that Conrad did indeed have an
eye on Paris and its literary trends. "How well he knew our writers!" Gide
enthuses.[88]

The prevailing tendency to demonstrate Conrad's connection to the
French language is most pronounced in Valéry's account of Conrad. He
recalls the shock he suffered when he first heard what he assessed as Conrad's "horrible accent" ["accent horrible"] while speaking English; contrasting Conrad's English with what he saw as his fluent French and his
"good Provençal accent" ["bon accent provençal"], Valéry concludes: "To
be such a great writer in a language that one speaks so poorly is truly a rare
and novel thing."[89] Valéry suggests that verbal-linguistic capacity indicates
a larger cultural affinity; going further, he identifies Conrad's thick accent as a sign of implicit resistance to the English language and English
literature. In Valéry's view, by dint of his foreign language skills, Conrad is
ultimately more a French writer than an English one; his rightful place is
in the lineage of French literature. He recalls contentiously grilling Conrad
on the putative superiority of the British Navy during the Napoleonic era.

Like Valéry, Jean-Aubry emphasizes Conrad's enviable command of
French. Unlike Valéry, however, he nowhere criticizes Conrad's English. A
great friend of Conrad and his first biographer, Jean-Aubry notes the active

role Conrad played in his own translations, often translating portions of his novels and stories himself. Although Jean-Aubry connects Conrad's nobility and chivalrous nature with his Polish heritage, he ends his essay with a polemical statement that echoes Marlow's oft-repeated "one of us" in *Lord Jim*: "[H]owever great an English writer that he was, he was one of us."[90] Indeed, Jean-Aubry's commemorative essay underscores Conrad's sympathy with French values and aesthetics as well as his "feeling for the French language and its resources, vocabulary, and style."[91] His decision to include several of Conrad's French-language letters in the memorial edition appears polemical and perhaps intended to cast doubt on Conrad's own claims about the relationship between his writing and the English language. "You can take it from me," Conrad famously wrote to British novelist and critic Hugh Walpole, "if I had not known English I wouldn't have written a line for print, in my life."[92] In Conrad's own view, he was not a writer who accidentally wrote in English when he could have written in another language; it was the English language that made a writer of him.

Much as they address Conrad's national identity and linguistic skills, contributors draw attention to his astonishing life and strength of character, using adjectives such as "bitter" ["âpre"] to invoke both Conrad's person and the characters that people his novels and stories. Gide's commemorative essay is exemplary in this respect: "And I think what I loved the most in him was a kind of native nobility, bitter, scornful, and somewhat hopeless, the very nobility that he lends to Lord Jim and which makes that book one of the most beautiful that I know but also one of the saddest and the most exhilarating."[93] In his essay, Gide directly connects Conrad the writer with Jim the character, once again emphasizing the relationship between his work and his life.

Nearly all of the contributors dwell on the importance of Conrad's path to literature via an exacting and virile métier; they commemorate a writer whose literary vocation they saw as the outcome of a younger adulthood characterized by hardship and generative loneliness. For many contributors, Conrad's years at sea spared him the superficiality and pretentiousness they find abundant in contemporary literature. As André Chevrillon declares: "He didn't emerge from a school of writing or a literary coterie; he wasn't searching for a new way to write."[94] In his contribution to the commemorative edition, Robert Francillon further addresses the generative element of Conrad's seafaring: "The unity of the life of Conrad the navigator and Conrad the novelist resides in an act of abandonment always renewed by the power of imagination."[95] For Francillon, it is in part Conrad's solitary nature that made him both an artist and a sailor; loneliness fed his singular vision. Likewise, in the view of the *immortel* Edmond Jaloux, Conrad's formidable life led him to reflect on the ways in which human nature is tested when "faced with unusual circumstances."[96]

In his memorial essay, André Gide writes: "No one lived more savagely than Conrad; no one then patiently, consciously, and wisely submitted life to such a transmutation into art."[97] In his parallel declaration of genius, Gide praises Conrad's talent for molding his life into his writing. With its emphasis on the connection between Conrad's writing and his seafaring years, Gide's essay summarizes the guiding spirit of all of the contributions. Fittingly, *Typhoon* is the most frequently invoked work in the volume.

Like Larbaud and Mac Orlan before them, for many contributors to the *NRF* commemorative edition, appreciation for Conrad requires a refined taste and the capacity to perceive hidden and rugged beauty beneath discernable surface flaws. Chevrillon's commemorative essay articulates this view and reiterates the widespread preference for his works about the sea:

> We could debate some of Conrad's books, reproach them for their length and sometimes disconcerting and complicated composition. But when he limits himself to sailors and the sea—what certainty of conception, what direct and easy narrative flow, what increasing grandeur of expression![98]

Even more critical of Conrad's literary techniques, André Maurois considers his later works as failures. He cites the example of *Victory*, which he later contrasts with earlier sea-oriented works such as the *"Narcissus," Lord Jim*, and *Typhoon*: "The Conrad of *Victory* could not have believed in his monstrous and romantic characters in the way that the Conrad of the *Typhoon* believed in his friends, the sailors."[99] In this view, Conrad's later works failed because he did not believe in them.

Written in English, Jean-Aubry's *Life and Letters* (1927) was published three years after Conrad's death; it was the first Conrad biography to appear. Its ten chapters of biography, supplemented by photographs and a collection of Conrad's letters, remains faithful to key notions expressed in the book reviews and in the commemorative edition essays. Jean-Aubry published Conrad's French letters separately in *Lettres françaises*, a controversial editorial choice, but omitted much of Conrad's later correspondence, including the letters that he wrote to Gide. In 1947, twenty years after *Life and Letters*, Jean-Aubry published in French a second, revised biography of Conrad entitled *Vie de Conrad* [*Life of Conrad*]. This book had no letters and was dedicated to Gide, although Gide is rarely mentioned in this revised biography either. In *Life and Letters*, Jean-Aubry echoes his commemorative essay by emphasizing Conrad's mastery of French, claiming in a footnote that: "Conrad's knowledge of French was perfect. He not only spoke correctly, with a good accent and with great fluency, but he showed later, as a literary man, a nice feeling for French style and a knowledge of the precise meanings of words which many Frenchmen might have envied."[100] Jean-Aubry's impulse to make much of Conrad's French and his four years in Marseilles hints at a longing, one shared by the contributors to the commemorative edition, to enjoy some kind of connection, or share something essential, with Conrad.

In *Life and Letters*, Jean-Aubry notes the significance of Conrad's years at sea and highlights the writing that draws from that period. In the absence of other historical documents, *Life and Letters* joins biographical analysis with selections from Conrad's fiction. For instance, he suggests that the *"Narcissus"* provides an accurate account of Conrad's life at sea:

> From this beautiful book [the *"Narcissus"*] and *The Mirror of the Sea* we know what Conrad's life was like, not only during the voyage of the Narcissus but during the twenty years he spent aboard sailing ships. The atmosphere, the dangers, the fatigues of that life become real to us; also its arduous beauty, which appealed intimately to Conrad, brought up from childhood, as he was, to be familiar with the sentiment of the sublime and with struggle against all odds.[101]

Jean-Aubry underscores the connection between Conrad's life and his writing, despite Conrad's insistence, most notably in *A Personal Record*, that his novels bear only a tangential relationship to real events; he explains that they were often fabricated out of a fragment of a story he had heard although, relevantly, in his view, this did not take away from his work's authenticity. In an author's note for an edition of *Typhoon*, he writes of the protagonist Captain MacWhirr as the product of his own "twenty years" of seafaring life albeit fictional: "If it is true that Captain MacWhirr never walked and breathed on this earth [. . .] I can also assure my readers that he is perfectly authentic. I may venture to assert the same of every aspect of the story, while I confess that the particular typhoon of the tale was not a typhoon of my actual experience."[102]

In *Life and Letters*, Jean-Aubry stresses Conrad's temperamental and yet unaffected nature, arguing that this nature led Conrad to write without pretense in the same devoted fashion with which he had sailed ships. His vocation is "unconscious," the result of "circumstances and the still secret impulse of his nature" and a continuation of his work at sea.[103] As in his commemorative essay, Jean-Aubry, in a footnote, emphasizes Conrad's fluent French.

Despite many differences, Jean-Aubry, like his *NRF* contemporaries, situates Conrad between nineteenth-century aspirations and twentieth-century paradoxes, casting him as a chronicler of noble, but typically outmoded, masculine feats, and fashioning him as a model of authenticity. The majority of Jean-Aubry's contemporaries discovered Conrad during or after the First World War, whereas his life and writing were rooted, they suggest, in the illusions and aspirations of the prewar period. Nevertheless, they contend that Conrad's early works, in particular those that detailed emotional and physical strength in the face of adversity, could function as a literary salve for readers still recovering from the war.

Venuti describes the process of forcing, through translation, foreign writing into familiar norms as a violent one that runs the risk of "wholesale domestication."[104] Conrad's French consecrators were drawn to the foreign elements of his writing. However, it was their domestic criteria for foreignness in the interest of which his consecrators evaluated Conrad's writing and privileged his early work. Yet if I speak of slanted or tendentious readings, I also suggest that correct and permanent readings are possible and that literary merit is easily decided. Conrad's case foregrounds the inevitably variable nature of literary consecration.

Part Two: "Unknown and Prestigious Shores"

Charles Forsdick has demonstrated that the interwar period was a period of complete renewal for French travel literature. He argues that this was particularly true in the 1930s, a decade that "witnessed rapidly multiplied contact between Europe and elsewhere before the postwar collapse of colonial dependency."[105] A number of interwar-era writers place themselves in dialogue with Conrad's work. Several literary readings and rewritings of Conrad at the time also express notable anguish and related sentiments of belatedness in the face of his seemingly inimitable life and work. Two of the most canonical interwar-era French novels, André Malraux's *The Royal Way* (1930) and Louis-Ferdinand Céline's *Journey to the End of the Night* (1932), both question whether a certain kind of authenticity-granting experience is still possible. Isabelle Guillaume argues that both novels, in which the search for new territory cedes to the search for otherness ("altérité"), are rewritings of *Heart of Darkness*.[106] In the fourth and fifth chapters, I explore *Journey to the End of the Night* in depth; for now, I note that Céline's novel takes place, in part, in Africa, just as *Heart of Darkness* transpires, in part, in an unnamed place that is understood to be in sub-Saharan Africa. Both Conrad's and Céline's novels are, as is also widely understood in both cases, informed by their own experiences in Africa.

Conrad's early writing provided a standard for interwar-era French writers of both fiction and nonfiction. He was often invoked in narratives that detail searches for endangered experiences such as those sought by Gide in sub-Saharan Africa. The novelist and reporter Joseph Kessel offers an exemplary reading of Conrad in *Marchés d'esclaves* (1933), a cri de coeur that he wrote while investigating the slave trade in the Arabian Peninsula and in the East African region known at the time as Abyssinia. He invokes Conrad—dead for nine years at the time of publication—at a moment in the book when he crosses the Red Sea to Hodeidah, a port city on the Arabian Peninsula. He recalls reading Conrad and desiring experiences of the sort that Conrad described. He draws particular attention to Conrad's story "Youth," and its drama of a young seaman who survives a tempest and then glimpses the horizon through disappearing clouds. He laments that, although he is on a ship on a benighted coast, he will never feel the excitement felt by the protagonist of "Youth," an excitement which he presumes Conrad once felt himself: "I remember that when I finished reading the story, a profound melancholy mingled with my admiration. I thought that I would never know the beautiful and pure joy experienced by Conrad, sailor of the last century."[107] Kessel's assessment of "Youth" involves a complicated mixture of admiration, melancholy, and anxiety.

But Kessel's despair is short-lived. Although modern travel first seemed to him to have robbed European men of the world's mysteries, Kessel manages to stumble upon what he deemed was real adventure in Hodeidah. He employs a rhetoric of discovery, combined with a nod to older modes of travel, to describe a moment when he is traveling, of necessity, in a simple boat: "Sea liners have become the buses of the ocean, I told myself, and how could I imagine that I could find myself on distant waves onboard a fragile vessel, and discover unknown and prestigious shores, the likes of which one sometimes lands on in one's dreams."[108] Kessel suggests that he has experienced something like the sailor in Conrad's "Youth" and dramatizes his account accordingly. In his account, his experience is particularly exciting because he did not believe that such adventures were still possible; if the protagonist of "Youth" must confront a tempest in order to see the Orient, then Kessel must confront Conrad—functioning here as a metonym for authentic and antiquated experiences—and keep writing. Kessel exhibits himself succeeding at finding such experiences, despite the unfavorable era. In this way, by experiencing the previously unattainable, he defeats Conrad and then deflates him, just as the protagonist in "Youth" combats and conquers the storm: "As the coast slipped away, Conrad's novella "Youth" came back to me."[109] Spatializing history, Kessel travels to what he paints as the past, to have experiences like Conrad.

Kessel's tribute to "Youth" casts it as the account of a supremely transformational experience; he identifies in the novella the prestige of difficult experience and the ways in which hardship can be understood to confer authority and guarantee authenticity. He suggests the anxiety Conrad inspires as a literary precursor insofar as he writes about experiences that appear to be out of the reader's reach. However, Kessel's challenge is less to prove that life-changing experiences of the kind Conrad fictionalized are still possible than to substitute himself for Conrad as the final representative of an imperiled world of adventure. Kessel extends no welcome when he invokes "Youth"; rather, he inserts himself into another bygone and imperiled world. In this view, the old world of adventure is indeed still disappearing, but he was offered the last chance to experience it before it vanishes forever. In the following chapters, I will demonstrate that this logic of belatedness and exclusivity is shared in other writing about travel from the interwar period.

French writers in the thirties were overall much kinder towards Conrad's later work than the gatekeepers at the *NRF*. Michel Leiris's adaptation of Conrad's 1915 novel *Victory* appears in the travel journal he kept while acting as a secretary and archivist for the Dakar-Djibouti ethnographic mission from 1931–1933. The Dakar-Djibouti mission lasted nearly two years and was the first mission of its kind to cross the continent of Africa;

it was funded by the French state in the interest of advancing ethnographic studies in a variety of regions in Africa from the West Coast to the East Coast. The mission was led by the French ethnographer Marcel Griaule, and included, among others, ethnographers, linguists, a musicologist, a painter, and a naturalist.

Leiris's "transgressively reflective journal," which he quickly transformed from a public document to a private journal, was published in 1934 in France as *L'Afrique fantôme* (published in English as *Phantom Africa* in 2017).[110] His command of English rather limited, Leiris had most likely read Isabelle Rivière and Philippe Neel's translation, which Gallimard had published in 1923. In 1933, stationed in Abyssinia towards the end of the twenty-one-month mission, Leiris rewrote the plot of Conrad's novel *Victory*, transforming Axel Heyst—the Swedish-English protagonist who lives in imposed isolation on the fictitious island Samburan—into a miserable colonist whose story involves a mental foundering, seemingly like that of Kurtz. In this and elsewhere, Leiris' adaptation of *Victory* is also redolent of *Heart of Darkness*. He registers his own fragile mental state: "Terrible depression. The real thing: colonial depression."[111] Indeed, although Leiris's lengthy adaptation retains the name Axel Heyst, he transposes him from the Dutch East Indies to colonial East Africa, consciously incorporating elements of the "present reality" ["présente réalité"][112] into the plot.[113]

Michel Leiris, the Surrealist-turned-ethnographer-turned-autobiographer, contributed frequently to the *NRF* in the 1930s. His lifelong obsession with masculinity colors his semi-autobiographical rewriting of *Victory*, a novel whose plot concerns, to a great extent, Heyst's extraordinary feats on his remote island. Leiris's adaptation is also informed by his interest in *l'art nègre*, which he championed as a contributor to Georges Bataille's Surrealist magazine *Documents* (1929–1930). As in Conrad's *Victory*, the prominent themes of Leiris's adaptation are failure and cynicism. In vivid detail, he narrates the humiliation of a man who seeks to retain his fragile and much valued dignity in the colony by avoiding sporting functions and social encounters. Both Conrad's isolated Swedish Baron and Leiris's colonial island dweller are "gentlemen" (the word is in English in Leiris's journal) and both characters' situations contest the implicit triumph suggested by the novel's title. Indeed, Leiris's sketch of Axel Heyst documents Leiris's growing disappointment at the end of the Mission when he contemplates: "[A] review of all my failures; acts, adventures, copulations gone wrong."[114]

Leiris's Heyst navigates the masculine behavior for which Conrad's protagonists won praise from *NRF* contributors. His adaptation intermingles his own experiences on the Dakar-Djibouti Mission with the misadventures of Conrad's Heyst in the Dutch East Indies. Like Conrad's Swedish Heyst, Leiris's English Heyst is a self-controlled man who breaks the rules of behavior demanded of him by his countrymen. He runs afoul with the bulk of his fellow colonials because he does not adhere to custom; he is friendly with the "natives" ["indigènes"] and mainly keeps to himself. The other colonists take him to task for his heterodox behavior: "Some say he's not 'a man'; he doesn't go out, he doesn't hunt, he is very lax with the natives, he gets flustered easily."[115] Although he has had opportunities for sexual relations, he has apparently not had any since his arrival in the colony. Like Conrad's Heyst, Leiris's Heyst is aloof, but also jocular and playful when he does socialize, prone to ill-advised jokes concerning such topics as masturbation.[116] His unusual demeanor and inappropriate joking leads the community to suspect that he is either homosexual or impotent. Heyst bucks the colonial community's guidelines for correct behavior and grows even more isolated because of it: "Most people saw him as a poseur: the better educated called him an aesthete. It was considered odd that he didn't ride and disliked hunting."[117] Leiris experienced similar alienation in his own community as he testifies in his journal only a few days before composing his adaptation of *Victory*: "Soon I will have been chaste for two whole years. Some people will call me impotent or say that I have no balls."[118]

In this passage, Leiris is particularly concerned with how the other members of the Mission perceive his deeply undesired chastity and his attendant feelings of shame. His concern with group reflection is mirrored in another journal entry, in which he envisions a possible misreading of his adaptation and offers a defensive apostrophe to the reader: "Let no one call Axel Heyst an aesthete, a madman, or an eccentric. He is just a semi-lucid man in a world of the blind."[119] Although both Conrad's Heyst and Leiris's Heyst are capable of robust self-mockery, neither can bear calumny; in *Phantom Africa* overall, a notion of honor evolves that is pinned both to self-esteem and other peoples' esteem; for Leiris's Heyst, the community functions as an evaluative group whom he must convince that he is a norm-obeying man and, thereby, redeem himself. Ultimately, Leiris's Heyst must die in order to be understood.

Edward Said has relevantly noted Conrad's affinity with Nietzsche, particularly with respect to *Victory* and Heyst's flawed "code of philosophic disengagement from life."[120] I argue that, with respect to such a code of disengagement, we can see just how much Leiris has rewritten; whereas in Conrad's *Victory*, the native East Indians remain in the background while a drama plays out among Europeans, Leiris's version brings indigenous people into the foreground. Conrad's British Lena is transformed into an indigenous woman with whom Heyst is enamored.

The rumors about Heyst that circulate among both the colonials and the indigenous people suggest that Heyst's impotence far exceeds the sexual sphere. However, a sudden flurry of events and discoveries in the colony ultimately confirm that he is indeed capable of convincingly conforming to normative masculinity despite the scornful judgment of his fellow colonizers. Unlike Conrad's Heyst, who is maligned for his Nietzschean independence and contempt, Leiris's Heyst faces ridicule and humiliation for general ineptitude. In Leiris's adaptation, a rumor starts that Heyst is having an affair with an indigenous sex worker. With the avowed hope of curing himself of his fear of coitus, Heyst invites the indigenous woman to his home; she leaves quickly, terrified by his sexual aggression as well as his spare room with its "overwhelming cleanliness and bareness."[121] Shortly thereafter, Heyst attempts suicide and fails because, forever bumbling, he cannot manage to shoot himself effectively; once again, even during a suicide attempt, he proves himself an incompetent colonist, as a familiarity with guns is one of the attributes of the "gentleman" he unsuccessfully tries to become. This episode echoes the episode in Conrad's *Victory* in which Heyst's gun is stolen due to his carelessness. Shortly after his suicide attempt, Leiris's Heyst dies in a massive epidemic. In line with Conrad's penchant for second-hand narration, Heyst's story is then seen through the eyes of an interested doctor. Here, Leiris introduces an avatar of Davidson, the second-hand narrator who tells Heyst's story in *Victory*. In an episode reminiscent of *Heart of Darkness*, the doctor searches Heyst's room, uncovering a photograph of a solemn young woman and a messy personal diary. The "fairly thick pile of separate pages, forming a sort of diary, rather confused and mostly undated," mirrors the piles of ethnographic notes which Leiris transcribes for the Mission.[122] Heyst's mostly undated papers include a variety of different kinds of writing. There are reflections on suicide as well as accounts of affairs that suggest that Heyst was not, after all, impotent. There are also optimistic notes about his plantation work,

work that could have elevated Heyst's reputation in the colonial community, work that will allow Heyst to "show that he, too, is a 'man.'"[123] The
diary also includes reflections on various intimate topics such as love and
sex and relations with indigenous women. Yet when the doctor interviews
Heyst's domestic servant, he counters that Heyst's only attempt at a sexual encounter in the colony was with the aforementioned indigenous sex
worker, who fled his house, terrified by his strange manners as much as his
barren and antiseptic living quarters. The doctor speculates that Heyst's
suicide attempt was precipitated by this failed encounter.

Leiris, like so many of his interwar-era contemporaries, believed that
sub-Saharan Africa was a place where authentic and character-building experiences could be had and that, therefore, travel would cure him of sexual
neurosis and what he saw as cowardice. He hoped that the Mission would
permit him to escape from what he saw as a stifling and degrading European life, a hope that had at its foundation the quite firm conviction that
living for nearly two years among sub-Saharan Africans from a broad variety of regions would prove both curative and restorative. He anticipated
returning from the Mission a more virile and sexually confident person.
Emawayish, the Abyssinian woman whom Leiris encounters and falls in
love with on his trip, is given (and rightly refuses) the absurd task of eman-
cipating him from what his journal describes as "the education I was given
[. . .] all the rules that merely ended up enchaining me, making me the kind
of sentimental pariah that I am, incapable of living a healthy life and copu-
lating in a healthy way."[124] In his semi-autobiographical rewriting of the
plot of *Victory*, as well as elements from *Heart of Darkness*, Leiris, like his
contemporaries, interprets Conrad's characters as lonely individuals who
confront themselves in extreme situations, just as his own "colonial depression" prompts him to confront his false expectations and personal failures.

In a 1951 preface to *Phantom Africa*, Leiris, now ["ceasing to aspire to
the romantic role of the White Man [. . .] like Lord Jim]," underscores the
dangerous solipsism of his younger self, impelled to travel to such distant
lands, because it "signified to him, not only a test, but also a lived poetry
and a change of scenery."[125] The 1951 edition, with its new preface and
notes, published almost twenty years after the initial publication of *Phantom Africa*, offers a rereading of both his adaptation and his earlier understanding of Conrad's work. If Leiris were to rewrite *Victory* at that later
date, he remarks in a lengthy marginal note, he would change the doctor's
account to reflect quite different insights:

If the doctor had reflected a bit further, he would surely have had more to say about the blow given to the "native" laborer renowned throughout the area for the enormous size of his virile member. He would have noticed how much Axel Heyst's reaction—this gesture of puritanical fury toward a man of color—showed him to be vaguely contaminated, despite the open mind that one might suppose he possessed, by one of the worst racist prejudices: the one that transforms black men, in the eyes of many white men, into dangerous sexual rivals who must be kept at a distance. And perhaps he would have suspected that, if Heyst succumbed to suicide, it is because this fear of turning out to be inferior—a sign of the elevated value he attached to his prestige, as well as his exaggerated self-concern—could not be dispelled without a radical conversion, in a way that would have, for example, let him see a woman only as herself, instead of reducing her to an instrument for him to experiment with or to prove something to himself with; a radical conversion, in sum, so that in the most general manner he would have been less anxious about *virility* and instead show himself to be more generous with pure and simple *humanity*.[126]

As I have illustrated, Lefevere uses the term "rewriting" to refer to translation as well as many other forms of adaptation, including critical work. The study of rewritings can help establish the factors influencing cultural production and reception; Leiris's belated analysis of his own youthful adaptation of *Victory* does indeed point at a specific mode of cultural production. In Leiris's adaptation, Heyst's interactions with indigenous people serve primarily to instigate self-encounter. He is particularly concerned with the opinions of fellow Europeans. According to Leiris's 1951 preface and marginal notes, a new Axel Heyst would concern himself far less with group perception, would not dwell on the sexual prowess of an indigenous laborer, and would not look to indigenous women to cure him of sexual neuroses. Overall, he would guard himself from looking at indigenous people in an instrumental fashion.

Edward Said has notably argued that Conrad's *Victory* served as a kind of "re-invasion of his past by Conrad."[127] Leiris's 1951 rereading of his earlier adaptation of a writer whose work nourished his childhood also discloses an autocritique. Indeed, Leiris's rewriting of *Victory* adapts Axel Heyst in order to reflect the unusual way in which Leiris stages his own masculinity. Relatedly, his 1951 preface is an implicit critique of his earlier reading of Conrad, a reading that echoes the obsessions and personal concerns of Conrad's early French consecrators. In his adaptation of *Victory*, Leiris highlights the dominant early French interpretation of Conradian heroes: men made noble and authoritative through rugged experience abroad, drawn by a writer who was authenticated by his maritime past, by his first métier.

Lefevere challenges readers to ask "who rewrites, why, under which circumstances, for which audience."[128] Interwar-era French writers, critics, and translators, many of them associated with the circle of appreciation constituted by the contributors and editors of the *NRF*, describe Conrad's characters as antiquated heroes who stand for a bygone world and now fading possibilities for heroism and adventure, the very stuff of authenticity in their view. Yet Leiris, in his 1951 preface and marginal notes, identifies this reading as flawed because it ignores both the indigenous people who are an ineluctable part of these rugged experiences, as well as the colonial contexts that permitted them. Here he offers another reading of *Victory*, positing the dangers that Heyst and Lena face precisely because they do not recognize indigenous people as people. It is therefore important to note that Leiris's adaptation, as well as his later preface and marginal notes, suggest that Leiris, in 1951, was not criticizing Conrad, but rather the readings of Conrad that ignore the human element of his fiction. It is only fair to note that current French- and English-language Conrad scholarship does not necessarily echo his interwar-era French consecrators. For instance, as Padimi Mongia notes with respect to Conrad's colonial fiction: "Conrad's interest in the white men who go soft in the heat and dust of colonial outposts is always attentive to the possibilities the colonial context makes available to these men."[129] She suggests, like so many of her counterparts, that Conrad was aware of his own position and, in the main, effectively captured some of the abuses of power that the colonial project entailed. However, debates about Conrad's view of colonialism are ongoing.

The younger Leiris, like his *NRF* counterparts, neglected this human aspect of Conrad's work, as well as his criticism of colonialism. However, in 1951, Leiris moved to center stage the indigenous people who stood in the margins of his adaptation. As I will show in the fourth and fifth chapters, Gide began an earlier parallel project later in the late twenties when he traveled to Africa in the footsteps of Conrad, but with more concern for the plight of indigenous Africans than the personal transformation of white men among them. Neither reading is a self-righteous critique of Conrad, but both offer the possibility of a reinterpretation, and both suggest that the interwar-era French reading of Conrad was due for revision, rejection, or reaffirmation. These works also anticipate the work of contemporary Conrad scholars who seek to further illuminate his writing through the lens of our own cultural moment. As Said has reminded us with regard to a number of writers, such investigations offer a confirmation of merit, not a dismissal: "I see them contrapuntally, that is, as figures whose writing travels across temporal, cultural and ideological boundaries in unforeseen ways to emerge as part of a new ensemble *along with* later history and subsequent art."[130] He asserts the value of reading Conrad "in all sorts of unforeseen proleptic ways," giving particular preference to later reworkings and "echoing answers."[131]

Casanova asks readers to "continually shift perspectives" by situating literary works within a literary temporality that is both historically and aesthetically defined but not reducible to either.[132] In his adaptation of a remembered translation, Leiris offers us a personal glimpse into how Conrad was read in France during the interwar period. It is no accident that Leiris chose a Conrad character to dramatize the unusual way in which his protagonist stages his masculinity. Considering the reception of Conrad in France, a new literary hero emerges, one perpetually transformed by rugged experiences, one whose life justifies and authenticates his work. Yet this hero is also an antiquated hero; the war years effectively complicated many of the things that once counted as heroism. If the First World War sounded the death knell for the heroic individual, Conrad served as both example and counterexample to this death. He became a hero in France after the war, but the possibility for such perceived heroism was anchored firmly in the prewar world.

Conrad's interwar-era readership made use of his writing in order to ask themselves if the kind of experiences he narrated were still possible and if one could still unproblematically transmute art into life as they believed he had. Conrad's early works in particular inspired a unique combination of yearning and nostalgia. The travel literature that followed this fascination with Conrad is replete with ambition for lived knowledge coupled with nostalgia for endangered experiences, for authenticity, for Kessel's "unknown and prestigious shores." For his French readers of the war and interwar period, Conrad inspired a generative blend of optimism and anxiety.

During the interwar period in France, Conrad was read, translated, and consecrated by members of the *NRF*, and others in proximate critical constellations, in a manner that reflected domestic aesthetic criteria. However, as Venuti argues, much is to be gained from identifying and decoding strategies of interpretation and translation. Said argues that adaptations and rewritings of Conrad honor the originals, leaving Conrad's writing "further actualized and animated by emphases and inflections that he was obviously unaware of, but that his writing permits."[133] He also makes a case for Conrad's undiminished relevance and likewise for the usefulness of returning to and drawing meaning from writers who "brush up unstintingly against historical constraints."[134] Later writers like Leiris can, as Said argues, "dramatize the latencies in a prior figure or form that suddenly illuminate the present."[135] Jean-Yves Tadié also notes that Conrad's narrative style is particularly well suited for a productive afterlife: "His movement is that of interrogation, not of realism, nor of certitude."[136] Conrad has much to tell readers about themselves. In the case of his interwar-era French readers, critics, and translators, there is clear evidence of Conrad's elasticity in the way in which he contributed to their self-definition as they read, translated, commented on, and otherwise adapted his work.

I have demonstrated how Conrad became a model for a group of interwar-era French writers who emphasized his work's origin in unusually exclusive and unrepeatable experiences.[137] I have explored the way in which an interest in authenticity and authority-granting hardship informs the imaginary of the writers among Conrad's early French readership. I will now explore how these two desiderata, authenticity and authority, are inscribed in *Death in the Afternoon*, Hemingway's 1932 treatise on the Spanish bullfight. Our look at Hemingway's opus thus begins where I leave off in this chapter, as if the young American writer had taken the French Conrad as a blueprint for traveling, and writing about travel. I will demonstrate, however, that Hemingway, albeit problematically, pushed local cultures, so absent from the accounts of Conrad's French consecrators, into the foreground.

We will also see the same interwar-era anxieties about a changing world play out in bad faith through Hemingway's insistence on a nostalgia whose object is ultimately coterminous with the present. Such nostalgia, which I introduced in the introduction as "anticipatory nostalgia," is radically different from the backwards looking nostalgia of Conrad's consecrators, and serves as a way for Hemingway to distinguish his writing and put heavy and strategic pressure on the gap between the time of writing and the time of reading. Hemingway will make much out of this inevitable time lag in the publication process; indeed, he will make it one of the chief motifs in his treatise and pair it with a marked hostility to his anticipated readership. The following chapters will further explore the ways in which ambition for authenticity, tethered to nostalgia, became the defining template in interwar-era literature about travel. It did so by means of distinct and widely shared conventions among traveling writers, for traveling, for writing about travel, and for writing about the people they meet while traveling.

CHAPTER TWO

Exposing the Secret: Hemingway's Authentic Spain

When Scribner's published Hemingway's *Death in the Afternoon* in 1932, critics struggled to understand why an acclaimed writer of fiction would devote the better part of a decade to what was, in part, an exposition of bullfighting, a sport widely condemned by the public as immoral. The idea for what would become *Death in the Afternoon* had gestated for eight years before Hemingway finally wrote the lengthy manuscript he had promised Maxwell Perkins at Charles Scribner's Sons. Initial critical response was guided by questions about the hefty book's "genus and species."[1] Early reviews demonstrate that critics found it difficult to label a book that combines 297 pages of exposition with an eighty-four-page glossary and eighty-one illustrative black-and-white photographs with detailed captions.[2] They searched for the book's organizational logic in order to make sense of this mass of information. In *The Bookman*, one frustrated reviewer bluntly summed it up as "an interlude of reporting and miscellaneous comment in a career chiefly devoted to fiction."[3] How should a book that foregrounded Hemingway just as it suggested that "it is always a mistake to know an author" be made sense of?[4] *Death in the Afternoon* baffled reviewers.

Questions about taxonomy persist in critical studies of *Death in the Afternoon* (hereafter "*DIA*"). I maintain, however, that scholars are wrong to consider the book as representing a radical departure from his earlier writing or else from other writing of the era about foreign climes and practices.[5] Indeed, I argue that *DIA* is more of a parallel project to *The Sun Also Rises* (hereafter "*SAR*"), published six years earlier in 1926, than an aberration. The connection between the two works is particularly salient if we examine the manner in which the trope of anticipatory nostalgia functions in both works as a guarantor of authority and authenticity. In his review of *DIA*, Malcolm Cowley adroitly notes that each work by Hemingway "has been an elegy."[6] Just like Jake Barnes in *SAR*, the Hemingway of *DIA* makes use of anticipatory nostalgia to distinguish himself from his readers as well as the other foreigners who have tampered with, for instance, "the way it used to happen at San Sebastian."[7]

Cowley tackles the question of the book's species by likening it to a travel guide; *DIA* is, in his view, a "Baedeker of the bullfight."[8] It is unclear how Hemingway classified his effort. Cowley's review notwithstanding, forty pages into his book, and in the middle of a lengthy passage about the beautiful cultural artifacts of Aranjuez, Hemingway apostrophizes the reader: "You can find the sights in Baedeker."[9] Yet, in chapter seven, Hemingway implicitly claims to have written a guidebook that will, from then on, best serve those who have already witnessed the practice: "There are two sorts of guide books; those that are read before and those that are to be read after and those that are to be read after the fact are bound to be incomprehensible to a certain extent before."[10] By directing the reader to see the event before finishing the book, Hemingway is implicitly suggesting that words cannot adequately capture first-hand experience when it comes to the bullfight. Furthermore, Hemingway continues, even if the reader does go to a fight, the one he will see will be decadent and irrelevant to the book's exposition insofar as the book deals exclusively with the normative classical bullfight. Going even further, Hemingway claims that individual instances are so unique that, even when he describes one, "it would not be the one that you would see."[11] At the very moment when Hemingway provides a wealth of technical information—what Edward Said fondly lauds as his "how-to-ism"—he suggests that much of it will ultimately be useless.[12] All of this might seem to defeat the purpose of the book, but Hemingway instead makes the bullfight's decline one of the principal stories he tells: a story that positions him as the ideal writer for the subject. *DIA* offers a qualified introduction to a deteriorating practice by a writer who had witnessed it during an era he is now idealizing, one that he emphasizes is firmly in the past.

Also manifest in Hemingway's demand that his readers go and see for themselves is a marked ambivalence about sharing his knowledge. Just as he, as I demonstrated above, questions language as a viable vehicle for sharing knowledge about the *corrida*, he also questions readers' competence. Concerns about readers' overall capacities are conjoined with the contention that only an elect few will be able to understand and appreciate the spectacle. Compounded with that is Hemingway's implicit claim that it is nearly impossible overall to convey essential aspects of Spain and the Spanish bullfight. This is particularly noteworthy in the mournful final chapter, where a description of Valencia is followed by the claim: "You do not know what hot is when you have not been there."[13] Once again Hemingway implicitly underscores the fallibility of language when communicating information or experience.

Hemingway describes people with *afición* or "love of bullfights," as he puts it in his glossary, as understated and aloof.[14] *Afición* is rare among non-Spaniards in both *DIA* and *SAR*; in the latter book, Anglophone groups travel to, and then proceed to ruin, the festival in Pamplona. In *SAR*, a visitor's capacity for *afición* is adjudicated by the Spanish innkeeper, Montoya. The arbiter Montoya singles out Jake as one of the select few with *afición*. Like Montoya, others with *afición* recognize each other in an understated fashion:

> When they saw that I had afición, and there was no password, no set questions that could bring it out, rather it was a sort of oral spiritual examination with the questions always a little on the defensive and never apparent, there was this same embarrassed putting the hand on the shoulder, or a "Buen hombre." It seemed as though they wanted to touch you to make it certain.[15]

Barnes is a model of the foreigner with *afición*; his Spanish is fluent and idiomatic. He avoids luxury, preferring to lodge in modest pensions. He eats with locals at humble restaurants and inns, romanticizing the hardships that Spanish people face. He loathes tourists, Americans in particular. He is nostalgic for the bullfights that he witnessed during earlier visits. Among his expatriate coterie, Montoya indicates that Jake alone has the right sensibility to appreciate Spanish culture and the *fiesta*, in addition to the bullfight itself. His relationship to the Spanish bullfight is suggested in spiritual terms; indeed, Alexandra Peat has termed Barnes a "modernist pilgrim."[16]

SAR, much like *DIA* after it, also suggests the difficulty of capturing the bullfight in words. In addition, it communicates the dangers inherent in talking about the bullfight to other non-Spaniards; for instance, Brett disastrously seduces the brilliant and vulnerable young matador Pedro Romero only after Jake talks him up.

It is possible that in both books Hemingway is atoning for his own role in adulterating the very spectacle whose lost purity he now mourns. Just as he casts Barnes in *SAR*, Hemingway, in *DIA*, casts himself as a sober initiate to the bullfight, earnestly traveling to the Iberian Peninsula with a self-imposed goal to write about death. However, in earlier letters, he begs friends and friends of friends to come with him to the San Fermín Festival of Navarre for bargain-rate fun. "Bullfighting is the best damn stuff in the world," Hemingway claims in a 1924 invitation to Howell Jenkins: "For Christ sake come on."[17] "Spain is the real old stuff," he advises, "you could have a hell of a good time here and spend hardly any money."[18] Hemingway's concern with affordability runs throughout his letters and nonfiction. As Hemingway biographer Michael Reynolds notes of 1925 in particular: "Wherever Hemingway looked [. . .] he saw dollar signs. Everything was for sale, its price clearly marked."[19]

Hemingway's later concerns and lamentations about the bullfight's adulteration both revisit and reproduce colonial and imperialist tropes. Renato Rosaldo has argued that such elegies to changed places make use of a deceptive pose of innocent yearning, hiding the "coming collapse" of places in the margins.[20] He relevantly explains what he defines as "imperialist nostalgia," the seemingly paradoxical impulse to destroy a culture and then mourn its destruction as the end of a way of life. I argue Hemingway's nostalgia for the earlier days of the bullfight is, at the same time, anticipatory nostalgia and imperialist nostalgia for his youth and a "pure" Spain. Rosaldo explains that such dual nostalgic longings form the backbone of imperialist nostalgia: "Indeed, much of imperialist nostalgia's force resides in its association with (indeed, its disguise as) more genuinely innocent tender recollections of what is at once an earlier epoch and a previous phase of life."[21]

In the second chapter, Hemingway explains his motivations for writing the book he presented to Charles Scribner's nearly a decade after he first grew frustrated with his Boni and Liveright contract. He represents the book as the product of his goal to craft a truthful account of bullfighting as a "real" subject, which for him meant one that involved both life and death. When he was still new to both writing and the bullfight, death was something he hoped to write about as a challenge and as a self-prescribed rite of passage. In the second paragraph of the treatise, a two-page stream-of-consciousness meditation on his views of writing, he states his goal: "I was trying to learn to write, commencing with the simplest things, and one of the simplest things of all and the most fundamental is violent death."[22] Indeed, Hemingway traveled to Spain after the First World War in order to witness such violent death, "one of the subjects that a man might write of."[23] He recollects his first trip to Spain when he was an apprentice writer and new to the bullfight, signaling the importance of conscientious beginnings for both vocations, just as he, as I will demonstrate, argues that both contemporary writing and the contemporary bullfight are characterized by decadence.

Ann Douglas suggests that young veterans of World War One were confident that it had afforded them riveting material for a novel. Indeed, this particular pattern of hardship conferring authenticity and authority is found in *SAR*, in which Jake is not a bullfighter, although he has quite literally been wounded at the site of manhood. His wound sets him apart from the rest of his coterie and affords him special insight into the bullfight, just as Hemingway believes that his experience as an ambulance driver during the First World War affords him, in part, *afición*. This is partially due to the nature of bullfighting as an art. As Hemingway explains it, bullfighting is "the only art in which the artist is in danger of death and in which the degree of brilliance in the performance is left to the fighter's honor."[24] Hardship will afford the spectator particular insight into the sport.

Spain provided the young Hemingway with ideal subject matter for his ambitions as a writer. In 1923, he described his discovery to William D. Horne:

> It isn't just brutal like they always told us. It's a great tragedy—and the most beautiful thing I've ever seen and takes more guts and skill and guts again than anything possibly could. It's just like having a ringside seat at the war with nothing going to happen to you.[25]

He embraced the tragedy with considerable passion. By the time he finished *DIA*, he had witnessed hundreds of *corridas*; he was a self-identified *aficionado*, a Spanish word he defines in the lengthy glossary as signifying "one who understands bullfights in general and in detail and still cares for them."[26] Polemically identifying himself as "part of the human race" that derives "pleasure and pride" from killing, he will explain the practice to an uninitiated audience from a position of knowledge and experience.[27] He will tell the unvarnished truth in frank language and steer clear of the euphemistic trappings of what Douglas has called the period's "high-minded idiom."[28] Relatedly, Hemingway claims that a love of killing is rare among writers, hence, he argues, the paucity of good statements on the subject: "Because the other part, which does not enjoy killing, has always been the more articulate and has furnished most of the good writers we have had a very few statements of the true enjoyment of killing."[29] Hemingway will breach this gap between those who write and those who love to kill, approaching the topic with solemnity. The bull, much like the marlin fish in *The Old Man and the Sea* (1952), is anthropomorphized into a noble and brave opponent. If this interest in representing death sets him apart from other writers, it also demonstrates how he wanted to be aligned with the Spanish people, rather than with what he casts as the more privileged viewers of the spectacle.

A number of reviewers remarked that Hemingway was catering to public interest by casting himself in *DIA* and making use of his person to strengthen what Comley and Scholes describe as his "will to textual power."[30] Both the presence of "the author" and the emphasis on the act of writing itself function to establish a connection between the narrator and Hemingway, the writer named on the cover. An implicit autobiographical pact, as Philippe Lejeune has defined it, is signed as he scatters direct references to his family and personal history throughout the book. Despite these enticements, however, *DIA* was a commercial failure; its reception confirmed Perkins' fears and made good on the prophesy of the copy editor who typed "Hemingway's Death" across the galley proof. Critics took Hemingway to task for the style and subject matter of his treatise. *DIA* contains many of the familiar aspects of Hemingway's prose: the repetition of simple adjectives such as "fine"; the homey, conversational parataxis; the nonidiomatic translation of foreign languages; the declarative sentences. But something else had surfaced as well: an explosive aggressiveness so pronounced that reviewer Robert Coates deemed the book "almost suicidal."[31] Other reviewers objected to Hemingway taking on anticipated detractors with foolhardy challenges. In a highly unfavorable review entitled "Bull in the Afternoon"—later the cause of a fist fight between reviewer and author—Max Eastman likened Hemingway's prose to the practice of "wearing false hair on the chest";[32] he speculated that Hemingway's style functioned as a compensation for sexual insecurity. On all sides, Hemingway stood accused of vulgar writing in the promotion of a sport that many Americans found indefensible.

Hemingway mailed his first letter to Perkins in 1925, seven years before the publication of *DIA*. Although he was technically still under contract with Boni and Liveright, he was responding to the editor's invitation to join him at Charles Scribner's Sons and publish another novel. However, Hemingway was already invested in a different project, "a sort of Doughty's Arabia Deserta of the Bull Ring, a very big book with some wonderful pictures."[33] In Hemingway's letter, he refers to the novel as "an awfully artificial and worked out form"; he agrees that a novel would likely sell more copies than a nonfiction book but "somehow," he confesses, "I don't care about writing a novel and I like to write short stories and I like to work at the bullfight book."[34] To Perkins he expresses his desire to write a book that would provide a wealth of information about Spain and the *corrida* without ever lapsing into what he cast as the studied artificiality of the novel. He was less concerned with establishing an engaging plot than with truthfully conveying information about a controversial cultural practice in a manner characterized by extensive formal innovation.

In correspondence from the twenties, Hemingway openly announces his commitment to capturing the bullfight in words. In 1925 he wrote an apropos letter to George Horace Lorimer, then editor of the *Saturday Evening Post*; in his letter he refers to his story, "The Undefeated," and its treatment of bullfighting. He writes specifically of his attempt, when writing the story, "to show it the way it actually is," and expresses confidence in the level of accuracy he ultimately achieved.[35] Hemingway's nascent book project was, in part, charged with the goal of offering the perspective of an insider. It would be "a real bullfight story, one written without bunk, from the inside by someone who really knew bull fighting."[36] Throughout *DIA*, Hemingway does indeed emphasize his participation in many *fiestas* and his presence at countless bullfights as if to offer credentials for registering and codifying what is presented as essential knowledge of Spain and the Spanish bullfight. Such recourse to experience, Thomas Strychacz has pointed out, results in a treatise that is "less a handbook to bullfighting than a guide to the multiple modes of performance undertaken by men."[37] In due course, Hemingway notes his ability to locate scalped tickets, select quality bullfights, and win local sympathy.

In letters from the early twenties, Hemingway expresses this commitment to portraying his experiences as accurately as he could. Hemingway had first visited Spain as a young foreign journalist and immediately wished to return: "In Madrid I lived in a bull fighter's boarding house and followed the bullfights all over Spain traveling with a cuadrilla of bull fighters. I'm going back again next summer."[38] As important as the information offered by *DIA*, is its emphasis on the fact that such information originated in the specific life of a specific person. Hemingway puts pressure on this prehistory and repeatedly refers to it. In chapter one, he suggests that it has heuristic value; the reader new to Spain and the bullfight will learn lessons from a writer who has not always been an expert. However, Hemingway moves away from the book's ostensible project of educating the reader in favor of a tour de force of aggression against the reader.

Hemingway maintains that it will be valuable for the reader to have an English-language introduction to the connected subjects of Spain and the Spanish bullfight. But the reader is soon confronted with a paradox; although *DIA* includes directions to local cafés dealing in last-minute tickets, an in-depth inventory of the fare at restaurants, a column of festival dates, and a host of Spanish lessons, Hemingway emphatically insists that he does not intend for his book to be read by tourists, in particular the cosmopolitan and rich ones he accuses of polluting *fiestas* with their manners and their money. The end of chapter three is an invective against wealthy American tourists in particular; he describes them leaving the fights squeamishly and then returning after they became popular only to raise prices and sully the general crowd: "In nineteen thirty-one I did not see one leave within range and now it looks as though the good old days of the free barreras at San Sebastian are over."[39] Hemingway identifies the foreigners as fellow Americans, remarking their "skull and bones-ed, porcelain-ed, beach-tanned" appearance.[40] Indulging in the kind of one-upmanship seemingly essential to interwar literature about travel, Hemingway stresses that his fellow Americans are, unlike him, necessarily belated. The descriptions of different fights and festivals that follow these screeds against American tourists ultimately serve to distinguish Hemingway from the reader; he seeks to establish that his own countrymen have imperiled the integrity of both Spain and the *corrida*. Mournfully, and in the spirit of both anticipatory and imperialist nostalgia, Hemingway forecasts the destruction of "a country you love very much," which he believes will lose its fragile essence due to the deleterious effects of an increase in Anglophone visitors.[41] The great days of Spain are already over in this account in which the author presents himself more as historian than guide.

Indeed, Hemingway assumes Montoya's suspicions in *DIA*. "What you will want at a bullfight [. . .] is a good public," he states, emphasizing the critical role the audience plays in determining the caliber of a bullfight and its adherence to high standards.[42] Indeed, the audience becomes a kind of analogue for his readership as an analogy between writing and the violent sport is developed in subsequent chapters and the act of writing is cast as a struggle between reader and writer. Just as upper-class American tourists destroy Spain and the Spanish bullfight, Hemingway, in the guise of "the author" sitting at his habitual chair at a humble pension, suggests that readers have the power to destroy a writer's work. Crucially, an ambivalent stance toward the reader informs *DIA*. Ostensibly functioning as an initiation, it ultimately, as highlighted by anticipatory nostalgia, rejects its readership, cancelling its initial welcome.

The bibliographical notes that conclude *DIA* outline Hemingway's project in that book as an attempt "to explain [the modern Spanish bullfight] both emotionally and practically."[43] This dual introduction is apparent from the passages in chapter one in which Hemingway recalls his response to the goring of the horses in the second and middle segment of the spectacle. This is arguably one of its most controversial aspects and also, in his personal experience, the one most disturbing to foreign spectators. His account of his first reaction to the goring of the horses allows him to "establish the fact that the reactions were instant and unexpected."[44] By this logic, the immediacy of his response suggests its authenticity. This immediacy informs the bibliographical notes in which he claims that the information that he imparts in *DIA* might differ in part from that offered by competing treatises on the same subject; he claims to have consulted 2,077 works about bullfighting but begs the indulgence of "competent aficionados" for narrowing this mass of information into "one man's arbitrary explanation."[45]

Hemingway deftly claims the authority that he sees conferred by his immediate experience; following his account of his response to the goring of the horses, he offers a lengthy history of the integration of horses into the bullfight. He continues in this vein, combining personal anecdotes with detailed exposition, as well as frequent digressions into alternately irrelevant and provocative material. He saw his expository style as tauromachian in nature and hoped to write a book that would resemble the subject he was explaining. Before he began work on the treatise, he explained this novel approach in his first letter to Perkins:

It is a long one to write because it is not to be just a history and text book [*sic*] or apologia for bull fighting—but instead, if possible, bull fighting itsself [*sic*]. As it's a thing that nobody knows about in English I'd like to take it first from altogether outside—how I happened to be interested in it, how it seemed before I saw it—how it was when I didn't understand it—my own experience with it, how it reacts on others—the gradual finding out about it and try and build it up from the outside and then go all the way inside with chapters on everything."[46]

In the approach inaugurated in chapter one, with his description of the goring of the horses, "outside" material is communicated through colorful anecdotes and frank, lively description, whereas "inside" material includes extensive information of practical use, such as the complex rules of the bullfight, for instance, or else a pointed explanation of the difference between *gambas*, *langostinos*, and shrimp. In this, Hemingway reverses the typical outside/inside dichotomy to put personal material on the outside and make general information the purview of the insider.

Examining the bullfight through the lens of traditional humanistic criteria such as symmetry, beauty, and honesty, Hemingway grants immediate responses primacy for judging the spectacle's value and morality; immediate responses permit him to evaluate the bullfight's moral character in a Rousseauist fashion. "So far about morals," he submits, "I know only what is moral is what you feel good after and what is immoral is what you feel bad after and judged by these moral standards, which I do not defend, the bullfight is very moral to me because I feel very fine while it is going on and have a feeling of life and death and mortality and immortality."[47] By this logic, the reader is only entitled to judge the bullfight's morality after he has witnessed entire fights and knows his "reactions to them."[48] Insofar as Hemingway answers the question of morality by immediate feeling as opposed to exposition and analysis, he is already limiting the profit readers can claim for themselves from his book.

We find a similar logic in his accounts of experiences that he suggests cannot be reproduced; these accounts necessarily serve to highlight Hemingway's implicit claim that he has, through exposure and research, reached a level of experience unattainable for the reader. Indeed, as the chapters unfold, his ostensible goal of initiating the reader is quickly abandoned, the whimsical and friendly persona replaced by a rebarbative guide who pointedly differentiates himself from his reader with his knowledge, exploits, and anticipatory nostalgia. Indeed, Hemingway's persistent demarcation of himself from the reader eventually comes to organize the presentation of information, and inform its strikingly different combination of approaches to his subject matter. In this, I identify the tauromachian logic of which Hemingway wrote to Perkins; the hapless but intrigued reader will be lured into the book by Hemingway's cape (his illustrative photographs, anecdotes, descriptions, and digressions) but then expelled from the ring by a rhetorical strategy of exclusion.

Hemingway begins this process of rejection when he submits that a person's capacity for *afición* will not be enhanced by instruction; in his view, a reader's position among the elect will be revealed at the first fight the reader watches. He argues the point with recourse to his own firsthand experience: "However I feel about the horses emotionally, I felt the first time I saw a bullfight; there are simply those who can appreciate it and those who cannot."[49] He sets limits to what he will be able to achieve in his project; indeed, he, in a sense, devalues his treatise as the majority of readers will presumably not yet have seen a bullfight, and will not know what their immediate reactions will look like, in addition to the fact that *afición* is far from a given. This logic courses throughout *DIA*, culminating in the "Some Reactions" section of the appendix, in which he pointedly illustrates what immediate reactions to the practice can reveal about a spectator's potential for *afición*.

The question of *afición* runs throughout *DIA*. Following Hemingway's logic, although his book is intended to serve as an exposition of the *corrida*, a reader might nevertheless prove incapable of profiting from it. He explains *afición* by analogizing it with wine connoisseurship. As is the case with wine, he argues, repeated exposure to the bullfight might reward the spectator with a deeper and more sophisticated appreciation, but only if his initial response is favorable: "A person drinking, not tasting or savoring but *drinking*, wine for the first time will know, although he may not care to taste or be able to taste, whether he likes the effect or not and whether or not it is good for him."[50] This analogy is returned to throughout the treatise as Hemingway frequently references his alcohol consumption; like Barnes, his *afición* is complemented by alcohol and other illicit pleasures. Prohibition had begun in 1920 and ended in 1933, one year after the publication of *DIA*. The passage analogizing *afición* with wine connoisseurship ushers in one of the principal characteristics of *DIA*: the inclusion of subjects other than bullfighting, an inclusion seemingly designed to startle the reader, while also foregrounding the breadth of Hemingway's ken. When, in the course of his exposition, he refers to other activities, be it hunting, sexual intercourse, or downing drinks at a speakeasy, it is with the tone of a seasoned veteran. "Do not look for beautiful women on the stage, in the brothels or the canta honda places," he advises the reader, casually intimating his acquaintance with the Spanish underworld.[51] His wide field of knowledge is legitimized and confirmed as its origins are in repeated experience. This logic subtends *DIA*; Hemingway's knowledge of Spain is unique, he suggests, in that it is culled from bars, brothels, cafés, and chance confidences. As an outcome of election, good fortune, and felicitous timing, Hemingway displays knowledge of subjects other than Spain, Spanish customs, and the bullfight, although his knowledge necessarily includes these things.

Hemingway teases his anticipated readership for its presumed inability to comprehend the stakes and importance of essential elements of the event. He suggests that this presumed inability is due, at least in part, to a lack of knowledge of the Spanish language while, at the same time, repeatedly signaling his own mastery of Spanish. The critical role played by Hemingway's understanding of Spanish, a complement to his *afición*, is clearest in the lengthy glossary. Extensive and detailed narratives telegraph Hemingway's view that translation is not merely the practice of finding equivalent words in English for Spanish ones; indeed, he moves quickly beyond the traditional literal versus paraphrastic dichotomy, implicitly claiming that no equivalent of any description exists for these Spanish words in the English language or, perhaps more significantly, in the American experience. The Spanish words included in the glossary indicate a way of life and a way of doing things; there is a word that indicates "the predominant sensation at a bad fight," and a word that expresses "the amount of popularity a bullfighter has in any locality."[52] In Hemingway's philosophy of language, different languages permit a person to mean unique things; each language can, in principle, convey things that other languages cannot, even when the same concept or thing is at stake. Such an approach to language is echoed in Hemingway's later writing as well. In his Spanish Civil War novel *For Whom the Bell Tolls* (1940), for instance, Robert Jordan decides that the word "dead" does not entirely line up with its "equivalents" in other languages: "Take dead, *mort, muerto,* and *todt. Todt* was the deadest of them all."[53] Hemingway is always attentive to the valences of the word in its original language and the inadequacy of "equivalents."

Defining the word *suerte* "according to the dictionary" early in *DIA*, Hemingway theorizes that:

> Suerte is an important word in Spanish. It means, according to the diction-
> ary; Suerte, f., chance, hazard, lots, fortune, luck, good luck, haphazard;
> state, condition, fate, doom, destiny, kind, sort; species, manner, mode,
> way, skillful manœuvre; trick, feat, juggle, and piece of ground separated
> by landmark. So the translation of trial or manoeuvre is quite arbitrary, as
> any translation must be from the Spanish.[54]

His solution in the glossary is to couch words in lived experience through stories and anecdotes. His definitions are often normative. In one telling example, he notes that *al alimón,* a particular pass in bullfighting, is used only to appease a naïve public. In line with his valorization of normative masculinity in the treatise, he, in another entry, advises that a good matador should possess *cojones* ("testicles"), although a cowardly matador might not. At times entries explicitly reference Hemingway's personal encounter with Spain and the bullfight. An exemplary entry is the one for *tacones* or "heels." Hemingway offers a literal translation of the word, but the entry is primarily a venomous diatribe about an ambulatory heel "ripper"; it documents the specific tricks of one particular Catalan heel-thief, whose right cheek Hemingway claims to have permanently scarred: "There is one sinister-faced Catalan heel ripper whom you can identify at all the ferias by a scar on his right cheek. I gave him that, but he is more of a dodger by now and you might have difficulty landing him."[55] The word *tacones* thus indicates, not only an equivalent word, but also an outsized act of retaliatory violence on Hemingway's part. If Hemingway is indeed telling a true story, it is a story about carrying out a vendetta in an extremely disproportionate way that suggests—despite the paean to Spain that is *DIA*—his assurance that he, presumably due to his American citizenship, will not face consequences for his violent act. (By recognizing this I do not necessarily judge by the terms of today; I simply point out what must be said).

By means of such personal entries, the glossary also becomes life writing; Hemingway effectively widens the definition of the word glossary. A number of the glossary entries are not even present as words in the body of the book; they are incorporated on their own merit, replete with personal anecdotes. The reader who uses the glossary only for consultation will thus miss several more of these entries that foreground Hemingway as much as they foreground Spain and the *fiesta de los toros* [bullfighting spectacle]. These entries emerge as a minor genre, a genre not of the book, but within the book. Stylistically, glossary entries deviate from the expository style that dominates the main body of the book. Hemingway suggests that writing involves a compromise between readerly expectations and the bold truth; the glossary appears as a kind of fruit of this compromise. Ultimately, however, he seeks to foil those readerly expectations, and the glossary further contributes to his rhetoric of exclusion. Indeed, the formal heterogeneity of the glossary contributes further to our overall sense that Hemingway's apparent aim is paradoxical; he wants both to initiate and reject the reader. His proprietary attitude towards his own apprenticeship leads to entries that telegraph exclusivity, just as they demonstrate his expertise; as much as they foreground Hemingway's command of the Spanish language, glossary entries foreground the formative events that led to what he presents as a deep and unbeatable knowledge of the practice and culture of the bullfight.

The glossary is also a place for elaboration and commentary that he began in the main body of the book; in this way, the glossary is also expansive and performs a nuancing and clarifying function. This is clear, for instance, in his discussion of male homosexuality. Indeed, an instructive place to tie words in the main body of the text to the glossary is given with a derogatory Spanish word for a gay man, *maricón*. In the main body of the book, Hemingway first uses the word in a discussion of Goya and El Greco and continues to elaborate:

> One time in Paris I was talking to a girl who was writing a fictionalized life of El Greco and I said to her, 'Do you make him a maricón?'
> 'No,' she said. 'Why should I?'
> 'Did you ever see more classic examples anywhere than he painted? Do you think that was all accident or do you think all those citizens were queer? The only saint I know who is universally represented as built that way is San Sebastian [*sic*]. Greco made them all that way. Look at the pictures. Don't take my word for it.'[56]

Hemingway's innuendo about El Greco's depiction of men is at first an insult, as he has compared him less favorably to Goya. However, further on, Hemingway describes telling the "girl" that El Greco can function to redeem literature by gay people, viciously pillorying a diverse canon of gay authors for their sexuality, as much as what he suggests are literary characteristics particular to gay men:

> If he was one, he should redeem, for the tribe, the prissy exhibitionistic, aunt-like, withered old maid moral arrogance of a Gide; the lazy, conceited debauchery of a Wilde who betrayed a generation; the nasty, sentimental pawing of humanity of a Whitman and all of the mincing gentry. Viva El Greco El Rey de los Maricónes [sic]. [The King of Maricones]'[57]

The extreme cruelty and homophobia of the above passage is amplified by the glossary where *maricón* gets a robust entry that routes the word throughout the concerns of the Spanish bullfight:

> *Maricón*: a sodomite, nance, queen, fairy, fag, etc. They have these in Spain too, but I only know of two of them among the forty-some matadors [sic] de toros. This is no guaranty that those interested parties who are continually proving that Leonardo da Vinci, Shakespeare, etc., were fags would not be able to find more.[58]

Expanding the word's meaning with a litany of derogatory "equivalences," Hemingway marshals his claims about bullfighters toward a theory of normative masculinity. The notion of "hegemonic masculinity" is relevant here, as are reminders from masculinities studies that "male privilege" must also contend with what is shut out, in this case, non-heterosexual men, a perhaps inadvertent reminder that masculinity is a hegemonic social construct. What is clear is that the glossary functions here like a second gasp of animosity, a digging deeper. And Hemingway, in the glossary, a self-proclaimed possessor of *afición*, stakes out Spaniards as equally biased as himself, and suggests that his own prose is likewise masculine.[59]

One of the other ways in which Hemingway seeks to prove his expertise in the Spanish language is by translating Spanish dialogue into non-idiomatic English. This can be seen in the glossary's "translation" of the word for *cartel*: "For instance, you ask a friend in the business, 'What cartel have you in Malaga?' 'Wonderful; in Malaga no one has more cartel than me. My cartel is unmeasurable.'"[60] In this example, the original Spanish is palpable in the translated sentences' language-specific deviation from Standard English and its retention of Spanish syntax. Hemingway's practice of translating (or seeming to translate) from Spanish into non-idiomatic English is "foreignizing" in Lawrence Venuti's terms. Drawing on the German late-Enlightenment thinker Friedrich Schleiermacher's own theory of translation (1813), Venuti proposes that translators adopt a "foreignizing method" that will "register the linguistic and cultural differences of the foreign text, sending the reader abroad."[61] Such translations highlight the foreignness of the original (the "source text") by signaling differences between the original and the dominant target language/culture.

Hemingway also foreignizes his translations by peppering his non-idiomatic translation with easily comprehensible Spanish words, just as he does in all of his Spanish fiction: "What do I want with exercise, hombre?"[62] Highly non-idiomatic overall, Hemingway's Spanish-in-English, as Gayle Rogers argues—looking more specifically at Hemingway's *For Whom the Bell Tolls*—"alternately absorbed and alienated generations of critics and readers," with such sentences that contain Spanish and/or followed Spanish syntax.[63] Similarly, Laura Lonsdale also wonders if the inclusion of Spanish and the English with Spanish in *For Whom the Bell Tolls* has not "perhaps alienated more readers than it has won over."[64] I will not speculate on this or relitigate it; I will also put to the side the issue of Hemingway's command of Spanish, something Rogers diminishes, suggesting that Spanish is a "language he knew partially," albeit one that served as "the grounds for his practice of creative translation and composition."[65] Even while acknowledging flaws in his written Spanish, Lonsdale suggests that Hemingway "had a fine ear for language, especially linguistic nuance" that led to "great subtlety in his semantic and syntactic incorporation of it into English."[66] Indeed, what is important about Hemingway's translations from Spanish is not necessarily their accuracy, but rather the ways in which they are marshaled towards a specific aesthetics of translation. Juliette Taylor-Batty, looking more specifically at Jean Rhys's work as an instantiation of a modernist aesthetic, writes relevantly of "translational style" in Rhys's Paris fiction, also dating from the interwar period:

> [T]ranslation becomes part of the compositional process [. . .] challenging the very boundaries between translation, adaptation and original composition. [. . .] Rhys's style is characterized not only by an effective creolisation of French and English, but by a frequent and disquieting sense of being 'already translated,' of being derived from some absent 'original' source text and language.[67]

Following Taylor-Batty, I argue that it is the work that the Spanish words or expressions and non-idiomatic translations do overall that is more important than the difficult-to-adjudicate question of linguistic mastery. Hemingway uses Spanish and Spanish syntax in the service of "translated style."

Hemingway's often aggressive rejection of readers, indeed his entire strategy of exclusion, is further complicated in chapter seven with the introduction of an imagined reader and interlocutor, whom he refers to as the "Old lady." At the same time, he introduces a character named "the author," with whom she will converse. The author, whose exact relationship with Hemingway, the narrator, is never clarified, will converse with her for nine chapters during which he will also outline the basic rules of the bullfight, as well as the *fiesta de los toros* overall. The Old lady performs a pedagogical role to the extent that she will ask the author the questions that a reader might also pose. To that extent, the inclusion of the Old lady also vouchsafes him an opportunity to respond to possible objections to his book. Indeed, throughout *DIA*, Hemingway defends his book from the criticism he anticipates from both critics and nonprofessional readers.

The Old lady is selected as an interlocutor after a staged interview with her and four unnamed men; like them, she has just attended her first bullfight. She is the only one among them who has enjoyed the bullfight, even the goring of the horses; due to this, she is invited to converse with the author about it. The reader learns little more about the Old lady than that she is American, unaccompanied, and an avid reader of popular literature. As she has enjoyed the spectacle even at its most violent moments, she appears to have a strong potential for *afición*. She will nevertheless be tossed out of the book in chapter sixteen, with no more knowledge about Spain, the *fiesta de los toros*, or writing—about which Hemingway, in the guise of "the author," will discourse for many of the chapters that include her—than when she first appeared in the book. At the very same time that she serves as an explanatory tool, she also functions as a foil to once again demonstrate that Hemingway's knowledge of the bullfight is singular and unattainable. Furthermore, when she is first introduced, the author invites her to Café Fornos in order to "discuss these matters at leisure."[68] However, he then interrupts their first dialogue with an aside, implying that the real discussion will not be with her: "We can discuss the fight, if you wish, and the Old lady can sit and look at the bullfighters."[69] The Old lady is distinct from this "we" who will discuss the bullfight. Although the author has only one concrete interlocutor in *DIA*, he appears to consider readers as interlocutors, however one-sided their dialogue.

The Old lady is described as a hypocritically pious woman, secretly drawn to the more salacious aspects of the spectacle, just as she hides her prurient curiosity behind humanistic homilies. By means of the Old lady, Hemingway registers not only his pervasive hostility towards the reader, but also his struggle with the elder generation—note that "old" is capitalized when he writes about the "Old lady"—embodied by his vitriolic rejection of New Humanist philosophy. The nine chapters in which the Old lady appears distinguish between ideal bullfights and the decadent kind, which, Hemingway explains, were pioneered at the beginning of the twentieth century by Juan Belmonte, a matador whose short legs led him to invent a style of fighting that privileged aesthetically rich cape work at the expense of dramatic and risky killing. The chapters also celebrate the globally dangerous life of the ideal matador from the ring to the bedroom; "*Más cornadas dan las mujeres*"—women gore more often than the bulls— goes the Spanish proverb Hemingway refers to repeatedly. Hemingway's philosophy of the *corrida* equates authenticity with danger and bravado; matadors risk venereal disease because syphilis is "a disease of all people who lead lives in which a disregard of consequences dominates."[70] The author-as-Hemingway submits that such disregard of consequences sets brave men apart, thereby fostering an elite. The author explains, in diction that is both archaic and rhythmic, the significance of danger for the kind of masculinity he praises: "Ah madame," the author explains, changing his register from vernacular to classic, "you will find no man who is a man who will not bear some marks of past misfortune."[71]

Robert Weber defends Hemingway's nonfiction from widespread contemporaneous criticism that he tries to cram too much into it. He turns to *SAR* to explain that the writerly approach of the fiction echoes Jake's contention that you'll lose it if you talk about it, whereas a spirit of generosity characterizes his nonfiction in which he openly provides information.[72] Yet, although *DIA* does indeed offer a quasi-encyclopedic amount of information pertaining to Spain and the practice and culture of the bullfight, coupled with nearly a hundred photographs with thoroughly detailed captions, it nevertheless echoes Barnes's disinclination to share. The tension between keeping the secret and explicitly explaining the bullfight is tangible in the author's reluctant and ill-tempered elucidation of the very information the treatise is, on the surface at least, meant to offer and explain. Such reluctance bodes ill for the curious Old lady. Indeed, the author meticulously registers her responses to his writing as he goes along, but he affords her no concomitant growth in knowledge. Hemingway's decision to include an obstinate reader is clearly strategic; from chapter to chapter, she plainly illustrates what he has all along been suggesting is the profound and insuperable difference between *aficionado* and non-*aficionado*, and, as becomes progressively clear, between the seasoned author and the belated reader.

Except for her gender and age, the Old lady remains generalized, as if she reflects a group sensibility; she makes occasional use of the first-person plural, as when she thanks the author for his unexpurgated explanation of bull seeding: "No one could say, sir, you place the facts in any but a straightforward Christian way and we find them most instructive."[73] In chapter sixteen the author announces her departure from the book: "She's gone. We threw her out of the book, finally. A little late you say. Yes, perhaps a little late."[74] However, the Old lady's rejection was apparent much earlier in the frequently anthologized excursus that ends chapter twelve: "A Natural History of the Dead." In this dramatized encounter, Hemingway, in the guise of "the author," offers the metafictional piece to the Old lady as a substitute for the dialogue that she enjoys but with which he has grown bored. "A Natural History of the Dead" is presented as something being written in real time, with the result that the Old lady will read along as the author continues to write what is, in effect, his answer to her demand for something "amusing yet instructive."[75] He offers her a graphic description of a bombed battlefield, which leads him to suggest war as a new field for natural history. In doing so, he takes a stab at Humanist philosophy, implying that nothing in that philosophy could explain or accommodate what he has seen and described. "A Natural History of the Dead," a darkly vivid account of one man's wartime experience, foregrounds, once again, the logic of an authenticity and an authority won by hardship. "The author" makes use of his experience to exclude both the Old lady and the reader.

In "A Natural History of the Dead," the author examines the clockwork argument for God advanced by nineteenth-century adventurer Mungo Park. Dying of starvation and thirst in an uncharted and uninhabited part of Africa, Park experienced a renewal of his faith and hope while contemplating a moss flower, reasoning that such a beautiful flower blooming in the wilderness necessarily implied a beneficent creator. The author suggests that such clockwork arguments—depending as they do on the belief that the universe is guided by a divine plan centered on human beings—are another casualty of the First World War: "One wonders what that persevering traveler, Mungo Park, would have seen on a battlefield in hot weather to restore his confidence."[76] With nothing to reassure him, and in defiance of Humanist philosophy's insistence on man's nobility, the author seeks instead to explore "what inspiration we may derive from the dead," offering a suitably gruesome depiction of the aftermath of a munitions factory explosion in Mina, Italy, that killed every woman inside.[77] The author draws particular attention to the sight of the female dead: "The sight of a dead woman is quite shocking," he writes, implicating the Humanist Old lady by including women in his depiction of a war theater.[78] His description of the female dead is particularly graphic: "It [was] amazing that the human body should be blown into pieces which exploded along no anatomical lines, but rather divided as capriciously as the fragmentation in the burst of a high explosive shell."[79] He registers particular alarm at the sight of women without hair: "In those days women had not yet commenced to wear their hair cut short [. . .] and the most disturbing thing, perhaps because it was the most unaccustomed, was the presence and, even more disturbing the occasional absence of this long hair."[80]

"A Natural History of the Dead" dips into metafiction when the author, using the conceit of a "present time" composition, foregrounds the difficulty of writing due to interruptions by the Old lady, whom he accuses of disrupting him with inane questions and demands as he writes. He expresses his annoyance in a frank manner: "Be patient, can't you? It's very hard to write like this."[81] The author's frustration with the Old lady plainly illustrates his distaste for writing for an audience he presumes devoid of *afición*. He excuses himself for his combativeness by suggesting that it is the inevitable result of writing for a nonideal reader.

The Old lady is not the first woman in Hemingway's oeuvre to appreciate the Spanish bullfight. In *SAR*, Jake, as I noted above, has *afición* and is able to understand the bullfight. He initiates Brett into it, and she is immediately enraptured. He lets her watch and discusses it with her afterwards: "I sat beside Brett and explained to her what it was all about."[82] Brett effortlessly understands the fight; indeed, she initially appears to bear the mark of election shared by aficionados and has already intuited what Jake explains to her. In a rhythmic paragraph, Jake describes her seamless initiation, alternating between "Brett saw how" with "I told her how."[83] But Jake merely provides the words for the aesthetic that Brett already understands by means of immediate feeling: "She saw why she liked Romero's capework and why she did not like the others."[84] Brett is a potential *aficionada* both because of her initial appreciation of the spectacle and because of her uncanny capacity to detect its nuances and stakes. She is a complicated precursor to the Old lady. She is less naïve, more appealing, and more masculine according to the codes of masculinity in the 1920s. She has a man's name and a tough sensibility; she is aloof in character, substituting her title "Lady Ashley" with her masculine first name, aspiring to become one of the "chaps." She is also self-motivated; she will find out herself what Jake will not tell her. Unlike the Old lady, she will get first-hand information about the erotic elements of the *corrida de toros*, albeit with disastrous results.

Montoya silently disapproves of Jake's friends; he is particularly upset when they engage with the bullfighters he hosts at his hotel. Unlike his coterie, Jake is identified as one with *afición* and he knows this: "He always smiled as though bull-fighting were a very special secret between the two of us; a rather shocking but really very deep secret that we knew about [. . .] as though there were something lewd about the secret to outsiders [. . .] It would not do to expose it to the people who would not understand."[85] Part of *afición* is, as this passage indicates, the capacity to silently identify fellow aficionados; language is downplayed as a useful medium for sharing information. Likewise, in *DIA*, the Old lady is instructed verbally and without profit. Unlike Brett, she is never cast as one of the elect, and appears an odd choice to help explain the bullfight and provide dialogue. Her questions reveal that her interest in the bullfight is misguided. A sexual motivation is attributed to the Old lady, who "never discusses things she has enjoyed even with her most intimate friends."[86] Her silence is not the guarded and respectful silence of an *aficionada*; it is rather the prurient flipside of prudishness.

As I have demonstrated, the hostility towards readers manifest in "A Natural History of the Dead" is mirrored throughout *DIA* towards other contemporary writers and critics. The final five chapters in particular intersperse lessons about bullfighting and writing with various forms of score settling. This is particularly pronounced in chapter sixteen, the final chapter including the Old lady: it contains the celebrated iceberg theory of literature, which advocates understatement. Taking aim at his fellow writers, he professes that specialization is ruining writing, just as it is ruining the *corrida*. Just as he maintains that aesthetic concerns should be secondary for *toreros*, he also suggests that they should be secondary when writing. As in good bullfighting, aesthetic concerns should not determine a work of writing: "Prose is architecture, not interior decoration, and the

Baroque is over."[87] Hemingway understands literary inheritance as an agonal process; only through unique experiences and knowledge does a writer
transcend his precursors and learn what he must take with him and what
he must "take his departure from."[88] Of the utmost service for the writer
is knowledge; a good writer will omit information, but he must nevertheless be knowledgeable about what he omits. The writer's purview should
be global and unlimited: "A good writer should know as near everything
as possible [. . .] but he should only show a part of what he knows."[89] The
iceberg is the model for this approach; it protrudes gracefully because only
one-eighth of it shows.

Despite his articulation of an aesthetic goal defined by omission, in
chapter twenty, the final chapter of the book, it is precisely the remaining
seven-eighths, all of the things Hemingway did not include, that dominate; in nine pages, he explicitly registers all of the things he omitted in the
first nineteen chapters. He both identifies and apologizes for these omis-
sions, draining the figurative water to expose the rest of the iceberg. In his
view, his lengthy but much-edited book is a reduced version of what he had
hoped to create. He avows his disappointment with the end result in the
first sentence of the final chapter: "If I could have made this enough of a
book it would have had everything in it."[90] The pages that follow Hemingway's admission of failure detail what he means by "everything"; the chapter, full of anecdotes, is a wide-reaching paean to Spain and the bullfight
and to his youthful days in Spain. Hemingway remarks that these detailed
anecdotes "should" be in the book but are not. Such repeated paralipsis in
chapter twenty contributes to the overall tension in *DIA* between inclusion and omission, between invitation and rejection. Certainly the latter
dynamic shifts in the elegiac chapter; now it is Hemingway's own failure if
the reader did not get everything he should have out of the book. He ends
the chapter, and thus the book, with a soupçon of defensiveness: "No. It is
not enough of a book, but still there were a few things to be said."[91] The author's aggressiveness mutates into nostalgic humility in the final chapter,
even if the past here wears a distinctly ideological face.

As demonstrated, the pronoun "we" makes scant appearance in *DIA*
overall. Hemingway privileges the "I" that experiences and vests it with
authority. In chapter twenty the pronoun "we" is used mainly in his nostalgic account of Spain; he makes use of it when recounting distinct experiences, for instance: "the Cathedral at Santiago and in La Granja, where we
practiced with the cape."[92] "We" is used to register the pathos of an aging

generation; in chapter twenty, "we" is associated with youth and an un-
spoiled Spain. By this logic, it is in retrospect that a group or a generation
becomes "we"; only by looking backwards at a presumably unrecoverable
past does "we" become "all of us ourselves as we were then."[93] Both "I" and
"we" are used as cudgels to further carve out the inevitable gulf between
author and reader on the basis of experience; as I have demonstrated repeatedly, Hemingway, with the tool of anticipatory nostalgia, makes the
uniqueness of his experience one of the principal stories he tells. Once
again, due to this emphasized gulf, he gestures to a possible failed initiation for the reader.

Hemingway shifts quickly between pronouns in *DIA*. One sentence
from an anecdote in chapter five shares two pronouns: "Seeing the sun rise
is a fine thing. As a boy, fishing or shooting, or during the war you used to
see it rather regularly; then, after the war, I do not remember seeing it until
Constantinople."[94] Following the semicolon, Hemingway foregrounds the
exclusive experience the war has afforded him; he moves from a widely
shared experience to a more rare one. By means of a shifting pronoun,
Hemingway telegraphs the rejection of fellowship characteristic of the entire book. The insistence that certain kinds of experiences are unrepeatable
is—as I submitted with respect to Kessel and Leiris in the last chapter—so
familiar a trope in travel writing overall that it might be overlooked. Yet
it is exactly the difference between the "I" in *DIA* and its projected reader
that allows for its unique structure. Hemingway's persistent attention to
the bullfight's decline, and to irrevocable changes in Spain, functions to
defend his authority when he describes earlier visits to Spain; not only
does he perforce know more than the reader, he also knows more than
the reader can ever hope to know. Furthermore, he requires an audience
whose comparative poverty of experience he can highlight to the point
that his treatise on bullfighting is, in part, a referendum on the reader.

As I have argued, Hemingway maps his hostility to his reader onto his
hostility with tourists, whom, due in equal parts to their financial power
and their boorishness, he credits with both the capacity and power to destroy the Spanish bullfight by bending it to their whims: "The bullfight is a
Spanish institution; it has not existed because of the foreigners and tourists,
but always in spite of them and any step to modify it to secure their approval,
which it will never have, is a step towards its complete suppression."[95] The
very people who will read his book are potential agents in the destruction
of the Spanish bullfight. Yet, to the extent that readers-as-tourists threaten

his beloved spectacle, they also afford him the possibility of anticipatory nostalgia, his point of departure in chapter twenty, and yet one more way in which he will emphasize his experiential advantage over them.

In her own anatomy of nostalgia, Svetlana Boym identifies two types of contemporary nostalgia: reflective nostalgia and restorative nostalgia. I classify Hemingway's anticipatory nostalgia as reflective to the extent that it eschews any attempts to rebuild a shattered past and instead "lingers on ruins, the patina of time and history, in the dreams of another place and another time."[96] In *DIA*, Hemingway puts particular pressure on the simple, indeed obvious, point that the world described in the book can be gestured at, but never entirely reconstructed. He insists that the spectacle's decline must mean that the reader will never see an ideal fight. Albeit in a hostile fashion, Hemingway acknowledges that he is participating in a long tradition with his backwards-looking gaze: "Historians speak highly of all dead bullfighters," he admits, just as he admits that bullfighting "has always been considered by contemporary chroniclers to be in a period of decadence."[97] Even his four-year-old son Patrick wistfully articulates this logic after watching his second fight: "Quand j'étais jeune la course de taureaux n'était pas comme ça" [Bullfighting wasn't like that when I was young].[98] It is forever late for the traveling writer and always too late for the reader; as I have argued, the rhetoric of belatedness is well worn in Hemingway's anticipatory nostalgia and his related "romance with the past," to borrow a description of reflective nostalgia by Boym.[99] Hemingway continues to acknowledge this logic of belatedness while nevertheless making strategic use of it.

Philip Young, studying Hemingway's nonfiction style, notes in it "a pattern of mannerisms and responses which give an illusion of reality that, in its completeness, reality itself does not give."[100] This is exactly the nature of reflective nostalgia as Boym outlines it: reflective nostalgia is "a meditation on history and the passage of time" that "cherishes shattered fragments of memory and temporalizes space."[101] Allen Josephs notes that the Hemingway of *DIA* is not merely nostalgic for the pre-decadent days of bullfighting, but also for his "discovery of Spain and the Spanish way of life which were best exemplified in *toreo*."[102] It is worthwhile to return to Rosaldo and his firm contention that the change in the meaning of nostalgia in the West is such that "feelings of tender yearning" are not "natural" or "pan-human" and "therefore not necessarily as innocent" as we might imagine.[103] In Rosaldo's view, the tendency to yearn for earlier eras and associate them with youth involves an ideological whitewashing of the occasionally problematic underpinnings of the nostalgic impulse. In this case, I point to Hemingway's own participation in the adulteration of the Spanish bullfight by means of, for instance, frequent visits with a posse of loud and disruptive friends and, if Hemingway's claim is factual, scarring a Spaniard's face, as I analyzed above.

Jean Starobinski has written of modern nostalgia that it designates "the return toward the stages in which desire did not have to take account of external obstacles and was not condemned to defer its realization."[104] Hemingway's nostalgia in *DIA* is, in part, nostalgia for the time before he realized that the fact of his presence at the *fiestas* changed the very atmosphere he so extolled. It is also nostalgia for a time when he was only one of only a small set of foreigners at the *fiesta de toros*, something that, as we have seen so many times, he insists sets him apart from his anticipated readership. In chapter twenty, Hemingway cautions once again that the bullfight is an imperiled spectacle; his readers, like the Old lady, will necessarily arrive belatedly. Hemingway's anticipatory nostalgia is very modern in the sense that he longs for Spain as a non-native; it is, in part, a refusal of his own home. Hemingway longs instead for an adopted home, a temporal elsewhere characterized by immediacy and authenticity. And yet "[m]emory," Hemingway acknowledges as he reflects on the history of bullfighting, "of course is never true."[105]

Hemingway's writing about Spain follows a recipe which privileges unique experience abroad and explicitly antagonizes the reader. *DIA* paradoxically emphasizes the singularity of its author through the description of a community spectacle. His introduction to the communally attended Spanish bullfight rejects both fellow travelers and future readers. *DIA* is both metatravelogue and metafiction; it offers detailed lessons on traveling and writing, yet ultimately invites the reader to do neither, paradoxically initiating the reader into a communal experience with an exclusionary rhetoric. Hemingway introduces an archaic ritual to his Anglophone readership by means of his enormous and innovative treatise; in doing so, he demonstrates a very modern way of thinking about experience and travel, one that echoes the anxious praise of Conrad's consecrators, as well as the work of the confident and whimsical fellow traveling writers whose work I will explore in the following chapter.

In this chapter, I have demonstrated the way in which *Death in the Afternoon* expresses hostility to the reader, much as it privileges authenticity and emphasizes the book's origins in lived experience; I have also called attention to the way in which Hemingway arrogates authority to himself due to such first-hand experience. While it is certainly true that first-hand experience is almost exclusively seen as an advantage when reporting on a place and its people and their customs, Hemingway has promised his readers a guidebook. But if the book will be outdated the moment he finishes, it cannot fulfill its function, as the reader is never invited to the rapidly declining spectacle and is rather told that the book—although it gives out dates, images, and even touts for businesses—will be as useless as it will be useful for him. With its competing gestures, projects, and conceptual markers, *DIA* edges on the philosophically impossible. It is a rejection in the form of an invitation insofar as it suggests that the reader go to Spain while also, frequently and most rebarbatively, reminding his reader that it will, ultimately, not be worth it. It simultaneously seduces and rebuffs. Here we leave off as we began the conversation: with the question of audience. From a philosophical, indeed logical, perspective, we can say that this book has no audience. It is for Hemingway scholars to pursue any biographical or aesthetic factors that might have led to him assuming this writerly stance, but clearly this is something of which there are very few in the history of literature as I know it: a book that suggests that the writer himself demonstrated hated towards what Conrad called, as seen above, his "public." Or perhaps it is better to speak of this in terms of a persona who writes such as to diminish his book's exposition.

Among the many elements of *DIA* that I investigate, the experimental glossary entries, in which synecdoche reigns, yield particular insight into the book's architecture and its commitment to authenticity. In the third chapter, I will likewise explore two interbraided instances of synecdoche in travel writing: the representation of foreign languages and speakers as well as reflections on language, both yielding insight into the quest for authenticity. Moving from Hemingway in Spain to a number of English traveling writers, I will survey this topic, giving particular attention to representations of indigenous peoples and their speech. I will examine how such reflections and representations cast the traveling writer on a quest as a cultural translator as well as, like Hemingway in his glossary, a literal translator. Such a dual approach—one that considers both statements on language and representations of indigenous speech—affords insight into important trends in this literature and illuminates conventions for the questing writer in his guise as a cultural expert and interpreter and arbiter of cultural authenticity. I will explore the way in which these writers echo Hemingway's exclusionary rhetoric in *DIA*, as they use their presumed authority to translate foreign cultures for a home audience.

CHAPTER THREE

"Speaking Native": The Sound of Authenticity

In this chapter, I look at work by Peter Fleming, George Orwell, Robert By-ron, D. H. Lawrence, and both Alec and Evelyn Waugh, in their measure as traveling writers in search of authenticity. Many of these writings, argu-ably part of an as yet unnamed canon, have been addressed in their capac-ity both as literature and political forums in highly convincing ways by, among others, Paul Fussell, Helen Carr, and Bernard Schweizer. However, the crucial role of spoken language in this body of work as a whole has yet to be addressed, although it offers the clearest throughline connecting the work in question. It is a fruitful object of study, one that will permit us to firmly identify steadfast conventions dealing with hardship, authority and authenticity, while also providing particularly fresh insight into the way in which our traveling writers perceived and described the indigenous people they met and spoke with during their travels. I maintain that ideological currents traverse language in a unique way at this time, making possible the richness of an extended study, one that will illuminate the interper-sonal stakes of their quests for authenticity.

In this chapter, I examine both meditations on indigenous language as well as representations of the speech of indigenous peoples, consider-ing ethical and epistemological implications, and identifying norms. I ex-plore a selection of sources from the notable interwar-era English traveling writers listed above in order to determine what kind of speech and what kind of words get included in this literature, from pidgin English to words writers perceive as untranslatable, to dialogue invented by the author for the purpose of entertainment. I question the status of these representa-tions of language and speech and demonstrate how, by and large, they detail a shared search for authenticity in putatively purer and simpler cul-tures. Following the lead of translation theorists who have investigated the commonalities between translators and ethnographers with respect to the goal of interpreting culture, I explore the relationship between representing the speech of indigenous peoples, and claims of cultural knowledge. I ultimately argue that our traveling writers, in their role as cultural translators, were prone to a tendentious interpretation of foreign cultures that so often, in the writers' search for authenticity, emphasized difference at the expense of engagement. What I ultimately find in nearly all of the works under consideration, is a normative "primitivism," as well as a singularist notion of language that casts any form of translation as inadequate.

These writers are united by era, high coincidence of literary style, and privilege. Most of them were graduates of notable secondary schools and universities and none of their trips were inhibited, with the exception of Lawrence's, by the issue of money. These writers contended with the social and political aftermath of the Great War, a war that contributed in part to what Jed Esty has aptly called the period's "minor-chord lament."[1] Nevertheless, these writers introduced a general levity to their work that clearly distinguished it from Victorian travel narratives and their plots of what Patrick Brantlinger has termed "sheer survival."[2] These traveling writers typically adopted a demotic idiom, one that incorporated several popular linguistic registers including slang, dialect, and, occasionally, profanity. This writing has no special claims on foregrounded narrators, but, as I argued in the introduction, it documents the advent of a traveler persona who combines accounts of travel with confessions and self-deprecating comedic passages. One of the essential elements of these works is the representation of speech by indigenous peoples, whether for the purpose of humor and local color, or else to suggest an insider status. By means of the practically obligatory inclusion of meditations on language, as well as the use of original or translated speech by indigenous peoples in particular, these traveling writers sought both to seize authority and demonstrate expertise. Such representation of language was arguably intended, in part, to satisfy the expectations of a reading public who would presumably find in it both entertainment and a confirmation of the widely held belief that there are insuperable cultural differences between peoples.

The *"mañana"* [tomorrow] and *"Como no, Señor"* [Why not, sir] spoken by his indigenous housekeeper are the two refrains that make D. H. Lawrence's 1927 late-life travel collection *Mornings in Mexico* a contrapuntal composition. *Mornings in Mexico* was written primarily in Oaxaca, Mexico, in the winter of 1924–1925. Oaxaca, of which he gives an account in the first four essays in the collection, represents another time period, another stage in evolution for Lawrence, who sought escape from modern life and industrialization in places where he and his wife Frieda believed they could live more harmoniously with nature. Although Lawrence force-fully expressed his alienation from England, he did not find his desired alternative way of living in Mexico, despite being inspired by a people who, as he saw it, privilege the "spark of contact."[3] In North America, he wrote to Earl Brewster of his search to find "new gods in the flesh," a goal born of his disillusionment with Europe writ large.[4] But Lawrence ultimately found himself ambivalent about a culture in which he saw the struggle for survival mixed with what he perceived as a kind of lethargy. Ultimately, he proposed that American-Indian consciousness is animated by strong nonintellectual currents alien to Western man.

Lawrence's untranslated "*Como no?*" [why not] and "*mañana*" suggest a people who rarely think beyond an eternal present: "*Mañana*, to the na-tive, may mean tomorrow, three days hence, six months hence, and never. There are no fixed points in life, save birth and death, and the fiestas. The fixed points of birth and death evaporate spontaneously into vagueness."[5] Untranslated speech undergirds Lawrence's leaning toward what he per-ceives and values as primitivism, and gives it a voice, and an "inevitable answer."[6] Rosalino, the young man employed by the Lawrences as a guide, is singled out to stand for Indian consciousness. "*Quién sabe, Señor?*" [Who knows, sir?] is how Rosalino responds to a question about their loca-tion.[7] Rosalino's aloofness and apparent lack of interest prompts Lawrence to generalize: "It is not becoming to a man to know these things.—Among the Indians it is not becoming to know anything, not even one's own name."[8] When Rosalino responds with "*Como no, Señor?*" to Lawrence's query about his desire to visit neighboring villages, he cruelly voices his annoyance by noting that the "Americans would call him a dumb-bell."[9] Later, when they arrive at a neighboring village, Lawrence is struck by the repeated response of "*No hay*" and again generalizes unfavorably: "*No hay* means *there isn't any*, and it's the most regular sound made by the pre-vailing dumb-bells of the land."[10] A definitive "*No hay*" from a village girl prompts Lawrence, eager for fresh fruit, to wager sarcastically that it is "a choice between killing her and hurrying away."[11] Such tendency to general-ize alerts us that, for Lawrence, the representation of the speech of indig-enous peoples can be oppressive, even damaging, at the very time that it is playful and inventive.

Lawrence characterizes Mexicans with a primacy that both intrigues and disappoints him. He finds in them a "complete absence of what we call 'spirit.'"[12] Pondering how Mexicans must see him and Frieda, he refers disparagingly to the European as "the white monkey." However, the Indian consciousness against which he pits it is also described in unfavorable terms. The theme of time is foremost here. In the chapter entitled "The Mozo," Lawrence further examines the difference that he perceives between the Indian's sense of time and the white monkey's sense of time: "The white monkey has curious tricks. He knows, for example, the time. Now to a Mexican, and an Indian, time is a vague, foggy reality. There are only three times, *en la mañana, en la tarde, en la noche*: in the morning, in the afternoon, in the night. There is even no midday, and no evening." Lawrence contrasts this with the "white monkey," whose days are "a horrible puzzle of exact spots of time."[13] Again, the Spanish words indicating time are left untranslated, with the implication that they are untranslatable. For the Mexican, in this view, time is not unique; each day replays the same structure and, Lawrence implies, there is no English equivalent for the Spanish words that convey this stasis. Later, in the same chapter, he writes of what he sees as the Mexican's lack of interest in money and again concludes that Mexicans live in some form of eternal present: "Strip away memory, strip away forethought and care; leave the moment, stark and sharp and without consciousness, like the obsidian knife. The before and after are the stuff of consciousness. The instant moment is forever keen with a razor-edge of oblivion, like the knife of sacrifice."[14] Lawrence signals the Mexican's orientation towards the instant moment by means of the untranslated Spanish terms that abound in the collection. He explicitly foregrounds language as one of the chief markers of cultural difference. By this logic, it is through mastering these Spanish words that he can, in part, buttress his belief that he has mastered the culture as well on his quest for authenticity.

The incommensurability that Lawrence saw between European consciousness and Indian consciousness is further explored in the chapter "Indians and Entertainment," where Lawrence makes the more general claim that the "consciousness of one branch of humanity is the annihilation of the consciousness of another branch."[15] Lawrence's account is only one in a series of "impatient acts of travel," yet his disillusion, foregrounded by his use of untranslated Spanish, is particularly characteristic of the disappointment of the prematurely late-life literary nomad as he quested for authenticity and sought to deepen his knowledge of humanity and competing belief systems.[16] Lawrence insisted, generalizing his experience, that to understand the culture, his own consciousness would have to die, as "the life of the Indian, his stream of conscious being, is just death to the white man."[17] Lawrence's response can arguably be understood, in part, as the response of an economically advantaged Englishman feeling shut out of a culture, one who blames his outsider status on what he depicts as insuperable cultural difference.

Alec Waugh had fought in the First World War, and the elation of survival is palpable in *Hot Countries*, his 1930 account of his visits to Tahiti, Siam, and Ceylon, among other tropical locales. Like most of his traveling contemporaries, he held the elder generation responsible for the previous war and for the one that he, among so many others, believed was forthcoming. His former idols were no longer wise and cultivated elders, but monsters complicit in the murder of young men. The putative primitivism that he encountered while traveling offered Waugh, like his fellow travelers, the promise of something different in essence from the Christian civilization that had succumbed to an unthinkingly brutal war. On his quest for authenticity, he favored what he deemed primitive cultures for what he saw as their immediacy and pacificity, as well as their rumored sexual emancipation.

As in Lawrence's *Mornings in Mexico*, in Waugh's *Hot Countries*, there are meditations on the temporalities of exotic locales. A significant example is when Waugh loses his watch in Tahiti: "Hours did not matter. When the sun rose you got up. When the sun was high you siestaed. When the sun sank you began to think of supper."[18] When Waugh fictionalizes autobiography in order to describe a real love affair with a Tahitian woman, he puts particular pressure on the woman's English. When Ray Girling, Waugh's fictionalized lover, wakes up next to a woman, drunk and headed to Tautira in a taxi, she speaks to him, saying, "you tired, you sleep."[19] Later, their fragmented dialogue continues:

"Tired?" She asked, at length.
He nodded. "A little."
"Then we go. You come with me?"[20]

Waugh explains that Tahitians' relaxed attitude to clock time is mirrored in their attitude towards sensual experience. His fictional Englishman leaves the Tahitian woman after a month, arguing that she attaches no particular sentimental feelings to the breakup of their union: "She would weep when he went away but though there is tear-shedding there is no grief upon the Islands."[21] Her identity appears as a reliably homogeneous essence, grounded in the climate of the islands, and manifested in her kind and frank speech. Her depiction as simple and devoid of attachment illustrates the dynamics of their colonial encounter; Waugh's quest for authenticity is, in part, a quest to reassert difference at the very moment of encounter. *Hot Countries*, even the title suggests it, involves a reading of Tahitian culture that emphasizes the "profound" difference between "brown and white," between a sensual people who copulate and a cultivated people who make love.[22] Waugh implicitly suggests that the speech of his Tahitian, much of which is reserved for intimate words, indicates a challenge to bourgeois sexual norms.

Waugh borrows from the library of writings about Tahiti, meeting readerly expectations even as he declares that "The South Seas are terribly *vieux jeu* . . . Long before you get to them you know precisely what you are to find."[23] Yet, it takes him less than a day to conclude that he has found the South Seas paradise, "the Eden of heart's longing [. . .] a fellowship that was uncalculating and love that was not possessive, that was a giving, not a bargaining."[24] His fictionalized Ray Girling praises a world where there are "no possessions" and "nothing that a woman can gain from love-making but love."[25] Overall, Waugh emphasizes what he sees as incommensurability between cultures, even when this leads to him painting Tahitians in a more favorable light than the English. In Martinique, Waugh engages in one of the clichés of translation to argue that one "cannot explain what snow is to a Marquesan."[26] Later he concludes that "[b]etween brown and white there can only be a brief and superficial harmony."[27] Here and elsewhere, Waugh popularizes Lucien Lévy-Bruhl's highly influential distinction between the primitive man and the modern man.

Evelyn Waugh was Alec Waugh's younger brother, and thus equally upper class. He was also one to ridicule the use of English by non-native speakers during his travels. The protofascist published his first travel book, *Labels: A Mediterranean Journal*, in 1930. Like Byron's *Road to Oxiana*, *Labels* is also partly fictional; Waugh did not want to reveal to readers his wife's infidelity, an infidelity that led to them divorcing shortly after his return. Like his brother, he reproduces the pidgin English of various peoples he encounters. He is alert for absurdities, faithfully reporting on a young Neapolitan girl who, after sticking her face into an exhumed corpse, reports that it "smell good."[28] However, his chief innovation is to include in his book the English version of various signs and historical markers in the interest of comedic material. A marker for the Abu Sarga Church, for instance, reads, in part, "cross alladvig Judes [*sic*] who betrayed our Lord" and "wich were are tow nice penals [*sic*] of carved wood."[29] What is most notable is certainly the absence of indigenous language, let alone indigenous people, in his work. That a best-selling travel book of the time could proceed like that, casts an eye on the consumers of travel literature, as well as the traveling writers themselves.

In the introduction, and as I will examine in depth in the subsequent three chapters, I argued that many travel narratives of the interwar period function as one-man shows. Here we see the ramifications of the one-man show; people are not essential in the travel narratives of this era. As for questions of translation, Waugh, an anti-quester, sidesteps them altogether. His work stands in the canon without a meditation on language or a representation of foreign peoples speaking; it is an outlier. Perhaps Waugh has explicitly chosen to leave indigenous people out of his narrative so that he does not have to confront these issues. In any event, as Jonathan Greenberg has argued, "in *Labels* as elsewhere Waugh's writing personality fills the frame."[30] Confrontations with alterity function here to refract the aesthetic and political concerns of Waugh himself; in the end, his explorations of "labels," of travel writers' shibboleths about popular traveling destinations, serves the self-study that characterizes so much of his travel literature and all too often, as I will explore further in the fourth and fifth chapters, casts indigenous peoples as props for a wider mirror of Western culture, as well as his place within that culture.

The example of George Orwell demonstrates that the inclusion of untranslated speech is one of the most significant ways in which the questers for authenticity foregrounded their own experience, particularly the hardship, which—despite the ironic distance from the heroic vocabulary of earlier travel literature—was still, as I have demonstrated with Hemingway, one of the main avenues for authenticity, narrative authority and aesthetic recompense. With respect to the rhetoric of displacement in the twentieth century, Caren Kaplan has noted how "disaffection or alienation as states of mind function as a rite of passage for the 'serious' modern artist or writer."[31] At times, this disaffection and alienation reflects the writer's own volition. George Orwell's 1933 *Down and Out in Paris and London*, although officially titled a "novel," is a semi-autobiographical account of self-imposed poverty in France and England, told as a form of political and sociological reportage. Orwell hoped to change the conservative reader's mind about class inequality by showing him the damage caused by what he perceived as the death of political ideals. Although he cautions at the end of the book that he hasn't seen more than "the fringe of poverty" and hopes readers will find it interesting "in the same way as a travel diary can be interesting," he still claims the authority that comes from hard experience, a claim for which some later critics would take him to task.[32] Critics remain likewise divided over whether Orwell's work occasioned the creation of a more progressive political consciousness for himself as much as for his readers. It is certain that he intended it to; Bernard Schweizer has illustrated the way in which Orwell "portrays his later sufferings in the lower-class contexts of Paris, London, Wigan, and Catalonia as a heroic act of self-sacrifice in the interest of social justice and personal redemption."[33]

Orwell's challenging experience of self-inflicted poverty has a language. His descriptions of life as a dishwasher in Paris are peppered with French. This untranslated French shares a common characteristic. The words he reproduces are, for the most part, slang words by means of which he shows his intimacy with a certain subset of French people. For Orwell, this language is the language of a people and, more significantly, an economic class, which does not shy away from representing things as they are. These untranslated French words suggest the contours of a rough life but also Orwell's intimate engagement with that life, in both its squalor and its freedom. They suggest that Orwell's self-imposed downward mobility has been successful and that he can speak with authority about the social underworld of Paris. Dennis Porter has noted that, for the traveling writer who visits places familiar, through a variety of media, to the general public, the "challenge" is to "prove his self-worth by means of an experience adequate to the reputation of a hallowed site."[34] In an ironic twist, Orwell's downwardly mobile spiral serves as one such adequate experience with respect to the Parisian underworld.

On the first page of *Down and Out in Paris and London*, the landlady of a Parisian slum hotel chastises a female lodger for smashing bugs against the wall of her room; she uses a wide variety of insults which Orwell leaves untranslated: *salope, vache, putain*. These insults do have English equivalents; it is possible and even likely that Orwell was concerned about avoiding the fate of *Lady Chatterley's Lover* and *Ulysses*, and used French to mask what might be seen as unacceptable or obscene language. But Orwell is clearly also emphasizing a caliber of experience by presenting the restaurant worker's world as outside the limits of conventional conversation, conventional morality, and conventional representation. He hopes to share "an object lesson in poverty" by recounting his encounter with the slum "with its dirt and its queer lives."[35] His intimacy with destitution, substance abuse, and sexual liberty, are experiences in France, but also in the French language. He was a bilingual quester.

Orwell uses a combination of untranslated and translated French to portray the other inhabitants of his hotel, in particular its eccentric characters who "lived lives that were curious beyond words."[36] One in particular, a young man named Charlie, tells the guests how he brutalized a prostitute a couple of years before. His account is delivered in translated and untranslated French: "'Figure it to yourselves, *messieurs et dames*! Red carpet on the floor, red paper on the walls, red plush on the chairs, even the ceiling red; everywhere red, burning into the eyes.'"[37] (Orwell's multilingual exposé was intended for a sophisticated readership, one that would be familiar with French). By the inclusion of untranslated French, the reader is called on to remember that this is a Frenchman speaking to other French speakers. His vulgarity and cruelty is summed up by his claim that the events in question took place on "'the happiest day of my life.'"[38] The combination of translated and untranslated French that characterizes Charlie's account roots him effortlessly in the Parisian underworld. And, to the extent that his speech is translated into an elevated register, readers also learn that he is an unusual dweller there.

When Orwell takes a job as a *plongeur*, a dishwasher, his experiences with menial labor are also experiences with the French language. His understanding of the vocabulary of the restaurant signals his insider status there. The reader is treated to a French lesson: "*Débrouillard* is what every *plongeur* wants to be called. A *débrouillard* is a man who, even when he is told to do the impossible, will *se débrouiller*–get it done somehow."[39] Orwell's language lesson, cobbled together from interactions with other staff in the restaurant, suggests that the French can be translated, if not by one word then by many. However, he continues to keep the words in French for the rest of his account of his employment, linking them together with descriptions of a harsh, and therefore authentic, environment where the work is as hard as the chances for getting fired are high. Inevitably incapable of escaping his class and personal privilege, Orwell's untranslated words illustrate the elements of poverty as they were made manifest to a self-described "lower-upper-middle-class" man whose experience, he argued, led him to embrace the tenets of socialism.[40]

The affluent Oxford graduate and anti-quester Peter Fleming makes it clear that the representation of indigenous languages was an acknowledged issue, a problem even; travelers of the interwar period were well aware that they were participating in a tradition. This is particularly true of *Brazilian Adventure* (1933), a travel narrative which Fussell speculates was "perhaps the most popular travel book between the wars."[41] In 1932, Fleming and a few friends traveled for several months in the jungles of central Brazil, without any prior knowledge of Portuguese or any of the indigenous languages spoken there, ostensibly to search for the missing explorer Percy Fawcett. Put broadly, *Brazilian Adventure* is the narrative of the expedition of Fleming and his friends as they travel down Amazonian rivers progressively farther from metropolitan areas. Although the trip was arduous, Fleming, as is his wont, adopts an antiheroic tone in *Brazilian Adventure*. In the first few pages he vows to avoid bombast along with grandiose claims to hardship:

> In treating of the Great Unknown one has a free hand, and my few predecessors in this particular field had made great play with the Terrors of the Jungle. The alligators, the snakes, the man-eating fish, the lurking savages, those dreadful insects—all the paraphernalia of tropical mumbo-jumbo lay ready to my hand. But when the time came I found that I had not the face to make the most of them. So the reader must forgive me if my picture of Matto Grosso does not tally with his lurid preconceptions.[42]

As will be clear, Fleming shares with his contemporary travel writers a tendency to debunk Victorian truisms and break with its traditions, distinguishing himself from other questers for authenticity. Nevertheless, he will conform to a new set of conventions.

Fleming targets Victorian travel writers by using capitals to highlight and deflate the clichés of the genre. He targets the almost mandatory claim by Victorian travel writers that they have mastered the search for "the Real Thing."[43] The writer who uses such vocabulary, he opines, "must lack both shame and humour."[44] He also denigrates the use of untranslated foreign words by previous travel writers:

> From my youth up I have lost no opportunity of mocking what may be called the Nullah (or Ravine) School of Literature. Whenever an author thrusts his ways through the *zareba*, or flings himself down behind the *boma*, or breasts the slope of a *kopje*, or scans the undulating surface of the *chapada*, he loses my confidence.[45]

Fleming suggests that the use of untranslated, italicized words, in addition to being potentially frustrating for the reader, is a tactic for travel writers

hoping to demonstrate authorial expertise and authenticity, "an affecta-
tion not less deplorable than the plastering of one's luggage with foreign
labels."[46] In this he is both in agreement and at odds with his traveling literary contemporaries who use untranslated words while, at the same time,
remaining alert for possible clichés.

And yet Fleming acknowledges that the use of untranslated words is
inevitable, that "self-denial is not altogether possible."[47] He offers three reasons for his decision, despite his own misgivings, to include these words.
The first—and this is a common justification for the inclusion of untranslated words—is that there are words for which he can find no linguistic
equivalent in English. These are, he argues, "impossible to translate," so he
offers a short introduction to these words when he first uses them and then
relies on the reader's memory "as not to repeat the explanation of their
meaning which accompanies their first appearance."[48] He also includes a
glossary where readers can find these words. The second reason for using
untranslated words, he argues, is that words exist for which there is some
form of linguistic equivalence, but the equivalence is either inadequate or
misleading. These untranslated words are thus "words of which a literal
translation is for one reason or another inadequate."[49] Thirdly, and here
Fleming underscores the ludic possibilities of untranslated material, there
are the words which he and his traveling companions decide to adopt—in
the original—in their *own* conversation: "a few words which can be translated perfectly well but which we, in conversation, never did translate."[50]
These are, he opines, the only reasons for which he violates his rule that
"italics should be heard and not seen."[51]

The glossary that ends *Brazilian Adventure* offers descriptions of words
that have no English equivalent because they "denote things unknown
outside Brazil."[52] Fleming has a variety of approaches when defining these
things. The glossary definition of "Mandioca," the cassava root, is defined
through a humorous analogy to home culture; it is a failed version of its
perceived home equivalent, a "disheartened potato."[53] Fleming's lengthy
translation of *mandioca*, with its reach back to England and English cuisine, plays to a home audience and its anticipated sense of humor. Fleming was also evaluative in his glossary; we see this in his translation of
"Mataburro," a game analogous to bridge, but "primitive."[54] Here Fleming
implicitly assumes that there is a widely shared notion of what it means for
something to be primitive and that the reader, while fascinated by other
cultures, understands that he is not primitive himself. The definition
for "Si Dios quize" is "if god wills," and Fleming's additional note to his

translation—"An indispensable rider to all Brazilian statements about the future"—underscores Fleming's claim that Brazilians in toto have a different conception of time.[55] This notion of different cultures functioning with a different sense of time is, as seen above, a frequent trope in this literature; it is often, as I demonstrated with Lawrence and Alec Waugh in particular, paired with broad generalizations about temperament and intellect.

That Fleming echoes his peers in this regard is particularly noteworthy in that he claims to be breaking from the many traditions that he maintains are characteristic of traditional travel narratives. He sees himself engaged in a unique project, one that could mark a break from the past, and create a new tradition. More specifically, he specifies that he will not seek authenticity and narrative authority from hardship:

> The hardships and privations which we were called upon to endure were of a very minor order, the dangers which we ran were considerably less than those to be encountered on any arterial road during a heat wave; and if, in any part of the book, I have given a contrary impression, I have done so unwittingly.[56]

Fleming honors his pledge to avoid making claims of authority and authenticity based on perceived hardships. In many other places in the book as well, he deflates the pretenses of past and contemporary travel writing, as well as his own claims to knowledge. As Tim Youngs has observed, such "assured self-deprecation [. . .] is typical of a strain of male-authored travel texts."[57] Nevertheless, as demonstrated while surveying the glossary entries, he implicitly asserts cultural mastery and is firmly convinced of the precision of his interpretive powers. In this, he does not succeed in distinguishing himself from contemporaneous quests for authenticity.

Robert Byron's travel writing blends comedic personal anecdotes with, among other related topics, art history and archaeology. In *The Road to Oxiana*, published in 1937, Byron, another young Oxford graduate, explores Italy, Palestine, Syria, Iran and, finally, Afghanistan. In general, Byron was ambivalent about colonialism, often critical but also complicit, benefitting from his privilege as an Englishman. Booth has argued that Byron was the most progressive of the English interwar-era traveling writers, maintaining that *The Road to Oxiana* "celebrated the possibilities for cultural renaissance and personal growth that could result from cross-cultural encounters."[58] Nevertheless, Byron takes his representation of indigenous speech in a new direction. Byron's traveling mate, Christopher Sykes, later revealed that the two had spent evenings abroad inventing the dialogue for *The Road to Oxiana*. Indeed, much of the book is fictional. Byron explicitly chooses to speak on behalf of foreign cultures rather than letting individual people speak for themselves. In fact, it is subsequently unclear if the speakers are not also invented along with the dialogue. This was perhaps his way to try and bypass the problems of foreign language and confusion about what to quote, particularly when continuing to write and rework the book for nearly a decade after his trip. The choice is also plausibly strategic, a way to offer the reader a rest from the long passages dealing with history and archaeology. Whatever his reason, these dialogues reveal what Byron thought would succeed with his audience: bizarre encounters and amusing misunderstandings.

In one telling example, they offer a fictional version of a potentially real Afghan ambassador's speech. The goal here is both twofold and single: the irregular grammar and mistakes function to suggest the ambassador's simplicity; they also create entertainment out of that simplicity. Byron's dialogue with the Afghan ambassador in Persia, Shir Ahmad, from whom Byron hopes to get permission to travel, is scored like a musical composition and scripted like a play. Lurking behind linguistic confusion are notions of cultural incommensurability, of people who do not and cannot think as Byron does. The obtuse official demonstrates his personal frustration by alternately shouting and whispering:

> Last year they ask me to go feast at Baladiya, how you say, at Municipality. I go. (*cr*) I go. (*m*) I stand by Mayor. Round him stand all mullahs. There is big crowd. (*cr*) Very big crowd. (*m*). All crowd, all, yes, young mens, old mens, (ff) even officers from Persian army, (*pp*) weep and weep and (*f*) smack chest, so, for remember death of Ali.[59]

Fashioned by two Oxford graduates both abroad and in England, the Afghan ambassador speaks English in a manner that reads like a botched literal translation.

Byron and Sykes do something interesting when representing Byron's own speech. Byron is represented as talking as if he was himself translating from a foreign language as his interlocutor is doing. He also does this, in part, to suggest that the Afghan ambassador cannot understand him unless he speaks in pidgin English, making use only of the present tense and dispensing with articles: "(f) 'So,' I say, 'Arab-men are relation of Ali, but do not weep for remember him. Persians weep, but they are not relation of Ali.'"[60] Byron's English, while speaking with the ambassador, is the English of a person who has only a little knowledge of the language, and reads as if it was translated from another language. For many theorists, writing that sounds like a translation, or is presented as translation, can be considered as such. I argue that the whole invented dialogue, in addition to being a fabrication, is a kind of pseudotranslation. Pseudotranslation permitted Byron to paint cultural misunderstanding in what he saw as a humorous fashion.

We can clearly see here how pseudotranslation functions similarly to translation. Lefevere's call to find out for whom a translator translates is relevant in the case of pseudotranslation as well. Gideon Toury (1995) posits that, in order to convince readers that a pseudotranslation is a translation, authors typically take the expectations of their readership into account. Byron and Sykes' pseudotranslation was for Byron's readership, in the interest of providing an engaging story, but also in the interest of gaining authority. In these translations, which cast the speaking other as amusing and not ruled by common sense, translational issues dealing with transfer across linguistic and cultural boundaries become quickly apparent. In pseudotranslation, just as with translation, the process is charged with significance; by not only depriving the indigenous other, the ambassador, of his own voice but actually giving him one not his own, Byron's pseudotranslation comes up against the same issues of inequality. Brigid Maher has spoken to the ethics of pseudotranslation in such contexts:

> Cultural appropriation is a very real concern in pseudotranslation. By disguising his or her voice as that of a member of another culture, the pseudotranslator is inevitably speaking *for* members of that group. This can be particularly problematic if that culture is underrepresented in public discourse in the target culture and thus has very little voice of its own. One runs the risk of propagating stereotypes, exoticizing the other, or simply drowning out authentic voices.[61]

Despite making use of complex literary techniques, and despite the frank response to a disjointed and fractured postwar reality, both of which led Fussell to declare that *The Road to Oxiana* had much in common with "such other masterpieces in the modern mode of rhetorical discontinuity as *The Waste Land, The Cantos, Ulysses*," Byron reproduced the predictable component of the English travel narrative, the comic native speaker.[62]

Even if, in the extreme case, the ambassador did not exist, we can still ask to what end this translation was created. The pseudotranslated speech meets expectations that the speech reproduced in interwar-era travel literature will be funny and compelling, but also barely adequate for the various situations at hand. As alien as the language may seem, it is a familiar alienness, one that plays to conventions that characterized questers. Examining the practice of pseudotranslation here, we can see that Byron and Sykes clearly saw themselves as belonging to a superior cultural system. Just as pseudotranslated speech can represent indigenous peoples in a comic fashion, pseudotranslation can also function as a strategy of containment, one that asserts the supremacy of the English language by ridiculing its use by a non-native speaker.

By employing similar modes of representing the other, which they thereby also bring into being, the writers I look at reinforce hegemonic theories of culture. They use "foreignizing" methods to represent the speech of indigenous people, but their immediacy is a fiction of power; foreignizing representations and translations can be equally hegemonic, as I demonstrated with Alec Waugh and Robert Byron. Foreignizing appears in their travel narratives as an unusual domesticating tool; it is a making manageable, a strategic recipe for narrative authority, aesthetic gain, and a marketable story. Indigenous people speak in this travel writing, but their translated or untranslated speech is subordinate to narrative and style. The speech that writers choose to represent is similar in theme; it works to suggest a unified culture that can be neatly summed up, understood, and mastered by the traveling writer in search of authenticity. Words are pinned to contexts with the quixotic understanding that there are discrete cultures whose various parts unproblematically mirror the whole, where an untranslated word can authorize a foray into cultural analysis and speculation. The differences among the heterogeneous groupings and interests that comprise any collective of people, and complicate any simple narrative about it, are typically repressed. Individual selections of language, translated, untranslated, and pseudotranslated, are summarized, analogized, and generalized as representing cultural mentalities.

Overall, this study confirms Toury's assertion that translation, both cultural and linguistic, is a rule-based activity, a cultural behavior that is guided by shared norms. Travel alone is still group travel: these writers shared their methods and manner of representing indigenous peoples and their languages; their determined search for authenticity and authority in foreign climes entailed tacit commitment to contradictory notions about masculinity, empire, and intercultural contact. The close relationship between translation and colonization is highly apparent in many of these writers' commitment to establishing cultural expertise and even dominance; indeed, I have identified ways in which translation is part of a relationship of domination in which the traveling writer searches for confirmations of difference instead of commonalities. The analysis of translation in this context contributes to our understanding of the complicated ethics and epistemology of travel and any claims about understanding a subjugated or differently advantaged culture, particularly in its entirety.

This study of representations of indigenous speech, as well as meditations on language, has shown us how the writers in question have navigated the complexities of the power relations involved in quests for authenticity via travel. It furthers our understanding of how they conceptualize foreign cultures and how they understand their relationship to the indigenous people they encounter on their travels. They were at once retrograde and forward-looking, belated and modern; they trafficked in new and experimental approaches while still beholden to traditional beliefs. The questing traveling translators traveled with their preconceptions and translated (or did not translate) accordingly. To that extent, however, they foresee the day when much travel writing, mirroring the (then) nascent field of ethnography, explicitly turned the telescope back onto the traveler, acknowledging his limited interpretive powers, highlighting the relativity of his cultural knowledge, and making transparent his privileged vantage point.

In this chapter, I have illustrated how a small canon of English traveling writers adopted the role of cultural translator, sharing conventions for representing the language and speech of the indigenous people they encounter. Making use of key concepts from the field of translation studies, I have given particular address to the issue of transferring meaning, whether of a word or of a culture, to a home audience expecting anomalies and surprises. This angle of approach is productive and brings new insight into the representation of foreignness in these works, ultimately identifying conventions that speak to a tendentious interpretation of a number of cultures at the heart of quests for authenticity. In the following chapters, I analyze a wide range of writing about travel in sub-Saharan Africa from a variety of traditions. These works will give us specific insight into the role of sub-Saharan Africa in our questers' imaginary.

CHAPTER FOUR

The Romance of Hardship: Questing in Sub-Saharan Africa

In the introduction, I established that the literature of masculine adventure written during the interwar period was unusually adherent to shared conventions for dealing with topics such as idealism, travel, and encounters with alterity. In the first chapter, I demonstrated how Joseph Conrad's traveling texts inspired a blend of optimism and anxiety in French writers of the era who saw his writing as anchored in a bygone and unattainable world of adventure. Both Joseph Kessel and Michel Leiris paint a world in which the prestige formerly attached to travel is now nearly impossible to win. In the second chapter, we saw Hemingway put a premium on hardship as a means to authenticity and narrative authority, while also expressing a counterintuitive but ultimately strategic anticipatory nostalgia. In the third chapter, the interwar-era English traveling writer stood in as a cultural translator, using his representation of indigenous speech and his meditations on language to further claim authenticity and authority. Such studies come together in this chapter, in which I investigate the romance of hardship in American, English, and French interwar-era nonfictional and fictional writing about quests to sub-Saharan Africa, a place of reputed hardship and, for reasons that I explore in what follows, fascination during the interwar years.

Interwar-era writers were not alone in looking to a diverse number of places in sub-Saharan Africa for answers about the past and the troubled present. Their quests parallel numerous contemporaneous positivist searches for answers about origins in the domains of both science and politics. In the two decades following the "Scramble for Africa" that culminated when European powers met to partition Africa at the Berlin conference of 1884–85, imperial ideology continued to dominate, but its particular formation was upended during the First World War, which redistributed power in many domains. In this context, after the war, sub-Saharan Africa became a choice destination for personal quests for a broad range of writers. Simon Gikandi notes how, in the period following the First World War, the wider public came to associate the African continent with "a certain kind of redemptive primitivism."[1] During this period of ostensible imperial decline, sub-Saharan Africa was seen as one of the last theatres of such "primitivism," and travel narratives about the region were a popular stage for its afterlife. Marianna Torgovnick argues that sub-Saharan Africa and the South Pacific functioned, in the 1920s and 1930s, as the destinations of choice for men anxious about their "manhood or health."[2] In her account, "'[t]he primitive' was widely valued as a way station or spa for men suffering from cultural alienation or psychic distress."[3] Sub-Saharan Africa was a privileged destination for travelers in search of health and community albeit one far afield from the watering places of earlier and contemporaneous sufferers. Writers traveled to sub-Saharan Africa in anticipation of adventure as well as antidotes for, and consolation from, the political dirges that haunted the interwar years.

Bivouacking in Central Africa during the Mission Dakar-Djibouti, Michel Leiris wrote one of many long letters to his new friends, Pablo Picasso and his wife, Olga Khokhlova. Near the end of the lengthy trek, Leiris warmly promises to "play Africa" with their son Paulo upon his return, clearly referring to an earlier request by Mme Picasso: "It would be a great pleasure for me, around Christmas, when we have returned, to play Africa with him and to play for you the role of the chatty explorer who, brooking no opposition [. . .] annoys everyone with his endless stock of stories."[4] Leiris does not explain to Mme Picasso what this game of Africa is, from where it originates, and how it is played. Yet he promises to play it with the child, as if Mme Picasso would tacitly understand what the game is. By general definition, a game is a physical or mental competition or diversion that groups players together in a series of rule-based activities. The players of the game are typically familiar with the rules before they play. Likewise, the game of Africa proposed by Leiris is already known to Paulo Picasso, who would like to go to Africa someday and wants to begin rehearsing now. Embedded within Leiris's affectionate offer lies the central argument of the present chapter—namely that interwar-era American, English, and

French literary representations of sub-Saharan Africa are effectively governed by a logic that grants authenticity and narrative authority based on hardship and affliction, however trivial or faintly calibrated. In the comfort of Pablo Picasso's villa in Southern France, Leiris and Paulo Picasso would play an exciting but familiar game.

I now strive to understand how quests for authenticity by way of hardship were so entrenched in interwar writing about travel in sub-Saharan Africa that even a heterodox writer might mock the trend but not easily reject it. A study of a broad range of interwar-era writing about sub-Saharan Africa permits assessment of the traditions and pressures that contributed to producing these ostensibly individualist but generally conformist narratives. Whether the product of casual travelers, ethnographers, novelists, colonials, or journalists, both fictional and nonfictional accounts narrate tribulations both trivial and serious.

Indeed, the formulaic aspect of the interwar-era narrative about sub-Saharan Africa authorizes us to juxtapose fictional with nonfictional accounts based on actual travels with a warrant provided by Kai Mikkonen, also referenced in the introduction, who draws attention to "[c]ross generic exchanges and borrowings" in this literature.[5] For instance, the inclusion of Céline's *Journey to the End of the Night*, as well as Evelyn Waugh's "African" novels *Black Mischief* (1934) and *Scoop* (1938), is possible precisely because I am concerned with the logic, adhered to or mocked, that grants authority and authenticity to the ill-fated, however welcome or illusory their suffering. I will demonstrate that, for interwar-era traveling writers, sub-Saharan Africa functioned as a tradition of thought, imagery, and vocabulary with which writers were intimately familiar long before they touched the continent's soil. As Céline's and Waugh's fiction originated in real voyages to sub-Saharan Africa, they can be juxtaposed with nonfiction and I will argue that they similarly narrate this travel in form as much as content. I will limit this study exclusively to writers who have actually been to sub-Saharan Africa. I will not, for instance, look at the popular and highly appropriative interwar-era genre of "*le Roman nègre*," novels that take place in sub-Saharan Africa with African protagonists, but written by white Europeans who had never been there.

During the interwar period, in Europe and in the United States, there was a significant increase in interest in sub-Saharan Africa, to which publishers and the reading public responded. In France, the tradition is strongest, no doubt due, in part, to French colonial power. At a formative moment, the opening in 1925 of the Institut d'ethnologie [Ethnological Institute] awakened ethnographic interest in the various peoples of sub-Saharan Africa. In the late twenties and early thirties, a fieldwork-oriented ethnography continued to emerge. In this environment, the newly renovated Musée de l'Homme [Museum of Man] reopened in Paris to great acclaim. Ethnography had earlier been popularized by the ethnographer Lucien Lévy-Bruhl, whose immensely influential and widely circulated book, *La mentalité primitive* (1922), (translated into English as *Primitive Mentality* in 1923), depicts sub-Saharan Africans in general as highly spiritual and prelogical. In Lévy-Bruhl's taxonomy, African peoples are free from the neurotic illnesses that Freud continued to detail at the time of the book's publication. *Primitive Mentality* is cast as a valuable source of information about different races by many of our French writers, including André Gide, Paul Morand, and Leiris. By means of popularized ethnography, academicians accompanied the avant-garde as it turned its interest to sub-Saharan Africa. Overall, writers, artists, and social scientists presented sub-Saharan Africa as a destination that promised new and provocative cultural knowledge, as well as self-knowledge by means of crucibles.

What historians have long termed "primitivism" won big in the interwar period with French Surrealists' fascination with sub-Saharan African traditions, including masks and music. *Négrophilie*, or "Negrophilia," was the word coined to indicate the topic as well as the level of fascination, although Negrophilia typically included African-American culture as well as African cultures. Artists, writers, and social scientists felt enriched by products and music from sub-Saharan Africa. As Mark Matera and Susan Kingsley Kent have noted, Negrophilia was a striking trend, "affecting everything from fashion advertising to the high art world."[6] In Switzerland, the Zürich Dadaists Tristan Tzara and Richard Huelsenbeck performed musical tam tams at Dadaist get-togethers, joining together to create their own homespun "African" rhythms. In the Dominican-English writer Jean Rhys's *Good Morning, Midnight* (1939), a Russian painter living in Paris shows the wayward protagonist Sasha some masks "straight from the Congo," specifying in the same sentence, "I made them."[7] In mainland Europe, sub-Saharan Africa spelt cultural appropriation, as much as it did new creative vistas for artists and social scientists in search of putative primitivism.

In England and in the United States, there was perhaps only a slightly less demonstrative appreciation of things African. One instructive literary

example is offered by the case of Evelyn Waugh and his "African" literature. In order to write *Remote People* (1931), a short account of his travels in
both East and West Africa, Evelyn Waugh received a generous commission
from *The Times* to cover the coronation, in then-Abyssinia, of emperor
Ras Tafari, also known as Haile Selassie. Although the commission was
for his coverage of the coronation, Waugh decided to write a whole book
about various parts of sub-Saharan Africa, arguably in order to satisfy his
readership's current cravings. *Remote People* would be one of four books
Waugh devoted to sub-Saharan Africa; in toto, he wrote two novels and
two works of nonfiction. I explore these in what follows, with attention to
his fascist sympathies

The putatively primitive world of sub-Saharan Africa was adored and
fetishized during the interwar period, but its contours, as described, do not
differ much from those of their forebears; our writers, in many ways, simply treat similar matters differently. They are in conversation with the Humanists and the Victorians; what the latter cast as threatening or dangerous, they paint as good and intriguing. They also adhere, like travel writers
before them, to a stagist conception of human evolution. The prevailing
interwar-era notion that hardship grants authenticity and narrative authority, a notion that I analyzed in the previous three chapters, is crucially
critical to interwar-era literature about travel in sub-Saharan Africa. Anxious as they are about sources of authority for their narratives, the majority
of which dramatize places few readers will have visited, traveling writers
foreground their narratives' origin in arduous travel. These narratives are
replete with accounts of ordeals and various forms of hardship that, as
the writers suggest, legitimate their status as credible narrators. This belief in an authenticity and an authority gained through hardship is one of
the major conventions shared by interwar-era writers overall, but it has a
particularly strong imprint on writing about sub-Saharan Africa, writing
in which the region stands, so often, as a paradigmatic place for trials and
subsequent self-knowledge. In the interwar years, sub-Saharan Africa was
by and large difficult to get to and, outside of colonized stretches, very difficult to travel through. These very hardships made it a popular destination
for writers in search of authentic experiences and personal transformation.

Sub-Saharan Africa is also a place to which traveling writers go in
order to recreate themselves, even if that project is doomed to failure. In
the same shrewd 1951 preface to *Phantom Africa* considered in the first
chapter, Leiris writes of his failed search for self-knowledge while crossing

the African continent in the early 1930s, arguing that the publication of *L'Afrique fantôme* can function "as a sort of confession":[8]

> The product of a state of mind I consider myself to have moved beyond, for me they are above all valuable retrospectively as a document showing what a thirty-year-old European man—enticed by what had not yet been termed "négritude" and compelled to voyage in such distant lands because to him it represented a lived poetry and a change of atmosphere, as well as a trial—felt when he traveled from west to east across black Africa before the war, as he found himself surprised (quite naively) at his failure to escape from himself, forced to recognize that the overly personal reasons that had convinced him to tear himself away from those he had been close to were precisely what made it impossible for it to be otherwise.[9]

Leiris acknowledges that his trip to Africa was motivated, in part, by personal fantasies. His later reckoning suggests that his desires and fantasies are, in addition to being founded on misguided hopes and fantasies, also the product of the collective ethos of the era. For Leiris, Africa writ large held the promise of self-knowledge, generative tribulations, and sexual emancipation. With respect to the latter, Gérard Cogez argues that Leiris's desire for an indigenous woman in particular is a foundational element of *Phantom Africa* but also that Leiris sought a wider remit as well: "Attracting the good will of the female sex overall is Michel Leiris's African dream, roughly sketched."[10]

As is demonstrated below, Leiris was not alone in making of sub-Saharan Africa a stage for his own personal concerns, conflicts, and affirmations. In *Travels in the Congo*, Gide's extensive account of a trip to French Equatorial Africa, he joyfully insists that he has discovered his lost youth during his travels. The physical challenges and lush atmosphere he encounters permit him to realize childhood fantasies about travel. Recalling entering a forest at the beginning of *Travels in the Congo*, he muses: "If I had been twenty my pleasure would not have been keener."[11] While entering the waters of the Congo, he echoes the last pronouncement: "My heart beats as if I were twenty."[12] He also casts himself as one of Joseph Conrad's apprentices, registering an acute existential longing that exhilarates him and which he sees as the source of what he experiences as spiritual and physical rejuvenation. *Travels in the Congo* indeed has an agonal aspect with respect to Conrad, similar to the one we saw in the first chapter, when Joseph Kessel confronted the challenge posed by Conrad's ostensibly inimitable life. Kai Mikkonen has drawn attention to such cross-genre filiation in Africanist literature more widely, noting the way in which "[t]he fantasy of fiction [. . .] authenticates travel facts."[13]

The romance of hardship so characteristic of interwar-era writing about sub-Saharan Africa generally begins at the point of departure. In this literature, for instance, life aboard a ship to sub-Saharan Africa between the wars usually takes on a dystopian aspect due to illness or drama with other passengers. Indeed, Georges Simenon, in a veritable homage to Conrad, dedicates an entire interwar-era novella, *45°* [*Aboard the Aquitaine*] (1936), to the drama that unfolds onboard a ship headed from France to West Africa. Gide dedicates *Travels in the Congo* to the memory of Conrad. Gide's journal also begins on a ship on which he experiences a severe case of nausea widely shared by his fellow passengers. Gide's traveling partner, Marc Allégret, made a telling documentary film in 1927, also entitled *Voyage au Congo* [*Travels in the Congo*]; it begins onboard with footage of sickly European passengers looking uncomfortably out to sea. Difficulties begin early in these narratives in the form of heat, illness, and fellow travelers.

The fascist Louis-Ferdinand Céline's *Voyage au bout de la nuit* (1932) [*Journey to the End of the Night*] also documents adversity onboard. The antihero Ferdinand Bardamu sails to Africa aboard the *Admiral Bragueton* for a dystopian journey within a journey that makes of his shipboard paranoia a microcosm of the entire novel, a voyage within a larger voyage. The southward passage with a full deck of bellicose colonial officers is already a travel nightmare cycle for Bardamu; he comes just short of getting himself killed by the officers before he even reaches the colonies: "A great moral carnival was in the offing aboard the *Admiral Bragueton*. The 'unclean beast' would not escape his fate. That was me."[14] Narratives about the difficulty of traveling to Africa begin with embarkation and quickly give way to a familiar litany of trials.

Evelyn Waugh was well versed in the art of ennobling crises in the interest of humorous entertainment. He both reproduces and mocks the formulaic recipe for gaining authenticity through adversity in his 1934 story "On Guard." The story treats a young man, Hector, who is leaving his fiancée Millicent behind as he heads to Kenya for a couple of years. He hyperbolizes his upcoming tribulations: "'I shall think of you all the time Out There,' said Hector. 'It's going to be terrible—miles of impassable waggon [*sic*] track between me and the nearest white man, blinding sun, lions, mosquitoes, hostile natives, work from dawn until sunset singlehanded against the forces of nature, fever, cholera. . ."[15] Millicent is not impressed by this derivative litany of horrors. Hector's adversity is too predictable for the young fiancée; it is a story she has heard before. In her view, he is exaggerating his future hardships in the hopes of impressing her, and encouraging her interest in his life abroad.

"On Guard" is a parody of narratives about sub-Saharan Africa that signpost trials and ordeals. Waugh further sends up this tradition by narrating Millicent's response to his letter:

> In this way two years passed. Letters arrived constantly from Kenya, full of devotion, full of minor disasters—blight in the seisal, locusts in the coffee, labour troubles, drought, flood, the local government, the world market. Occasionally Millicent read the letters aloud to the dog, usually she left them unread on her breakfast table.[16]

In this parody of the more solemn accounts of travel to Africa, young Millicent is simply bored of the story of Africa—a good indication of just how common it was at the time. "On Guard" was published in Harper's Bazaar in 1934, only two years after Leiris wrote to Olga Khokhlova about playing the game of Africa with her son. As these examples show, conventions for traveling in and writing about sub-Saharan Africa crossed national and linguistic boundaries.

The premium on illness in the interwar-era African travel narrative suggests, in part, that what one has gone through is significant because it means that one has paid a price. From this perspective, the writer experiences Africa's available trials to the fullest extent by making his own body central to the narrative. Interwar-era accounts of travel in sub-Saharan Africa are replete with accounts of illness, at times quite grave. In *Journey to the End of the Night*, Céline also shows how illness, as well as hospitalization, can be exploited for personal gain in addition to narrative authority. In Céline's novel, this use of illness is first seen during the First World War, but it takes on its true force in Africa. Bardamu wants to escape from Africa through illness and the hospital, just as he had escaped from the war into the hospital:

> Every night I went to my no doubt unfinished shack, where my skeleton of a bed had been put up by my depraved boy. He set traps for me, he was as sensual as a cat, he wanted to become part of my family. I, however, was

haunted by other, far more pressing preoccupations, especially by my plan to take refuge for a while in the hospital, the only armistice within my reach in that torrid carnival.[17]

In the Africa of the interwar-era narrative, the hospital offers the only vacation; the hospital is the escape from the escape. Bardamu's less crafty compatriots, meanwhile, entertain each other with fever contests, which honor the patient with the highest fever. Mocking the doxa, Céline takes a shot at the one-upmanship so prevalent in interwar-era accounts of illness in sub-Saharan Africa.

A medical doctor at the time when he wrote *Journey to the End of the Night*, his first novel, Céline grants Bardamu discerning insights about illness. In 1915, Céline, on medical leave from the war, went to West Africa with plans to make a fortune. He returned to France penniless and was repatriated on medical grounds. Written in a terse and frank tone, his letters and postcards from his time in West Africa foreground physical hardship. He earnestly documents his state of health, referring to his extreme intolerance of the heat in particular. A terse first postcard to his father references a budding fever. His second postcard home contains a lapidary note innocent of punctuation: "Tremendous heat Louis."[18] In a third postcard, slightly more prolix, but also without punctuation, he complains: "very hot here very bad crossing I embrace you."[19] Subsequent epistles succinctly mention heat, illness, and quinine consumption. Anticipating Bardamu's experiences in *Journey to the End of the Night*, the young Céline casts West Africa as antithetical to the European body and rails against the climate.

However, Céline distinguishes himself from his literary contemporaries when he opts not to trade physical hardship for authenticity and narrative authority. For Céline, as seen in his early epistles from Africa, there is nothing ennobling about illness or hardship. Bardamu, telegraphing Céline, suggests that writers who ennoble hardship win only a pyrrhic victory; his blunt point is that health is more important than a story. Céline got significant literary material out of his trip to West Africa, but, in the African section in *Journey to the End of the Night*, he resolutely refuses Bardamu compensation of any description for his hardship. The novelist gets a section of a novel out of his travels; Bardamu gets nothing. As Roderick Cooke argues, although there is seemingly some indication of knowledge gained by Bardamu in Africa, "true wisdom or well-being remain[s] elusive."[20] Indeed, there is ultimately neither progress nor enlightenment for him during his nightmarish sojourn. In this, Céline explicitly outlines the dominant formula associating suffering with wisdom and vision, while explicitly countering it. In doing so, he writes against the era's grain but without offering it a real challenge. Céline's Bardamu has only the ironic nobility of cowardice to challenge his era's traditional romance of hardship.

A kind of generative loneliness is at play in literature about travel in Africa from the interwar period. In *Out of Africa* (1937), Isak Dinesen details her loneliness on her farm:

> At times, life on the farm was very lonely, and in the stillness of the evenings when the minutes dripped from the clock, life seemed to be dripping out of you with them, just for want of white people to talk to. But all the time I felt the silent overshadowed existence of the Natives running parallel with my own, on a different plane. Echoes went from one to the other.[21]

There is loneliness and melancholy on the farm, loneliness for those who travel in a big group like Leiris, and loneliness for those accompanied by people indigenous to the region. Dinesen's desire for white company is indicative of her lack of interest in attempting meaningful dialogue, however imbalanced, with indigenous Kenyans. Throughout *Out of Africa*, she engages with indigenous people in their capacity of helpmeet, storyteller, or object of curiosity.

Other representations of loneliness abound in interwar-era travel narratives about sub-Saharan Africa. As I submitted, it is an anticipatory but generative nostalgia that dominates this literature. Indeed, the low point of the journey often appears as the high point of the resulting book; trials are meant to confirm the book's unique character and grant the writer a singular perspective. Loneliness, seen as one of the greatest challenges posed by travel, is also cast as a guarantor of individuality. This is one of the ways in which travel writing of the interwar period dramatizes its origins. Foregrounding a generative loneliness, writers suggest their unique vision, their difference. The authority granted by loneliness trumps that of general sadness in terms of the implicit levels of prestige shared by these traveling writers. Dinesen writes about her loneliness but not the cause: the philandering husband who abandoned her. Indeed, the unhappy saga that underpins *Out of Africa* is left out of the book; accounts of it are relegated to biographies about Dinesen. It is at the core of the book, and yet sentimentality is left out of *Out of Africa* as much in Dinesen's oblique references to her ex-husband as in her lighthearted account of her lover

Denys Finch Hatton and his untimely death. Dinesen maintains an almost jocular tone with regards to her personal life. As I demonstrate and elaborate in the following chapter, the England-born, Kenya-raised aviator Beryl Markham does the same, as does Barbara Greene, Graham Greene's cousin and traveling companion.

With these examples in mind, I conclude that, while adopting a large portion of the Africanist codes shared by their male counterparts, women writing about traveling in Africa shared some conventions all their own and put less emphasis on hardship. In this case, these codes also include the omission of information about their sentimental lives. However, the paucity of work by women made of interwar-era literary writing about sub-Saharan Africa a nearly homosocial project and I thus only speculate when speaking of a women's tradition. I remind the reader that two of the three women I look at in both this and the following chapter, Dinesen and Markham, respectively Danish and English by birth, were actually living in, and not merely visiting, colonial Africa, a fact that arguably contributed to the lighter tenor and more familiar tone of their work as well as its absolute imbrication with colonialism. I also nod to Effie Yiannopoulou, who attempts such a study of women's writing about Africa, arguing that Dinesen and Markam, along with May Crawford—a missionary whose African travelogue, *By the Equator's Snowy Peak: A Record of Medical Missionary Work and Travel in British East Africa*, was published in 1913 (outside the time frame and genres under discussion)—can be fruitfully brought together:

> [T]he inflated subjects of these spatial and temporal journeys navigate their differing courses across a distant land and culture in a self-preserving act of remembering. They aspire to secure a love for the self by means of confessing a love for Africa. In venturing a perilous crossing into the uncharted borderlands of cultural otherness, each text in turn reproduces feminine positionalities that bring to bear the feminine desire for colonial (self) love upon the theory of "colonial fantasy." [. . .] No longer introspective chartgraphings of the self but colonial texts in dialogue with the racial other, these women's texts act as cultural negotiating arenas where the borderline between the personal and the collective (or else difference and identity) ceaselessly redraws itself.[22]

In these women's works, the genre of travel literature thus becomes a cultural practice. Further scholarship has looked at other women traveling through Africa, such as the Australian Mary Gaunt, and the Englishwomen

Mary Hall, Anne Dundas, Rosita Forbes, Jocelyn Murray, Katherine Fermin, HRH Mary Louise, and Katherine Fannin, intrepid but also often problematic travelers, colonists, and missionaries, but not traveling writers, i.e. writers with an expanded literary oeuvre that goes beyond their travel writing.

Tim Youngs, reviewing Patricia W. Romero's *Women's Voices in Africa* (1992), a collection of a century of women's travel writing in Africa, sums up the doxa about women and travel writing at the time, arguing that feminist critics treating women travelers have, to a large extent, concerned themselves with:

> [T]he questions of differences between men and women travellers, asking for example, whether women are more sympathetic to the natives they meet; whether they focus more on mundane and domestic matters which men fail to notice; and whether their narratives reveal signs of their subjugation under patriarchy.[23]

In 2001, less than ten years later, Sidonie Smith deftly reoriented this trend in *Moving Lives*, with particular interest in women travelers and transportation, a concern of this book overall, as I will demonstrate below with Beryl Markham and two-seater planes. Smith suggests that technology can be a metonym for the evolutions of new epistemologies of travel and mobility in women's travel literature:

> Moving by foot, plane, locomotive, or automobile, the woman traveler assumes a place in history of that technology of motion [. . .] But she may also define the meaning of a particular mode of motion in new and different ways and, in doing so, disentangle travel from its masculine logic. [. . .] For even as the traveler-narrator finds herself negotiating the cultural construction of femininity as sedentary, degrading, and constraining [. . .] she may reimagine her relationship to technology and rethink its history, even as it remakes her.[24]

We will explore this statement below, juxtaposing Markham in particular with male traveling writers dealing with aviation, and tying both more firmly to the hardship-equals-authenticity-and-authority equation.

Joyce E. Kelley's *Excursions into Modernism: Women Writers, Travel, and the Body* (2015) tackles the role of gender in early twentieth-century transnational travel narratives and fiction about travel as well as letters, newspaper articles, diaries, and photographs, attempting to put together an alternate canon of transatlantic women's travel writing. Kelley argues that privileged women of the period sought to redefine themselves through travel, often pairing inward with outward journeys. Although there is scant overlap of objects of study, Kelley's work has been helpful for my treatment of Isak Dinesen and Beryl Markham, particularly to the extent to which they highlight "the novelty of a woman moving into a foreign space where Western women seldom go."[25] I do not follow her assertion that the nineteenth-century "masculine 'discourse of discovery'" is dispensed with in women's early twentieth-century travel writing, at least not in the case of Isak Dinesen and Beryl Markham, both of whom, as I will explore further in what follows, engage in the myth-making of the cultural "expert" who will "explain" Africa to readers with totalizing statements.

Returning more generally to the books under consideration, the supposed hardships and dangers writers face in sub-Saharan Africa are connected to the activities that traveling writers pursue. Narratives about East Africa, for instance, often pay tribute to the dangers of hunting. Writers in East Africa, often on safari, are particularly devoted to this topic. The figure of the rugged white hunter, often born in Africa, or else a long-time resident, is an essential figure in interwar-era writing about East Africa, as I have demonstrated with Isak Dinesen and as I will show with Beryl Markham. A figure of great virility and towering sexual prowess, the white hunter is the resident expert, the successful master of East Africa. He has mastered Swahili and knows the geographical terrain, the animals, and the dangers, although he himself is impervious to the latter. In literature about East Africa from the interwar period, the white hunter is also an arbiter of other travelers' morality, particularly those who have recently arrived in the continent. He is cast as both morally and physically superior to any visitor to Africa. Hemingway was quick to identify and uphold this view. In "The Short Happy Life of Francis Macomber," one of the two major stories Hemingway fashioned out of his safari in East Africa, the fictional white hunter Robert Wilson identifies the ethical dimension of the Macombers' marital strife and Harry Macomber's subsequent transformation. Wilson intervenes in the couple's marriage only to casually seduce Mrs. Macomber; he does not, however, let this tryst interfere with his moral assessment of either of them: "Wilson looked at them both. If a four-letter man marries a five-letter woman, he was thinking, what number of letters would their children be? What he said was, 'We lost a gun-bearer. Did you notice it?'"[26] Following the logic that adversity and hardship grant authority and authenticity, Robert Wilson's ruggedness and hunting prowess guarantee his superior moral fiber; he is the ultimate traveler, although he never properly goes anywhere; he is the virile moral presence that the interwar-era traveler might look up to or from whom the traveler might gain by association.

In this literature, the East African white hunter is an incorrigible seducer and also potentially syphilitic. At the same time, he is a fiercely independent and principled thinker who is almost universally liked and admired. In describing the white hunter Bror (Baron Blixen, Isak Dinesen's ex-husband), Beryl Markham fondly recalls a larger-than-life character: "He is six feet of amiable Swede and, to my knowledge, the toughest, most durable White Hunter ever to snicker at the fanfare of safari or to shoot a charging buffalo between the eyes while debating whether his sundown drink will be gin or whisky."[27] Markham does, however, recognize the clichéd aspect of her mythologizing description:

> Beyond this concession to the fictional idea of what a White Hunter ought to look like, Blix's face yields not a whit. He has gay, light blue eyes rather than somber steel-grey ones; his cheeks are well rounded rather than flat as an axe; his lips are full and generous and not pinched tight in grim realization of what the Wilderness Can Do. He talks. He is never significantly silent.[28]

These two examples suggest that Markham both can and cannot think entirely outside the dominant paradigm of the white hunter, cast as the ultimate authority through his perceived bravery.

Markham was one of a small coterie of pilots who flew across Africa in the early years. Aviation is another site of danger and prestige in interwar-era writing about travel in sub-Saharan Africa; early models of two-seater planes figure prominently in this literature in which, in Sidonie Smith's words, "the airplane becomes a topographic machine, extending the borders of empire, including the empire of the Western subject.[29] Markham's *West with the Night* documents her childhood in East Africa and her brilliant career as a professional pilot, beginning with game hunting and culminating in a record-setting jaunt across the Atlantic. In *West with the Night*, she insists that flying has given her a special understanding of the

African continent, one created not only out of the sublime views that flying afforded her, but also out of the loneliness and danger involved in early aviation. The adversities that attended pilots during the first years of aviation are a central part of her book. Similar accounts of aviation in sub-Saharan Africa during the interwar period are offered by the Frenchman Antoine de Saint-Exupéry in *Night Flight* (1931) and *Wind, Sand, and Stars* (1939) and by his compatriot Joseph Kessel, in *Vent de Sable* (1929). There is a Conradian element to these pioneering pilots' excitement and pride in their first command. In their accounts, they bank on the prestige of danger and foreground the value of their métier for securing the singularity of their vision. They share an elevated sense of their place in the history of transportation and a feeling of camaraderie with other elite pilots, born out of their shared risks.

Flying appears to reproduce for interwar-era travelers the prestige that Conrad's interwar inheritors found in earlier modes of sailing. Indeed, Markham explicitly compares the early days of aviation to sailing ships before steam.

> For all professional pilots there exists a kind of guild, without charter and without by-laws. It demands no requirements for inclusion save an understanding of the wind, the compass, the rudder, and fair fellowship. It is a camaraderie *sans* sentiment of the kind that men who once sailed uncharted sea in wooden ships must have known.[30]

In describing their adventures in aviation, interwar-era writers and pilots such as Markham, Saint-Exupéry, and Kessel expressed an anticipatory nostalgia for the early days of flying in two-seater planes. But, as in other interwar-era writing, indeed very acutely in Hemingway's *Death in the Afternoon*, such nostalgia has a strand of one-upmanship; these early planes are associated with a past that is always already out of reach; in their writings, they anatomize a stage of aviation that will have been surpassed, or would soon be surpassed, by the time their accounts are published and read.

Markham's comparison of airplanes to sailing ships is also an elegy to those dangerous, heady days in two-seater planes:

> After this era of great pilots is gone, as the era of great sea captains has gone—each nudged aside by the march of inventive genius, by steel cogs

and copper discs and hair-thin wires or white faces that are dumb, but speak—it will be found, I think, that all the science of flying has been captured in the breadth of an instrument board, but not the religion of it.[31]

Markham again puts pressure on the nearly mystical excitement that attends the early period of a mode of travel. Here she anticipates nostalgia for a mode of transportation that is still very much in its infancy.

Early writers and pilots did not fly without anticipating the next stage of travel, and hence, like interwar-era French readers of Conrad with his early work, the death of early forms of travel, often those deemed more intimate and dangerous. This is clear in the following quote from Markham, who bemoans the inevitable increase in plane travel:

> One day the stars will be as familiar to each man as the landmarks, the curves, and the hills on the road that leads to his door, and one day this will be an airborne life. But by then men will have forgotten how to fly; they will be passengers on machines. . .And the days of the clipper ships will be recalled again—and people will wonder if clipper means ancients of the sea or ancients of the air.[32]

Like our constellation of Conrad's consecrators, these pilots in sub-Saharan Africa nod to former modes of transportation in their narratives. They were aware of participating in a special moment in the history of transportation and widely shared what might be thought of as a kind of pioneer's pride in the face of dangers.

Airplanes also granted their passengers a form of distinction by affording a unique view of Africa, one not available to the general traveler. Dinesen, writing about flying with her lover Denys Finch Hatton, muses: "Africa, in a second, grew endlessly big, and Denys and I, standing upon it, infinitely small."[33] She recalls that her greatest pleasure was flying over her farm. She recognizes this as an unusual privilege, one that grants her access to singular views not accessible to other people, whose stationary and urban existence she likens to slavery: "It is a sad hardship and slavery to people who live in towns, that in all their movements they know of one dimension only."[34] This privilege is also granted to dying Harry at the end of Hemingway's "The Snows of Kilimanjaro" when he is rescued by a pilot in a two-seater plane that has no room for his wife, and treated to a final, splendid view of Africa's tallest mountain, Kilimanjaro.

Much like adversity, the experience of war allowed writers to claim an enhanced experience in sub-Saharan Africa. *Journey to the End of the Night* begins as Céline's apathetic Bardamu enlists in a war of futility and atrocity, his reckless choice presented as the result of casual indifference, ill-advised impulses, and ennui. Whatever his reason for joining, however, his enlistment and consequent participation in the war will come to distinguish Bardamu's perspective from those who have not served, precisely because the experience has harmed rather than ennobled him.

Perhaps the most surprising complements to this authority conferred by war are the equally crucial stories of failure in sub-Saharan Africa, stories that also, even when recounting vulnerability, adhere to the logic that hardship grants authority and authenticity, as I examined above. Thus, Isak Dinesen recalls how she struggled to keep her prized but doomed farm in her possession despite innumerable obstacles: "It is a heavy burden to carry a farm on you. My Natives, and my white people even, left me to dread and worry on their behalf, and it sometimes seemed to me that the farm-oxen and the coffee-trees themselves were doing the same."[35] Yet, per the formula established in the previous chapters, the hardship Dinesen suffers in Africa is her story of Africa; it is the story that she alone is authorized to tell. The past tense of the first sentence in *Out of Africa*, "I had a farm in Africa," broadcasts her triumphant failure. Overall, interwar-era writing about sub-Saharan Africa routinely features failures: the failure of Dinesen's enterprise Karen Coffee, Hemingway's failure to shoot a lion, Leiris's failure to seduce an Ethiopian woman, and Bardamu's failure to achieve enlightenment. Failure-as-hardship grants authenticity and authority in these narratives. In her account of her farm, Dinesen foregrounds the dependence of indigenous people on the success of her farm, telegraphing herself as benevolent foreigner rather than a settler. I explore this process further in what follows.

Many traveling writers in sub-Saharan Africa chose the comprehensive genre of the journal in the interest of authenticity. Gide's *Travels in the Congo* and *Back from Chad*, both of which detail his tribulations and occasional incompetence, were written in journal form. Following Conrad's footsteps, in the 1920s, Gide spent nearly a year in French Equatorial Africa and explicitly published his journal without revisions, in the interest of guaranteeing the authenticity and authority of his account and observations. Numerous journal writers like Gide and, perhaps most notably, Leiris, made explicit that their work was unaltered before publication.

Morand's *Paris-Tombouctou* (1928), a self-described documentary account, narrates his travels across French West Africa. It is also in unmolested journal form. Morand explains that his book contains a collection of notes taken only for himself, notes which he then published under pressure from his friends and his publisher. He suggests that this makes the journal more authentic in its observations, as it was not written with readers in mind, and he thus had no plausible reason to confabulate. In a telling section, Morand eschews the opportunity to exaggerate or embellish when he arrives in Timbuktu. Despite the deflationary reports of travelers dating back at least to Mungo Park, Morand expresses surprise that he is disappointed by the ancient West African city. He recalls centuries-old accounts of Timbuktu and laments that the reality contradicts them: "Where are the gleaming domes, the caravans with the sacks of gold powder and ivory of which the books spoke?"[36] Ultimately Morand adds his name to the long list of travelers disappointed by the remains of the once-imperial city. In the economy of the literature I look at, this also is hardship. Indeed, once aestheticized, hardship claims even the most privileged of losses.

As demonstrated above, it is axiomatic of Western travel writing from earlier centuries that at least some of what the traveling writer engages in abroad is meant to earn him respect and admiration when he publishes his account of it. In interwar-era writing about sub-Saharan Africa in particular, the writer must find things to show; the failures must trail behind feats, and failure is yet another form of hardship. Where this is not the case, writers nevertheless nod to the convention. Leiris, for instance, casts his failure to meet a sexual goal as shameful. *Phantom Africa*, as I demonstrated in the first chapter, documents, in unadulterated, first-draft form, his twenty-month expedition across Africa with the Mission Dakar-Djibouti. In it, Leiris, seemingly going against the grain, foregrounds conventions for travel in Africa by consecutively failing them. For instance, Leiris feels that he would have to seduce an African woman in order to succeed at the goal he set himself at the beginning of the trip. This normative prurience comes to a head in a sexual obsession he develops while in Abyssinia, where the Mission stopped for two months to do research. Leiris details the shame that he felt when he problematically touched the arm of an Abyssinian woman he desired but was unable to take further what he perceived as a flirtation with the possibility of a sexual encounter. By a now familiar logic, failure generates narrative and Leiris rehearses the logic of hardship just as he foregoes it.

Like other travelogues of the era, Leiris's *Phantom Africa* is paradigmatic in the way in which its guarantees its immediacy with its diary form and Leiris's prefatory remark that he would, for the sake of honesty and scientific accuracy, publish the journal as he wrote it, untouched and unexpurgated, practically without revision, "a document as objective and sincere as possible."[37] This was a pyrrhic victory for a married man who, although he did not technically commit adultery, had intended to, indeed, had arguably attempted to do so, counting his lack of success in this regard as one of his principal failures as a man. Due to that, and other seemingly unprofessional and even salacious passages, *Phantom Africa* was considered a potential threat to the future of the nascent discipline of ethnography.

The Mission, which had employed Leiris as a secretary and archivist, was one of the first extended fieldwork missions of its kind. Other Mission members, in particular Marcel Griaule, the Mission's chief ethnographer, feared that the future of the practice of "fieldwork" [*enquête de terrain*]— and its popularity with government agencies who were always eager for the kind of information fieldwork trafficked in—would be threatened by Leiris's blending of social science with ambivalent depictions of a variety of cultures, intermittent self-obsession, and sexual musings about indigenous women. Griaule worried that *Phantom Africa* would take away from what he saw as the Mission's successes: making contact with the West African Dogon people and collecting (often by thieving) over thirty-thousand artifacts for the main ethnographic museum in France, the Musée de l'Homme (known, before 1937, as the Musée d'Ethnographie du Trocadéro). Critics such as Marianna Torgovnick (1990) and Marjorie Perloff (1998) have addressed this threat before, but nowhere is it engaged so forcefully as when Ruth Larson (1997) argues that it is precisely an interest in exposing ethnographic practices that guides Leiris: "Leiris's daily observations of his and his colleagues' activities are important less for their evocation of a fugitive continent than for their presentation of an inexperienced field worker's initiation into the abusive colonial politics of early French ethnography."[38] In this book, I do evoke the representation of a fugitive continent, but I nevertheless join Larson in her argument that Leiris does articulate anti-colonialist stances in *Phantom Africa*, if not to the same extent as the older Leiris.

Nevertheless, as Phyllis Clarck-Taoua (2002) also notes, Leiris and the Mission Dakar-Djibouti were fully imbricated with colonial practices and benefits:

While it is true that Leiris offers a self-consciously subjective account of the Dakar-Djibouti Mission's journey across the continent, this does not ultimately decenter his European cultural assumptions and initiatives. [. . .] Leiris's repeated accounts of the interactions he and Griaule had with the natives with whom they did business rather quickly establishes the fact that they were sent in the pocket of the colonial administration. They visit one colonial administrator after the next.[39]

This is a deft analysis of, for instance, the cruel imbalance of power in financial transactions (when it is not outright theft) between the "Frenchmen who pay almost nothing for sacred objects" and the villagers who "hand over their possessions—often under coercion."[40]

Just as significantly, Leiris was recognized by Sébastien Côté (2005) as an important contributor to debates about the very possibilities and ethics of ethnography. From *Phantom Africa*, Côté argues, Leiris shows the fragility of ethnographic discourse and suggests that there is a lesson here: "How can ethnography claim to give an objective account of a given culture when a life of introspection has not been enough for a single man to give an account of himself."[41] Leiris gives occasion to both heralding and bemoaning the nascent discipline.

In the last couple of decades, several scholars, including scholars of literature, anthropologists, and cultural critics, have lobbied to have *Phantom Africa* translated into English. *Phantom Africa*, translated and published in English in the United States in 2017, has been reevaluated and praised precisely for the very reasons it was criticized in the first place; that is, for exposing the cultural imperatives subtending ethnographic work and foregrounding the difficulty of separating objective study from personal interests and motivations. James Clifford is perhaps the best known of the pre-translation rehabilitators. In *The Predicament of Culture*, he emphasizes the revolutionary character of Leiris's massive tome when read against the ethnographic tradition, in particular its insights into the complicated stance required by participant-observers conducting fieldwork, as well as its innovative juxtaposition of high and low registers. *Phantom Africa*, published almost immediately after Leiris's return to France, was seen by a number of colleagues as a mess of unhelpful truths detailing behavior that they generally saw as beneath the dignity of the practitioners of the evolving discipline of ethnography. But it is precisely this mess that Clifford welcomes in his essay "Negrophilia:"

What emerged, anything but a proper history, was a diary recording observations, research problems, encounters with Africans, idle thoughts, moods, speculations, dreams (waking and sleeping), draft prefaces, notes for a novel—"data" relevant to the subjective states of an ethnographer in contact with a problematic, "phantom" reality.[42]

Clifford welcomes the bold heterogeneity of Leiris's journal. In the same essay, he categorizes *Phantom Africa* as "a unique specimen of surrealist ethnography," reminding us that Leiris began his career as a Surrealist poet and suggesting that this plays a part in his unique perspective.[43] He notes the way in which the book brings together diverse styles and schools, before declaring that it was "perhaps the most striking hybrid to emerge from the interwar-era encounter of the literary avant-garde and academic anthropology."[44] Clifford juxtaposes Leiris's hybrid style with the linearity of scientific writing, valuing it precisely because it is not a "proper history" and instead explores "ethnography's interpersonal frictions, its alternations of feverish work and depression, its implication in both tribal and colonial politics."[45] Leiris's work offers an implicit evaluation of the discipline of ethnography, in particular the relationships that the ethnographer creates with the people he studies, and presumably lives among.

Leiris appears to follow a different logic of inclusion from his contemporaries. Yet what strikes the reader is just how acutely Leiris's epic journal resembles the larger canon of non-ethnographic interwar-era literature about sub-Saharan Africa. Indeed, *Phantom Africa* is exemplary in the way in which it adheres to the basic interwar-era formula for writing about sub-Saharan Africa; the interwar-era African plot is highly visible in Leiris's contested journal. By his own admission, Leiris joined the mission in the interest of personal and erotic liberation, as well as authentic contact with African peoples, including sexual contact. But the note of disillusion that informs his pursuit of these goals is familiar, as is his gradual realization that the putative primitivism he was chasing did not exist. He reflects on this ruefully in the introduction to *Phantom Africa*:

What did he find?
A few adventures, study that excited him at first but which soon showed itself to be too inhuman to satisfy him; a growing erotic obsession; an increasingly large emotional emptiness. Despite his disgust with civilized

people and urban life, he finds himself, by the journey's end, wanting to go home.[46]

Leiris quickly realized that he could not transform himself simply through contact with people deemed primitive. He also began to suggest that the quest for authenticity among alien cultures was a bogus and deeply problematic desideratum, given, in particular, the way in which it pits the ethnographer against the cultural other in an imbalanced nexus of power. Leiris is perhaps unique in seeing quite through the Africanist catalog I have established thus far, one that he nevertheless conforms to, making much out of hassles and disappointments. Although the vagaries of ethnographic social observation and the shibboleths of fellow questers for authenticity are central topics in *Phantom Africa*, Leiris also gives an account of how he tried to make what he believed would be life-changing contact with indigenous peoples and just how decidedly he failed at that already fraught task. *Phantom Africa* is paradigmatic in the way in which it accounts for the failure of all of Leiris's conventional projects in Africa, especially the quest for authenticity. His disillusion with Africa is, in a manner, exemplary; it is an interwar-era drama of failure that centers on the familiar problem of making real intercultural contact. Leiris is not alone as he tolls the bell for a primitivism that he himself continues to practice, mixing anecdote with speculation, leaping from the personal to the universal, from hardship to authenticity and authority.

CHAPTER FIVE

Writing and Cultural Translation in Sub-Saharan Africa

In travel writing about sub-Saharan Africa from the interwar period, the very act of writing is generally cast as antithetical to the peculiar character of the area. A broad number of travel narratives foreground the difficulties and incongruities involved in writing in or about the region. In this way, writing also serves as one of the hardships so often emphasized. The very practice of writing is also at times a subject that writers mine for the kind of anecdotes that would play to their anticipated readership. For Isak Dinesen, settler and entrepreneur, the act of writing is first of all antithetical to her experience of Africa insofar as any time she spends writing is time stolen from her beleaguered farm. She also casts writing as an act that she believes makes her incomprehensible to the indigenous people she employs. In *Out of Africa,* she depicts herself writing in the evening as her farmhands watch. She describes their confusion, attributing it to their belief that it is concern over the farm that makes her write. She offers a theatrical and racializing description of her farmhands watching her write: "They would come in, and stand for a long time watching the progress of it, and in the paneled room their heads were so much the colour of the panel, that at night it looked as if they were white robes only, keeping me company with their backs to the wall."[1] Here Dinesen also implicitly reiterates the loneliness that characterizes her stay on her farm on which, she writes, Europeans and indigenous peoples inhabit parallel universes. Written language, she suggests, only serves to seal the distinction between herself and her various servants, whom she associates with oral traditions.

In another instance, Dinesen maintains that her cook Kamante does not believe that her loose-leaf manuscript is a book, because it is unbound, unlike the books on her shelves. Her attempts to enlighten him fail on all accounts: "A few days later, I heard Kamante explain to the other house-boys that in Europe the book which I was writing could be made to stick together, and that with terrible expense it could even be made as hard as *The Odyssey*, which was again displayed. He himself, however, did not believe that it could be made blue."[2] Passages like this illustrate how the subject of writing becomes a source of anecdotes that highlight presumed moments of cultural difference in which the indigenous person is cast as simple and bound by different laws of reason.

Like writing, reading and books are frequent subjects in these narra-tives. As Dinesen notes, the scarcity of books inflates their value and even the experience of reading itself: "In Africa, when you pick up a book worth reading, out of the deadly consignments which good ships are being made to carry out all the way from Europe, you read it as an author would like his book to be read, praying God that he may have it in him to go on as beautifully as he has begun."[3] André Gide brings a generous library with him to French Equatorial Africa, the contents of which he details reading throughout *Travels in the Congo* and *Back from Chad*.

In this literature, books read in America or in Europe do not have the same ontological status that books have in sub-Saharan Africa; books in Africa are too precious, too rare, the source of too much excitement. In *Out of Africa*, Dinesen explicitly states that books as such also have a dif-ferent relationship to lived experience in Africa than they do elsewhere: "Books in Africa play a different part in your existence from what they do in Europe; there is a whole side of your life which they alone take charge of; and on this account, according to their quality, you feel more grateful to them, or more indignant to them, than you will ever do in civilized coun-tries."[4] Reading a book in Africa is cast as a kind of interpersonal experi-ence. Books are also invested with a mysterious worth by virtue of what writers paint as the opacity of their meaning to the indigenous population. Dinesen forcefully asserts that her indigenous workers evaluate narratives differently from European people: "Coloured people do not take sides in a tale, the interest to them lies in the ingeniousness of the plot itself."[5] Addi-tionally, the projected loneliness of the interwar traveling writer in Africa is in part a factor of his solitary appreciation of books.

In *West with the Night*, Beryl Markham claims repeatedly that she is not a true writer, that she is not foremost a literary person. Writing about her life is a challenge, she maintains, as she has lived in colonial British East Africa since she was four and has had no formal education.[6]

She confesses that she has no inner sense of a literary vocation before divulging that *West with the Night* is the outcome of a friendly challenge to write about her life: "'You ought to write, you know. You really ought!'"[7] Markham protests that she is no ordinary writer in that she will merely follow the vagaries of memory: "After all, I am no weaver. Weavers create. This is remembrance—revisitation; and names are keys that open corridors no longer fresh in the mind, but nonetheless familiar in the heart."[8] In Markham's view, she has a unique story to tell about East Africa because she has spent the majority of her life there. She nods to the wealth of books already devoted to Africa overall: "Africa must be all things to all readers [. . .] to a lot of people, as to myself, it is 'home.'"[9] Accordingly, she considers naming her book "Africa is my Home." Markham's intimacy with East Africa is the intimacy of the colonial locked into a hierarchy of power that gives her a significant advantage over the indigenous people of East Africa; it is an intimacy explored on her terms.

Indeed, in *West with the Night*, Markham notes that there are just a few ways in which the continent can be truly and adequately experienced. One of these ways is the extended stay, something with which Markham was intimately acquainted: "But the soul of Africa [. . .] is its own, and of such singular rhythm that no outsider, unless steeped from childhood in its endless, even beat, can ever hope to experience it, except only as a bystander might experience a Maasai war dance, knowing nothing of its music, or of its steps."[10] For "bystander" and "outsider," I argue that we must read, at least in part, the disparaged tourist. Like so many of her fellow traveling writers from the interwar period, Markham claims to have a singular perspective. In her view, her book's authenticity is guaranteed both by the length of her stay and her level of involvement in operations there.

Louis-Ferdinand Céline envisioned *Journey to the End of the Night* along similar lines, hitching the authority of his writing to his own lived experience, including his trip to what was then the British Cameroons. In what he unsuccessfully hoped would be his last interview, he discusses his recently published book with Pierre-Jean Launay in *Paris-soir*: "It's not literature. So? It's life, life as it is."[11] By the same logic deployed by Markham, Céline's experience is more authentic precisely because it takes place in a colonized region that affords him power over indigenous peoples. It is for this reason, Céline suggests in the interview, that his book is free of artifice and is more a record of life itself than the product of artificial emplotment. Such claims situate Céline as a kind of internal exotic in French literature as he teases the boundaries of the French language through his attempt to translate his real-life experiences into a novel that, although it is a novel, is not, as explored above, literature.

Overall, interwar-era traveling writers in sub-Saharan Africa sought to claim authority by dramatizing the origin of their writing. Just as novels have been presented as manuscripts or found documents, these travel narratives advertise how they came into being; indeed, the story of their coming into being is one of the principal stories they tell, and it functions as a framing conceit. Traveling writers foreground the vagaries of the composition of the book itself and they gather authority by referring back to themselves and their experience. In doing so, the tone is typically informal and dynamic. By and large, these traveling writers of the interwar-era Africa share a vernacular tone when narrating their travels. Their narratives often incorporate several popular linguistic registers, including slang, regional dialect, and profanity; the presence of these different registers sets them apart from other, typically "higher," forms of literature. Indeed, it was Céline's use of popular registers in *Journey to the End of the Night* that lost him the prestigious *Prix Goncourt* in 1932. In the aforementioned interview, he notes, "I write like I talk [. . .] And then, I'm one of the people, the real people. I did all of my early schooling and the first two years of my later schooling as a delivery boy for a grocery store."[12] In his declaration, Céline shows his subscription to a very familiar conception of the narrative authority granted by hardship, in this case, class-based hardship.

Years before the publication of *Out of Africa*, Isak Dinesen similarly told an interviewer that she was going to write a book about Africa "in which all the things are true, where everything that is told truly happened."[13] *Out of Africa* is indeed dominated by a tone of positivistic certainty in its observations, particularly with regard to the indigenous population. Dinesen's cultural observations about Africans emphasize behavior she deems primitive; for instance, *Out of Africa* is replete with a series of totalizing polarities such as: "Natives dislike speed, as we dislike noise, it is to them, at the best, hard to bear."[14] Due to her extended stay in Africa and her employment of indigenous peoples, she affords herself the liberty to speculate and make generalizing observations: "Amongst the inventions of civilization which the Natives admire and appreciate are matches, a bicycle and a rifle, still they will drop these the moment there is any talk of a cow."[15] Dinesen's pronouncements on race were increasingly severe and prejudicial. This is apparent in *Shadow on the Grass*, a later memoir of Africa, but also blunt and in full evidence in *Out of Africa*:

> The dark nations of Africa, strikingly precocious as young children, seemed to come to a standstill in their mental growth at different ages. The Kikuyu, Kawirondo and Wakamba, the people who worked for me on the farm, in early childhood were far ahead of the white children of the same age, but they stopped quite suddenly at a stage corresponding to that of a European child of nine.[16]

Although she started a mandatory school for children on her farm, Dinesen believes that indigenous Africans' ability to learn is stunted in their childhood. This belief, informed by assumption about European racial superiority, goes hand in hand with Dinesen's practice of interpreting and explaining indigenous people to the reader, stationing herself as a fluent cultural translator.

Dinesen classifies Africans into what she sees as the ages of man, with Christianity as the ultimate and entirely schematic goal. Once again, I can identify a chronotopic framing, the fruit of a spatial notion of time that permits her to hook the past to a particular geography to such an extent that Africans are figured as ancestral: "The minds of the young Kikuyu may now be walking on the shadowy paths of our own ancestors, whom we should not disown in their eyes, who held their ideas about the Transubstantiation very dear."[17] Here beliefs held by indigenous peoples are set apart chronologically from those held by both writer and presumed reader.

Totalizing statements about the character of indigenous people are scattered throughout *Out of Africa*: "All Natives have a strong sense for dramatic effect";[18] "All Natives have in them a strong strain of malice, a shrill delight in things going wrong, which in itself is hurting and revolting to Europeans";[19] "there are times when coloured people cannot make themselves clear to save their life."[20] Dinesen repeatedly employs what Albert Memmi calls "the mark of the plural," whereby a colonized subject is "never characterized in an individual manner; he is rather entitled only to drown in an anonymous collectivity; natives are all one way; natives are all the same."[21] Furthermore, Dinesen represents Africans as simple at the very moment when she, in a facile fashion, also characterizes them as inscrutable: "I reconciled myself to the fact that while I should never know or understand them, they knew me through and through."[22]

A similar tension is found in Gide's *Travels in the Congo* and *Back from Chad*. Like Dinesen, Gide paints indigenous peoples as juvenescent and outright claims that they are burdened with simpler, prelogical mentalities. Although Gide takes on a native pupil, Adoum, to educate on his travels, he echoes Dinesen's crude ambivalence about the overall possibility of any compatibility between Africans and what he sees as Western progress. Passages which detail the abuses of colonialism and the concessionary companies are intermingled with passages that question indigenous Africans' capacity for ratiocination: "It seems as though their brains were incapable of establishing a connexion between cause and effect (and I noticed this constantly during the whole of our journey)."[23]

In writing about Africa from the interwar period, the act of misunderstanding generates anecdotes. These anecdotes often concern the ostensibly humorous events that result from what the writers identify as the indigenous person's confusion about the writer or his culture. It is precisely the African's confrontation with the baubles of modernity that allows writers to provide readers with no end of ostensibly humorous copy about the differences between indigenous Africans and Europeans. A popular trick was to play a song on a phonograph and record reactions to it. To generate such anecdotes, the journalist Albert Londres brought a phonograph and jazz records with him to Africa on the trip that produced *Terre d'ébène*.[24]

Evelyn Waugh's writing about Africa is also replete with accounts of cultural misunderstandings, particularly when he documents Africans' encounters with Western practices and products. His novel *Black Mischief* (1932) grew out of the cultural misapprehensions he documented in his previous travel book *Remote People* (1931), an account of travel in Abyssinia at the time of Haile Selassie's coronation. There was a strong appetite among the reading public for stories about the 1930 spectacle that Waugh covered for three London papers. At the time, Abyssinia was the lone self-ruling Black nation in East Africa and an equal member of the League of Nations. However, in *Remote People* and *Black Mischief*, Waugh treats the event less as a sacred coronation than an ad hoc invention created for the benefit of the international press. In *Remote People*, for instance, the Abyssinians themselves are left out of the coronation:

> Eventually, about fourteen hours before the ceremony was due to start, numbered tickets were issued through the legations; there was plenty of room for all, except, as it happened, for the Abyssinians themselves.

The rases and Court officials were provided with gilt chairs, but the local chiefs seemed to be wholly neglected; most of them remained outside, gazing wistfully at the ex-Kaiser's coach and the tall hats of the European and American visitors.[25]

Waugh implicitly questions the Abyssinian's capacity for politics, painting the coronation as both absurd and corrupt.

The parodic coronation of the dubiously qualified, Oxford-educated African leader Seth in *Black Mischief* borrows heavily from Waugh's observation of the Abyssinian ruler and the juxtaposition of traditional cultural artifacts with hastily assembled modern amenities that he reported on at his coronation. In the novel, Emperor Seth attempts to introduce contraceptives to his fellow countrymen by means of some informational posters which duly misrepresent the product at hand: "See: on left hand: poor man: not much to eat: but his wife she very good, work hard in the field: man he good too: eleven children: one very mad, very holy. And in the middle: Emperor's juju. Make you like that good man with eleven children."[26] In this way, his countrymen interpret the Emperor's newfangled contraceptive devices as virility charms. Seth's experience with contraceptives suggests a desire to make Azania like contemporary England and share its relatively low birthrate. His fascination with Western culture never leads to any concrete results. The indigenous people continue to interpret Seth's imported contraptions according to their own framework: for instance, a local family adopts a car as a home.

Rita Barnard suggests that it is "all too easy [. . .] to show that Waugh's novels are jam-packed with racial stereotypes."[27] She argues that:

> [A] critic who proceeds to list his outrageous ethical lapses may be doing exactly what the novelist intends her to do: delivering an all-too-obvious rebuke, which the author, for complex and even perverse reasons, has set out to provoke in the first instance.[28]

Barnard writes about the "use of racist tropes," arguing that such use is "surprisingly multivalent and frequently verges on the parodic."[29] However, in the end, although the joke is on the Englishman, the depictions of indigenous Africans cast them as instrumental, a means to understand one's own culture and place within that culture. Indeed, indigenous Africans function as a prop to advance Waugh's own anthropological analysis, to reorient his colonialist gaze back at himself just as he reinforces it. In this way, despite the differences in their projects, this gesture links Waugh with Michel Leiris and his self-anthropology on the Mission Dakar-Djibouti.

Following a pattern seen above, many of these travel narratives are littered with anecdotes that show indigenous Africans struggling with technology. In *Out of Africa*, Dinesen sets aside a whole section of these anecdotes in a chapter entitled "From an Immigrant's Notebook." In one anecdote, Dinesen's servant Ndwettie wants to know if she and Denys have flown their airplane high enough to see God and if they ever will fly that high. "'Really I do not know,' said Denys. 'Then,' said Ndwetti, 'I do not know at all why you two go on flying.'"[30] These kinds of anecdotes are marshaled by Dinesen to buttress her racist claims that indigenous peoples' capacity to assimilate ideas is not the same as that of Europeans.

Although interwar-era writing about travel in sub-Saharan Africa generally does not trade in wonders, it contains more than a novel's share of scandals and surprises resulting from what is presented as the guileless mentality of the indigenous people. These anecdotes perform the function of creating what wonder there is and serve writers' agendas to represent adult Africans behaving and cogitating like young children. They also, as I have noted with respect to interwar-era writing about travel more generally, greatly prefer the status quo; they worried that the effects of Western modernization would destroy the Africa of their visits and they lament what they see as already destroyed by Europeans. But this is not out of concern for the welfare of indigenous Africans. They prefer what they understand as cultural primitivism, the easy foreignness that offers them colorful anecdotes, while also providing a forum for cultural speculation.

This preference for what they saw as primitivism is apparent in the few accounts of rumored cannibalism in these writings. It had been a long time since anyone of any description, writer or scientist, had offered an account of cannibalism, but the rumor still runs throughout the writing. Cannibalism lends literary Africa a necessary element of horror and danger; its inclusion in the book is a textual strategy. Cannibals infuse this writing with an element of the fantastic and pseudoscientific. In *Black Mischief*, a feast follows the death of Emperor Seth, the would-be modern emperor of the imaginary East African country Azania. It is only after the feast that Basil Seal—the young Englishman Seth enjoins to carry out his project of modernization—realizes that he has eaten his girlfriend in the communal stew. Prudence is the choicest meat available in Waugh's reworking of the classic cannibal story. The practice of cannibalism surfaces as a rude vestige of primitivism in the late Emperor Seth's modern sub-Saharan African state.

Cannibalism suggests the nightmare aspect of the European dream of sub-Saharan Africa in which the primitive, the childlike, the unconscious, and the sexual thread together. Occasionally the writer is a dupe in his obsessions and his fixed ideas about Africa, a dupe in terms of what he is willing to believe. Self-studying Leiris, for instance, borrows a tablecloth from an African chieftain and then proceeds to soil it with food on a luncheon outing. Leiris and his colleagues assume that the chieftain from whom they borrowed it has given them something of value. But, in an episode that highlights the troubled epistemology of travel, as they attempt to clean the wine off of the cloth, they discover dried fecal matter on the other side: "In the morning, we depart with the chief. As we are about to go, I shake out the sheet that one of the locals lent us to use as a tablecloth the night before. It had seemed so white that we were upset at having slightly stained it with red wine, but now I find some dried shit on the other side."[31] This anecdote highlights the unreliability of Leiris's and his fellow ethnographers' interpretive authority, and underscores the possibility of solipsism in cross-cultural encounters.

Like Leiris, traveling writers in Africa craft anecdotes out of the times when they feel foolish; once again the low part of the experience functions as the high point of the story. Dinesen admits that, at the beginning of her stay in Africa, she believed a playful Swede who told her there was no word for the number nine in Swahili and that it therefore didn't exist: "When I began to develop my ideas to other people, I was stopped, and enlightened. Yet I have still got the feeling that there exists a Native system of numeral characters without the number nine in it, which to them works well and by which you can find out many things."[32] She is not informed about this by an African, however; she believes the Swede because she is in Africa. It is important, here and elsewhere, to consider how writers negotiate the implicit vulnerability travel entails, and find textual strategies to safeguard their authority when recounting incidents that might be embarrassing or shameful.

In his 1929 *Terre d'ébène*, which documents his journey in colonial French Africa, French journalist Albert Londres reports on Africans who do not understand mail-order catalogues and, because of this, order themselves children's clothing because it costs less.[33] Memmi outlines the predicament of the colonized subject who finds himself rejected as different and scorned if he tries to assimilate: "Indeed, a man straddling two cultures is rarely well seated, and the colonized does not always find the right pose."[34] Indeed, colonized Africa has elements of the "spoiled" city that, in modern times, was perhaps first and best captured by Gustave Flaubert in *Voyage en Égypte* [*Flaubert in Egypt*], published posthumously in 1881. The "spoiled" city is a once-cherished place no longer pure due to the noxious effects of visitors who have damaged its presumed innocence. Within the "spoiled" city are its citizens, spoiled, in this literature through contact with Western cultures. Colonized places, with European people controlling the resources and the people, are "spoiled." However, more writers see this as an aesthetic fact than a political one and are rarely critical of the colonial ideology itself.

Gide also remarks the nefarious effects of colonialism on his sensibilities. What he sees as the culturally hybrid Africans in the towns frustrate his expectations: "These town people, moreover, are spoilt—less simple, I mean, and consequently less interesting than those of the bush."[35] For Gide, as for others, Africans should follow African traditions; to him, there is something unnatural and disconcerting about the "town people." The notion that African people are primitive is normative for Gide; if Africans do not act like archetypal adult children then they should. If Africa is to represent the primeval self, then African people must be and remain simple and even as if preserved in time, showing little of the results of contact with European people. After encountering a couple of touts in Cameroon who are not entirely honest in their dealings, he suggests that it is colonization that has made them dishonest: "These two are the wretched products of a large town (Yaoundé); they are thieves, liars, and hypocrites, and would justify the irritation certain colonists feel against the blacks. But that is just it—they are *not* the natural products of the country. It is contact with our civilization that has spoilt them."[36] People, like countries, are "spoilt" through contact with Europeans. Ultimately Gide concludes that the negative traits of the Africans he meets are rooted in European dominance. Even though Gide would later rail publicly against the crimes of the West African concessionary companies, it is difficult to determine if Gide saw himself as necessarily complicit with colonialism due to his travels. That he was is certainly difficult to contest.

Swift turns to racism are scattered throughout Gide's Africanist books. Although he takes Europeans to task for their deleterious effect on indigenous Africans, he nevertheless proceeds with the tacit conviction that they are, seemingly without exception, less intelligent than their European contemporaries: "When the white man gets angry with the blacks' stupidity, he is usually showing up his own foolishness! Not that I think them capable of any but the slightest mental development; their brains as a rule are dull and stagnant—but how often the white man seems to make it his business to thrust them back into their darkness."[37] Anecdotes about Adoum, Gide's young aide-de-camp, are often the jumping off point for generalizations about the intelligence of indigenous Africans: "I see nothing in him [Adoum] that is not childlike, noble, pure, and honest. The whites who manage to turn creatures like him into rogues are worse rogues themselves, or else miserable blunderers."[38] In this view, Europeans, by dint of being of superior intelligence, are derelict when they change the character of indigenous people. That the white man has the power to change character is, in part, the result of his perceived superiority. In Gide's view, such superiority necessitates a certain caliber of behavior. He scripts his own white man's burden; the European, in Gide's view, must be both model and guide and behave in a dignified fashion for the indigenous people. This will, in Gide's view, allow them to retain both the childlike simplicity and the intuitive morality that he describes them possessing.

Gide assigns himself the responsibility of understanding sub-Saharan Africans on their own terms, ultimately reasoning that what he sees as their prelogical cerebration makes them incompatible with, and incomprehensible to, people of European descent: "The people of these primitive races, as I am more and more persuaded, have not our method of reasoning [. . .] Their acts are not governed by the logic which from our earliest infancy has become essential to us—and from which, by the very structure of our language, we cannot escape.[39] Gide also warns readers to avoid comparison with the European man. Thinking that he is advocating for the people he meets on his journey, Gide opens up yet another racist meditation: "But people are always talking of the Negroes' stupidity [. . .] I do not want to make the black man out [to be more] than he is; but his stupidity, if it exists, is only natural—like an animal's. Whereas the white man's as regards the black has something monstrous about it, by reason of his superiority."[40] In this and elsewhere, while doubting the African's intelligence, Gide also takes aim at the European's. The European's intelligence is not necessarily more attractive; it is also uniquely capable of corruption. In addition to performing a cultural translation of Africa and Africans, Gide lists the misdeeds and the disasters enacted by Europeans in their own countries.

Gide bases his theories and generalizations on his observations of Adoum, whom he credits for exposing to him to the mentality of Africans overall. But the European mind, he suggests, is incapable of engaging Africans on their own terms, even when making human gestures towards them. What he sees instead is misfortune and beauty:

> Adoum is assuredly not very different from his brothers; none of these traits belong especially to him. Through him, behind him, I have come to feel a whole race of suffering humanity—a poor oppressed people, whose beauty, whose worth, we have failed to understand. . .whom I wish it was in my power never to leave. And the death of a friend would not grieve me more, for I know that I shall never see him again.[41]

Gide here acknowledges the way in which the Africans he encounters have been abused by the practice of colonialism, a practice ill suited to favor the capabilities of the colonized. Going further, he suggests that it is the Europeans' fault that they failed to meet Africans on their own terms. Gide counts his ability to do so as a lucky anomaly, and he trumpets this success with the hyperbolic language that he uses to describe the sorrow he feels when he says goodbye to Africa.

As hinted at above, corruption is not inherent to Africa in Gide's view; it is brought into a pure Africa from Europe. Conversely, Africans will retain what he sees as their native nobility only if they stay the way he assumes they have always been. Gide's preference for what he imagines was a purer Africa—even an Africa with fewer amenities—highlights the political ramifications of the notion of authenticity. Gide's perspective is also complicated by his aesthetic concerns and expectations. He is disappointed as well when the residents of a particular village are not physically attractive to him. Gide elaborates this concern, writing from Egypt in 1939:

> No, I no longer have a real desire to fornicate, or at least it's no longer a need as it used to be in the happy days of my youth. But I need to know that I could if I wanted to—do you understand that? I mean that a place doesn't interest me unless it offers multiple opportunities to fornicate. The finest monuments in the world can't replace that—why not admit it frankly?[42]

It is certainly impossible not to put into question whether such motivations underpin other writers' travels as well. Such confessions as Gide's are rare. However, we can certainly see such objectifying and sexual appraising in many of the works that I consider, as I explore in depth in what follows.

Overall however, for Gide, the critical moral division among Africans is between those who live in towns and those who live in the bush, a possible corollary, as I explore further in the next chapter, with Graham Greene's distinctions between the colonized people who live on the coast and interact with European men and what he perceives as the unadulterated and simple people who live inland. Underpinning all of these dichotomies is the principal distinction between those in contact with Western civilization and those who are not, between "evolved people" ["peuples evolués"] and intact people ["peuples intacts"], as Leiris later conceived it, doing his best, but not succeeding, to avoid a stagist dichotomy that invariably privileges a later stage.

Leiris was, to some extent, concerned about the instrumental use of indigenous people in the French colonies. Together, Leiris, with Griaule, had protested the use of indigenous people at the 1931 Exposition coloniale internationale [International Colonial Exhibition] that had brought hundreds of Africans to Paris to inhabit a model of the village Djenné in the Niger Delta, a region colonized by the French. As Matera and Kent have noted, "it was the grandest, and one of the last, in a long line of exhibitions celebrating the colonial civilizing mission and showcasing modern technological innovation."[43] At the time, Leiris believed himself to be on the right side of history. The same can be said with respect to much of his behavior in *Phantom Africa*. For instance, he recounts how Griaule and others bought and freed enslaved people. At the same time, however, he minimizes the practice of slavery itself:

Tomorrow, Griaule is expecting a dealer who will offer him a slave for sale, already the mother of a little boy and now pregnant. We will bring about her liberation as soon as possible. The anti-slavery idea only half pleases me. The bourgeois world gets indignant but I don't see that there is such a great cause to be scandalized by the existence of countries where the slave trade is currently practiced, when one thinks, for example, of the situation of workers in our own societies. Eternal hypocrisy. . . This opinion of mine has earned me the disapproval of the other members of the Mission.[44]

Leiris's "look to your own house" stance is on full display here. He would not stand for exploitation in Paris, but he relativizes it in Africa by analogizing it with a false equivalent.

In *Out of Africa*, Isak Dinesen's exhorts: "Love the pride of the conquered nations [. . .] and leave them [the indigenous people] to honor their father and mother."[45] Dinesen criticizes the contemporaneous execution of colonial projects without criticizing the overall ideology of colonialism. For instance, she calls on European visitors to Africa to leave certain social structures, in this case spirituality and religion, intact, and offers a sketch of what she believes is a more humane form of colonialism. She nevertheless does not critique the project of colonialism overall; indeed, she is the grateful recipient of many of the advantages colonialism offers to white women and men. She professes to care deeply about the indigenous people among whom she lives, and even suggests that she is making their lives better through education both formal and informal, yet she sees their capacity to learn capped at age nine. She both encourages and contributes to local efforts at education, but also rejects the results with a mixture of liberalism and racism so common among writers in the era of high colonialism.

Céline's Bardamu pointedly refuses the conventional view of the mental difference between Europeans and Africans. The only difference between black and white in *Journey to the End of the Night* is opportunity; there is no suggestion of a difference in mental evolution. He suggests that whites also have the advantage of privilege: "[A]ctually, they're just like our poor people, except that they have more children, less dirty washing, and less red wine".[46] Although Céline's illiberal, anti-Semitic, and racist views were developed at this time and would culminate in his collaboration with Vichy France, some critics have sought to defend his approach, arguing that he was more misanthrope than racist, casting him as an equal-opportunity offender. The writer Will Self describes Céline's literary projects as characterized by "invective, which—despite the reputation he would later earn as a rabid anti-Semite—is aimed against all classes and races of people with indiscriminate abandon."[47] But this is to ignore, relevantly for our project, the power involved in representation, the power to form opinion and enable racism, by providing what he saw as justification for it, championing before the Second World War for an alliance between France and Nazi Germany. In a 1938 profascist pamphlet entitled *The School of Corpses*, he asks: What is the true friend of the people? Fascism is."[48] Rosemary Scullion has done much to link the fascism of his wartime pamphlets to his early fiction, arguing that Céline's "volatile oscillations" between political views can be "linked to the ambiguity underlying nascent forms of fascist ideology that emerged in interwar Europe," ultimately linking him with other fascist interwar writers such as Wyndham Lewis.[49]

Overall, Céline's *Journey to the End of the Night* concerns itself less with indigenous Africans than with the fate of the European in Africa, beginning, as I demonstrated with other writers, with the long ship journey that carries Bardamu and his fellow passengers south. As a doctor, Bardamu's eyes are particularly focused on medical abnormalities, and he observes physical and moral decay among his countrymen: "From that moment on we saw, rising to the surface, the terrifying nature of white men, exasperated, freed from constraint, absolutely unbuttoned, their true nature, same as in the war."[50] This "biological confession" ["aveu biologique"] is observed and detailed throughout Bardamu's difficult stay in West Africa.[51] Europeans in Africa are of scientific interest due to their rate of decay, their inevitable physical destruction.[52]

Journey to the End of the Night contains neither the ludic anecdotes nor the earnest praise of indigenous Africans that fills so much writing about sub-Saharan Africa from the interwar period. As with all of the places he goes in the novel, Céline's iconoclastic Bardamu troubles competing literary depictions of Africa. In doing so, and precisely by pointedly rejecting them, he affirms the power and reach of the many conventions that characterize writing about sub-Saharan Africa.

Criticism of the overriding structure of colonialism rarely emerges in writing about Sub-Saharan Africa during the interwar period. Although nearly all of the countries our writers visited were colonized—with the questionable exception of Liberia and Ethiopia, which had remained independent during the Scramble for Africa—this structure itself is rarely put into question and is even (Waugh is the best example) openly lauded. A particularly strong connection between the traveling writer and colonialism is drawn in Evelyn Waugh's explicitly fascist and pro-colonialist journalistic effort *Waugh in Abyssinia* (1936). The book covers the period when Waugh favorably documented Italy's takeover of Abyssinia in 1935, reporting for the fascist paper *The Daily Mail*.[53] In a 1938 letter to the editor of the New Statesman, Waugh pushed back against accusations of fascism and rejected the use of the word overall, arguing that "we are in danger of a [. . .] stultifying use of the word 'Fascist,'" a word that he laments has been used to describe "colonization," "military discipline" and "patriotism," "an abuse of vocabulary so mischievous and so common, that it is worth discussing."[54] This letter had the reverse effect of that intended by Waugh and only led to further accusations. When there is criticism of colonialism, it typically falls on individual colonials, or else on the abuse of colonial prerogatives, but not on the system itself. Although Gide, something of a counterexample, actively criticized colonial excesses in French Equatorial Africa in his journals, and spoke publicly about them before the Chambre des députés [Chamber of Deputies]—a significant legislative body in Third Republic France—his views on Africans as people do not differ much from his contemporaries'.[55] When Gide and, notably, Londres, object to the abuses of colonialism in their writing, they single out particular articulations of colonialism to criticize, not the global and patronizing structure. The real problem of the colonies lies in France, Londres opines in *Terre d'ébène*, not in the colonial administration. He reproaches not colonialism but "the method" ["la méthode"].[56] Indeed, even those who oppose colonialism tend to stick to a more travelogue-based approach to their accounts of various negotiations of power, emphasizing instead, as I have shown, the picturesque, the comical, and the grotesque. Their exposure to the pervasive effects of colonialism tends to result more often in parody than critique.

Interwar-era travel writing about Europe often includes references to both erudite Baedeker guides and popular itineraries. The traveling writer in sub-Saharan Africa boasted fewer comforts, fewer precursors, and fewer trains. In most cases, however, the writer in Africa benefitted from the advantages offered by a colonial infrastructure. Like many of his fellow writers, Paul Morand hopes that *Paris-Tombouctou* will rectify the resulting chaos, by serving as a guide for future visitors. Much like Hemingway in *Death in the Afternoon*, he includes practical advice at the end of his book and recommends itineraries in the preface, even referring to specific timetables for transportation. As with Hemingway, Morand's method itself appears to be a convention: even as you write a travel book and include directions, claim that your book is the last one possible of the era. Although he offers a book replete with details that would allow the reader to follow his [Morand's] unusual itinerary across West Africa, Morand establishes that it is, first and foremost, his own itinerary, one that was unique to him when he completed it. He envisions a new tradition of writing about Africa, a tradition whose starting point would be *Paris-Tombouctou*.

The problem of preparing for a trip to sub-Saharan Africa is thematized in many travel narratives of the interwar period. As William Boot, the would-be journalist in Waugh's *Scoop*, gets ready to go to the fictional country of Ishamelia, he discovers that preparations are but a routine with its conventions. The list of things to bring to Africa already exists; he can purchase his "kit" at a local store. This twentieth-century routine of preparation is a throwback to the famous, extensively packed kits of nineteenth-century explorers, such as John Speke. When Boot visits a department store to purchase his kit, he is sold an expensive greenhorn's dream, filled with miscellanea:

> William had acquired a well, perhaps rather overfurnished tent, three
> months' rations, a collapsible canoe, a jointed flagstaff and Union Jack, a
> hand-pump and sterilizing plant, an astrolabe, six units of tropical linen
> and a sou'wester, a camp operating table and set of surgical instruments,
> a portable humidor, guaranteed to preserve cigars in condition in the Red
> Sea, and a Christmas hamper complete with Santa Claus costume and a
> tripod mistletoe stand, and a cane for whacking snakes. [57]

Boot's kit deflates the notion of Africa as an untrammeled wilderness; it contains every creature comfort and even a Union Jack. The issue of health is not overlooked; the kit includes an operating table and a set of surgical instruments. Boot will leave England with an absurd, yet predictable, set of objects.

Boot's kit, with its rations, introduces another nearly perfunctory element of the interwar-era travel narrative about sub-Saharan Africa: the drama of food. Food is another site of defiant non-assimilation. In this literature there are frequent references to the food left uneaten, either because it is the food of the indigenous people they are taking account of, or else because it is European food that the indigenous people have not adequately prepared. For instance, Dinesen, who refers to herself as an immigrant, vehemently refuses to sample local dishes. Like most of our traveling writers in Africa, she has her own cook. Relatedly, fond of what they present as playful juxtapositions, writers often ask indigenous people to successfully prepare European delicacies. This practice can be autocratic and coercive; for instance, Dinesen amuses herself by teaching a Muslim Somali how to buy champagne. She describes how she took a young servant named Kamante under her wing and taught him to make particularly elaborate and rich dishes. Kamante was, she specifies, famous through the region for his cooking, although he never ate it himself. She ridicules Kamate for his preference for his own cuisine and compares him to a dog offering up a bone when he brings her samples of his own food: "Here even his intelligence failed him, and he came and offered me a Kikuyu delicacy—a roasted sweet potato or a lump of sheep's fat—as even a civilized dog, that has lived for a long time with people, will place a bone on the floor before you, as a present."[58] Writers generally avoid the cuisine of indigenous peoples and concentrate instead on teaching them how to cook European food and source the right products. Dinesen rejoices in her effectiveness at teaching Kamante to make her version of European cuisine.

For those on a safari or trek, or else far from colonial centers, the tinned dinner was an essential part of their diet in Africa. Tinned Christmas dinners appear frequently in this literature, typically consumed at unseasonable moments. In *Journey to the End of the Night*, Robinson, the corrupt Kurtz-like figure Bardamu follows into the bush, leaves behind only a staggering quantity of canned "Cassoulet à la Bordelaise." This strikes Bardamu as both a blessing and a curse: "But plenty of that I assure you. I threw up whole tins of it."[59] Ersatz European cuisine is foregrounded as a source of hardship.

Like food, drinking is an essential element of interwar African travel narrative, one with its own set of conventions for representation. In "The Short Happy Life of Francis" the eponymous protagonist quickly learns that the appropriate afternoon drink in East Africa is a gimlet, it being the convention that one must have a strong drink in the afternoon. In *Journey to the End of the Night*, the director of the company where Bardamu seeks employment suspects him of sexual perversion because he neither smokes nor drinks. Hard drinking is one of the rules of Africa, as Bardamu learns on his near-fatal voyage south on the *Admiral Bragueton*. On that ship rowdy colonials persecute him for his abstinence. Heavy drinking is one of the tests that the interwar-era traveling writer in Africa often has to "pass."[60]

Leiris wrote retrospectively in reference to his journey with the Mission Dakar-Djibouti that he saw in travel a way to escape the constraints of a bourgeois Parisian life and embrace new freedoms:

> Tired of the life he was living in Paris, thinking of travel as a poetic adventure, a method for concrete knowledge, a test, a symbolic way of stopping aging by running through space to deny time, the writer, who is interested

in ethnography because of the importance that he attributes to this science regarding the understanding of human relations, takes part in a scientific mission that crosses Africa.[61]

Leiris recalls an escapist vision of an Africa that promises a curative effect. He travels in part because he is unhappy in Paris, but also to have the kind of experiences that are not possible to have there. Since the industrial age, most travel is cast as a journey from an ugly place to a more beautiful one, an uptight place to a freer one, and a complex place to a simpler one. In Leiris's case, travel also represents a possible move from dissatisfaction to self-knowledge.

Along with behavioral freedom comes privilege. As Lévi-Strauss earlier noted, the Western traveler changes social classes when crossing borders, traveling not only in space and time, but also typically upwards in a social hierarchy. Indeed, there is often a pastoral quality to travel narratives about Africa, as even a European of modest means becomes wealthy and thereby sees himself as entitled to the kind of service he could never afford at home, often including carriers, servants, cooks, and more. Self-importance is also generally inflated in Africa, as the traveler often rejoices in unprecedented attention.

Such significant transitions to higher economic classes often also lead to various possibilities for sexual interactions with Africans. Céline's Bardamu marvels at the African prostitutes he encounters:

At nightfall the native hookers came out in strength, wending their way between clouds of hungry mosquitos armed with yellow fever. There were Sudanese girls as well, offering the passerby the treasures under their loincloths. For extremely moderate prices you could treat yourself to a whole family for an hour or two. I'd have liked to flit from twat to vagina, but necessity obliged me to look for work.[62]

Even Bardamu, an unemployed Frenchman, understands the power of what little money he has with respect to possible sexual encounters. While erotic emancipation is often one of the promises of travel overall in this period, sub-Saharan African people in particular are cast as highly sexual and uninhibited.

I have noted that these writings contain their share of vernacular language, including slang and curse words. This is particularly true of the male writers; perhaps a sign of the times, women tend to foreground their grit through physical feats. Céline allows the porous structure of fiction about Africa to demonstrate his savoir-faire of prostitution and hard alcohol. In part, this widening of registers is a legacy of the First World War as well as literature about the war. A soldier's swearing and crudeness is less stigmatized and more likely to be tolerated than a non-soldier's swearing. It is indulged, presumably, because it is often associated with bravery, indicating, as it does, the adversities that the soldier has faced. Swearing is thus one of the conventions of writing about sub-Saharan Africa that can be tied to the battlefield. In addition, this writing about travel also follows the precedent set by combat novels—of which *Journey to the End of the Night* is arguably a later rewriting—in which conventional language was replaced by colloquial speech. This colloquial speech ostensibly serves to deflate rhetorical pretension. As Mary Jean Green has noted with respect to Céline, "[his] characteristic language would hardly have been possible without the precedent set by the combat novels, which opened respectable fiction to colloquial speech and even vulgar slang."[63] The introduction of crude language both grants authenticity to the writer and situates his work historically. But, in this, the extreme language also adheres to convention, even at its boldest. It is the conventional sound of authenticity granted by means of some familiar form of hardship.

Language is necessarily yoked to a certain caliber of experience. In *Journey to the End of the Night*, it is Bardamu's dubious hospital roommate Sergeant Branledore (a name which suggests the verb *branler*, French slang for masturbation) who teaches the important practice of swearing to his young acolytes in the hospital:

> After a week in this new hospital we realized that we would absolutely have to change our image, and thanks to Branledore [. . .] [o]ur speech had indeed become vigorous and so obscene that the ladies sometimes blushed, but they never complained because it is generally agreed that a soldier is as brave as he is wild and cruder than there is any need to be, so much so that his bravery can be measured by the crudeness of his language.[64]

Branledore teaches his acolytes that crudity equals bravery. He implies that swearing is a patriotic act and teaches his underlings how to play their part in the military and demonstrate their bravery with their language.

In *West with the Night*, Markham notes the white hunter Baron Blixen's tendency to swear. She does not swear herself, but she includes language spoken by male pilots and white hunters. She swears without having to swear herself, thereby demonstrating her mettle without sacrificing her decorum. Nor does she borrow from the tradition of the combat novel. Nevertheless, Africa does breed frankness for Markham; she implicitly suggests that living among indigenous peoples has changed the way she thinks. Dinesen articulates a similar logic in *Out of Africa*: "White people, who for a long time live alone with Natives, get into the habit of saying what they mean, because they have no reason or opportunity for dissimulation, and when they meet again their conversation keeps the Native tone."[65] In Dinesen's view, living among indigenous Africans has granted her a certain frankness and honesty.

As I detailed in the third chapter, along with mastering a local language, speaking English in the way in which indigenous people are perceived to speak it is a topos of interwar-era travel writing more generally. However, it gains particular force in writing about travel in Africa. Isak Dinesen addresses this practice with respect to her principal servant Farah: "instead of correcting him I took to using the same expressions when I talked to him."[66] From her letters it is clear that she was somewhat ambivalent, if only for vanity's sake, about what she perceived as a necessary task. She wrote home that living almost exclusively among indigenous Africans had made her sound "like Friday in *Robinson*."[67] On the other hand, many writers proudly demonstrate their ability to carry through this enterprise.

For Markham, as is also the case with Graham Greene in the next chapter, understanding Africa was, in part, a process of recognition. She recalls this sensation of familiarity in *West with the Night*: "The distant roar of a waking lion, rolls against the stillness of the night, and we listen. It is the voice of Africa bringing memories that do not exist in our minds or in our hearts—perhaps not even in our blood. It is out of time, but it is there, and it spans a chasm whose other side we cannot see."[68] Markham suggests that Africa is familiar to her as it is part of the communal past. Making use of an appropriative rhetoric, she conjectures that Africa belongs to humanity at large as the place of universal origins. For Markham, Africa is the familiar interior, the past, childhood.

Writers traveling to Africa during the interwar period often claimed to know the continent before they arrived, so armed were they with stories and phantasms. These phantasms inform their narratives, even if they bear no relation to what they see there. Constellations of predetermined notions served to orient narratives and meet readerly expectations. As Céline's Bardamu scoffs on the ship heading to Africa, fully aware of the borrowed and belated mythos of his journey: "We were heading for Africa, the real, grandiose Africa of impenetrable forests, fetid swamps, inviolate wilderness, where black tyrants wallowed in sloth and cruelty on the banks of never-ending rivers."[69] These writers traveled to and returned from a very familiar "real" Africa and, in this case, renewed a grotesque vision of indigenous people that has its origins in the Victorian African travel narrative with its symbolic enactments of monstrosity. Céline scrapes away what he sees as the contemporary tourist friendly image of Africa, to find what is familiar yet, at the same time, nothing like the "emasculated Africa of travel agencies and monuments, of railways and candy bars."[70] When Bardamu anticipates Africa, "Africa in the raw, the real Africa," he is drawing from an older and familiar repertoire, just as he presents his project as unique and himself as full of ironic bravado.[71] As Walter Putnam has noticed, Céline "relishes in marshaling out the stock imagines of earlier colonialism and exaggerating the stereotyped, hackneyed store of exotica that has fired the Western imagination about Africa since Antiquity."[72] The African episode in *Journey to the End of the Night* is a palimpsest of Africanism.

Recalling Africa is nearly as formulaic. There are several conventions for recalling Africa after one has left the continent. First of all, many writers claim that it is not possible to evoke the experience, as memory will, of necessity, fail. More significantly, memories are represented as being locked into another language and another mentality. Dinesen describes this failure of memory in *Out of Africa*:

> I have not heard from Lulu, since I went away, but from Kamante I have heard, and from my other houseboys in Africa. It is not more than a month since I had the last letter from him. But these communications from Africa come to me in a strange, unreal way, and are more like shadows, or mirages, than like news of a reality.[73]

Dinesen's African servants are, from this perspective, caught in another era and time is, once again, spatialized. The world she left behind needs her, the European writer, to bring it back to life quickly. If not, it will remain trapped behind her, lost in the distant history that Africa represents for her. Without her presence, her servant Kamante loses his identity: "Where the great Chef walked in deep thought, full of knowledge, nobody sees anything but a little bandy-legged Kikuyu, a dwarf with a flat, still face."[74] Only Dinesen can animate her former cook in all of his complexity. In her view, his full nature needs her presence to express itself.

Elegy is a necessary element in interwar-era narratives about Africa. Flaubert's notion of the "mélancholies du voyage" has a part to play here; writers submit that nothing remains unchanged and note that an awareness of transience is one of the sad beauties of travel. Numerous writers suggest that you should never visit the same place twice. I argue of interwar-era traveling writers more generally that, although they often note cultural decline, they believe they were there when it was still worth traveling, when things were still basically unadulterated. This is apparent, for instance, in the title of Waugh's 1946 collection of travel writing from the interwar period: *When the Going was Good.*

At the end of *West with the Night*, Markham ponders the necessary belatedness of travel writing. "Blix would see it again and so should I one day. And still it was gone. Seeing it again could not be living it again. You can always rediscover an old path and wander over it, but the best you can do then is to say, 'Ah yes, I know this unforgettable valley, the valley no longer remembers you.'"[75] In "The Snows of Kilimanjaro," Harry makes use of Africa for the ultimate elegy; he looks back at the time he spent there not from the perspective of home, but rather from death itself: "But he had never written a line of that."[76] By the time the reader gets there, he will be too late; the books document a place that is constantly changing, putting the writer into a superior and unattainable position. It is from this, in part, that they settle the question of prestige, the prestige of unrepeatable experience.

So, these writers suggest, you cannot really return to the same place for the very reason that everything will have changed in a marked fashion, almost always for the worse. By the time they write, they deem it already too late. Only once one is away from Africa can he put it into perspective. Perhaps predictably, Céline's iconoclastic Bardamu also pays homage to this convention of nostalgia by sending it up with another, making grotesques of indigenous Africans. Recalling his time in Africa, he writes: "Are there still black people sweltering and pustulating in that cauldron?"[77] The exaggerated nostalgia proper to interwar-era travel narratives about Africa is transformed by Céline into exaggerated expressions of humor and disgust: "I'll long remember those ten days going up the river. . . Huddled in the bottom of the canoe, watching out for muddy whirlpools, picking furtive passages between enormous drifting branches, nimbly avoided. A labor for convicts on the lam."[78] Bardamu's Africa looks good only in comparison with war. As a man he meets sailing up the river notes: "[Y]ou'll be better off here than in the trenches."[79] Bardamu ultimately mocks the conventional generative nostalgia of the interwar-era travel narrative.

In the end, Africa is Africa remembered away from Africa. The return home rewrites Africa as much as Africa rewrites home. Waugh's third "nightmare" in *Remote People* is his return to England and its pubs and his encounter with "real" savages in a savage land: laddish men and flirtatious women in a defamiliarized atmosphere noisier than "the market at Harar."[80] For Waugh, the worst aspect of home is that his prickly bachelor friends do not give him the reverential treatment due to a traveler who has proved himself abroad. In lieu of such treatment, they have simply forgotten him. In this attempted comic reversal, England itself has become the strange and uncomprehending place.

Overall, interwar-era writing about sub-Saharan Africa involved generous but formulaic codes. The subgenre, if you will, demanded personality, eccentricity, and digressions, but it accommodated these features at the price of a certain uniformity. Travel writing from the interwar period is unusually inclusive overall. This is true of the narratives I consider in this book; they combine essays, autobiography, history, social criticism, statistics, and moral homilies, among other elements, and often spend scant time on Africa. Writing about travel also became writing about writing and writing about personal topics. I have shown how several of the books under consideration stage self-discovery in Africa. In *Phantom Africa*, Leiris explicitly enacts his personal virility tests throughout the extended Mission Dakar-Djibouti.

Traditionally, travel writing's perennially marginal position in the world of letters has been seen to grant its practitioners license, indeed to encourage, formal and thematic innovation. Writing about travel in sub-Saharan Africa from the interwar period in particular involves the fashioning of a literary persona by means of perpetual detours into diverse and often ostensibly unrelated subject matter. It is addressed to a home culture and meets expectations and settles scores accordingly. Overall, interwar-era writing about sub-Saharan Africa is not exclusively about travel; nor is it exclusively about sub-Saharan Africa. It resonates with Jean-Jacques Rousseau's peripatetic philosophy, a philosophy that that leads to works comprised of observations and thoughts gathered en route.

In an almost aggressive polyvalence, interwar-era writing about travel in sub-Saharan Africa navigates steadily between the subject and the world, the particular and the universal. The writing is difficult to define generically; writers write about travel, although they do not, with the exception of Hemingway and Morand, encourage their readers to travel; their books will likely not function as guidebooks. The narrator's ostensible uniqueness and freedom is essential to the formula of the interwar-era book about travel in sub-Saharan Africa. Consequently, interwar-era traveling writers stage themselves at the same moment that they are offering data about human diversity. Interwar-era travel books demand reference to an experienced author. As a 1952 broadsheet [*prière d'insérer*] for *Journey to the End of the Night* declares: "The author debuts in full maturity after an extremely rich and varied life."[81] This declaration echoes the popular French image of Conrad, both in its prestigious excuse for Céline's relatively late start in literature and in the equation it draws between the quality of a writer's life and the quality of his writing.

When Hemingway won the Nobel Prize in 1954, he declared that there were three people who deserved it more than he did. In a letter to General Charles T. Lanham, he mentions Isak Dinesen as one of them. At that time he was also working on a second book about Africa, *True at First Light*, which would be published posthumously. Dinesen wrote to Hemingway to congratulate him, lamenting that the two had never met: "It is a sad thing we have never met in the flesh. I have sometimes imagined what it would have been like to be on a safari with you on the plain of Africa."[82] To a certain extent, we can imagine how that safari might have been narrated. Despite its apparent uniqueness, interwar-era writing about travel in sub-Saharan Africa stems from the same model, one characterized by a whimsical yet elegiac tone, an inclusive structure, and an emphasis on the prestige offered to the writers by means of what they saw as generative hardship.

It is instructive to consider what happens to these many conventions during and after the Second World War. One clue comes from Markham. Towards the end of *West with the Wind* she describes Africa in the early forties: "Adventure for Nairobi came in celluloid rolls straight from Hollywood and adventure for the other parts of the world went out from Nairobi in celluloid rolls straight from the cameras of professional globe trotters. It was a good time to leave."[83] Hollywood's Africa was invading Markham's Africa. She had no choice but to retaliate. After becoming the first woman to fly across the Atlantic, Markham, in search of new challenges and climes, hit Hollywood, where her dramatic past granted her an offer of employment from Paramount studios. Paramount had a motion picture called *Safari* on the stocks. In the film, the romantic hero, a white hunter, scouts elephant from a biplane in East Africa. Markham accepted the position of technical advisor in order to assist in the production of an African hunting expedition in the film.

Safari centers on said hunting expedition in Africa, during which the beautiful heroine, whose aviator sweetheart had been killed in Spain, seeks security and peace of mind as the wife of the rich, titled sportsman financing the expedition. But the heroine encounters a white hunter and confirms the tradition by walking out on her fiancé, and into the white hunter's arms. Markham earnestly ensured that producers, actors, and costumers painstakingly observed the rules of Africa as she told them about her childhood in Kenya. She assisted in the flight scenes, helped the actors with their Swahili dialogue, and ensured that the heroine had an appropriate wardrobe.

Hollywood was on its own quest for authenticity, and Markham thought herself well positioned to provide it. Having grown up in Africa, she was now ready to fabricate it; she knew the rules of narrative about Africa, how things were done and how they were not, what was foregrounded and what was not. Markham's perspective was highly marketable. Like travelers, producers wanted a vision of Africa, the veracity of which they could be sure. The producers of *Safari* anticipated a popular audience that would demand some level of authenticity; Markham could provide that.

The interwar period produced traveling writers who predicted, some in good faith, others not, the end of their style of travel. In part, this was due to their desire to distinguish themselves; as well, all of the writers considered here knew that change was coming quickly and very likely through war. They then played with this tragic element, prematurely living their epoch's nostalgia and early voicing its inevitable elegies. They decided in advance that this would be the last era of real travel and this view informs the very structure of their writing, determining what is included and how it is narrated. For the writers studied in this chapter, sub-Saharan Africa is a paradigmatic place to have an authentic experience. As I have demonstrated, these writers, for the most part, claim contact with putative primitivism and assume the role of cultural translator for their readers. Although writers so readily telegraph the uniqueness of their accounts, the books resemble each other in a striking number of ways. The fact that there were such powerful conventions for writing about quests in Africa is what made it so easy for Waugh to parody them, Leiris to make games out of them, Céline to mock them, and Markham to contract them out to Paramount. They and their traveling writer peers followed a strict recipe for inclusion in their writing about sub-Saharan Africa. They returned from a familiar Africa.

In the following chapter, I narrow my focus to concentrate on two travel narratives about sub-Saharan African travel from the mid-1930s: Ernest Hemingway's *Green Hills of Africa* (1935) and Graham Greene's *Journey without Maps* (1936). I argue that they must both be considered as quest narratives and, by doing so, unlock the particular manner of masculine self-confrontation that brings together the morose Englishman and his blunt American counterpart. It is for this reason and for precise scrutiny that I have gathered Greene and Hemingway together and separated them from their fellow traveling writers. I now build on this chapter's exploration of the tropes that characterize travel narratives about Africa during the interwar period, and draw particular fortification from the fruits of our investigation into aspects of self-staging in these narratives. As will be clear, both Greene and Hemingway search for self-knowledge, attempting to meet themselves *à travers* sub-Saharan Africa.

Considering the import of the historical context of the mid-1930s, I will argue that personal and aesthetic concerns characterize both books, neither of which deals exclusively with Africa, and neither of which foregrounds encounters with indigenous people. In this and the previous chapter, I have identified the solipsism manifest in all of the books' representations of indigenous sub-Saharan African people. In the next chapter, I analyze how Greene and Hemingway navigate this solipsism, particularly with respect to the indigenous people who work for them; I pay particular attention to the way in which Greene represents his encounters with the indigenous Africans who carry his tent and provisions, as well as Hemingway's depiction of his interactions with his Maasai helpers. At the same time, I consider the ways in which both writers claim authority for their books by means of accounts of hardship and declarations of authenticity joined, in a way that is familiar by now, with a sense of premature belatedness and anticipatory nostalgia.

CHAPTER SIX

The One-Man Show: Greene, Hemingway, Sub-Saharan Africa, and the End of the Interwar Period

In *Journey Without Maps* (1936), hereafter referred to as *JWM*, Greene documents his pursuit of self-knowledge in Liberia, the unmapped and uncolonized West African republic across which he and his cousin Barbara Greene trekked 350 miles. Hemingway's *Green Hills of Africa* (1935), referred to hereafter as *GHOA*, documents the Hemingways' expensive safari, in what was then referred to as colonial East Africa, an undertaking financed by the magazine *Esquire* as well as a $25,000 gift from Pauline Hemingway's wealthy uncle Gus, who specified that it was a contribution for Hemingway's next book. Although Greene organized his own Liberian trek, while Hemingway opted for a structured safari in Kenya and Tanzania, the books that document each journey echo the geographically specific stock of conventions investigated in the previous two chapters.

Such conventions—including the quest for hardships, the rhetorical use of nostalgia, the solemnity, the occasional excursus into seemingly unrelated material, and the emphasis on perceived primitivism—filiate their projects. Although both writers afford their readers an account of a specific region, they also offer more general meditations on the continent of Africa writ large, which is, for both of them, an idée fixe wider in scope than any particular region, as I demonstrate. Both *JWM* and *GHOA* take from and contribute to the literary tradition of books in which travel in Africa is cast as an opportunity to peek at a collective, if ultimately illusory, past. In the final account, both writers inadvertently foreground the fraught history of travel in Africa, as well as their place in that history, through their determined search for hardship, unique experiences, and dramatic encounters with alterity. Of principal concern will be Greene and Hemingway's quests: the former to attain historical and self-knowledge, the latter to write a "true story" that will compete successfully with fiction. I consider the contemporaneous pursuit of such highly disparate desiderata in two wildly different destinations and contexts. One could of course make the obvious point that the books are unlike each other in terms of length, style, and more; this is inarguable. But the conceits and concerns that they do share are remarkable enough for us to scrutinize them together in order to learn about a specific fashioning of masculinity, a paradigm for confronting alterity, and a perceived path to authentic adventures among authentic people.

I will demonstrate that *JWM* and *GHOA* share a strikingly similar narrative and thematic approach despite the different destinations, nationalities, and stated literary projects of the two writers. Although they head to vastly different areas on the African continent, both Greene and Hemingway end up fiercely proximate in the literary Africa explored in the previous two chapters. Both of their books are also characterized by a markedly similar admixture of appropriative rhetoric, personal revelation, and confident cultural analysis. Their shared aspirations and assumptions justify us in situating them together at a decisive moment in a long and fraught history of travel writing about the African continent. As seen in the previous two chapters, such firsthand accounts typically offer a combination of autobiographical material and material that is prioritized precisely because of its eccentricity. But they accommodate this combination by means of a seemingly paradoxical conformity to a romantic primitivism that is constituted, in part, by adherence to notions of racial superiority. As Miller has argued, "[t]he history of Africanist discourse is that of a continuing series of questions imposed on Africa, questions that preordain certain answers while ruling others out."[1] That Greene and Hemingway's journeys to sub-Saharan Africa were well scripted before they even left is more than apparent. The script of Africa is familiar to both writers, who travel with a shared arsenal of vocabulary and phantasms.

Traveling writers of the interwar period defined themselves through their choice of destination, often choosing the United States or the Soviet Union to glimpse at the future. As Greene asserts, "[t]he motive for a journey deserves a little attention," arguing that it is "not the fully conscious mind which chooses West Africa in preference to Switzerland."[2] Greene's interest in understanding large-scale violence, as well as his "impatience" with his own era, complement his belief in a collective past visible in sub-Saharan Africa.[3] As seen in the previous two chapters, answers about the past were often sought in the African continent. Greene polemically pits his choice of destination against the Soviet option: "There are others, of course, who prefer to look a stage ahead, for whom Intourist provides cheap tickets into a plausible future, but my journey represented a distrust of any future based on what we are."[4] Greene's declaration serves as an introduction to one of the notable themes of his book: the decline of modern life and the related need, in his case, for regeneration. Africa stands for the past that will help him understand the present and create the future. Greene relatedly associates the continent with childhood memories, generative memories that he believes will—in concert with the psychoanalytic tools he had picked up during recent rounds of psychoanalytic therapy—help him to decipher Africa.

In *GHOA*, Hemingway gives a cursory nod to the starvation and resulting migration of peoples that shadow his East African safari. As the car passes a group of people walking with their possessions, he refers obliquely to "the famine."[5] For Hemingway, the rain that threatens the displaced Tanzanians signals the close of the hunting season. In a similar manner, Greene's travels from the colonized country of Sierra Leone into the uncolonized Republic of Liberia are cast more as a journey into himself than a study of African independence. The Republic of Liberia, founded in 1847, was struggling to safeguard its independence from neighboring colonies during the 1930s. At the time of Greene's visit, the republic was still quelling the violence that had erupted between the indigenous Kru people and the ruling class, composed of formerly enslaved people from the United States. Also scrutinizing the context of Greene's trip, Bernard Schweizer reports that "Liberia had acquired notoriety in the late 1920s through allegations that the country's governing elite (descended from slaves in the United States) had itself encouraged slavery and forced labor."[6] Nevertheless, any interest that Greene had for reportage evaporated as he treated Liberia as a site for self-discovery and ignored the political reality.

Both Greene and Hemingway meet the challenge to provide innovative material by foregrounding their own outsized personalities; it can be argued that both *GHOA* and *JWM* are one-man variety shows. Both were released with an active publicity campaign, both appear as a response to readers' demands for more autobiographical work, and share notably similar content, as will be demonstrated below. In his 1936 review of

JWM, fellow traveling writer Peter Fleming explicitly stacks Greene's book against Hemingway's recently published *GHOA*, noting that both writers cast themselves as the principal attraction of their books by making use of "a highly individual style and a highly personal attack."[7] For both writers, the emphasis must be on the trials they faced while traveling. Dysentery, for instance, which both writers suffered, offers them the opportunity of demonstrating bravery and endurance. With its reputation as a difficult place to travel, Africa promised a great number of crucibles that, in turn, could provide compelling subject matter for books and magazine articles.

Whereas *JWM* starts with Greene's travel plans and documents his departure from England, *GHOA* begins in medias res, halfway through the hugely expensive sixty-day safari. When compared with *Death in the Afternoon*, *GHOA* is less overtly pedagogical and, unlike the earlier book, makes use of novelistic conventions. In the foreword, Hemingway presents his book as the outcome of his attempt to write a "true book" about a "month's action."[8] To the extent that the foreword underscores Hemingway's hope that *GHOA* will "compete with a work of the imagination," it invites comparison with engaging works of fiction.[9] Of Africa, he assumes that the "action" will be the kind of experience that only it can provide. Africa, cast by Hemingway as a land of beginnings, offers him notable challenges by means of which he can prove himself adept and capable. In his view, this book could only have taken place in Africa; furthermore, he suggests that his book will be truer than competing narratives precisely because Africa is, in his view, a place where one can experience very explicit and unique hardships.

Hemingway's assertion that he will attempt to write a "true book" recalls the kind of questions about authenticity explored throughout this book. Once again, challenges and hardships are cast as ingredients for authenticity and narrative authority. From his own words, Greene travels to Africa in search of aesthetic gain and powerful knowledge, including knowledge about himself, his past, and his place in time. He explicitly proclaims that the various forms of difficulty and adversity that he will face will bring him both self-knowledge and engaging material. Greene is loath to appear complicit with the exploitative colonial powers that were rapidly industrializing the continent at the expense of the welfare of the indigenous people. He depoliticizes the trek and situates its source, rather than in either idealism or *realpolitik*, in the extensive course of psychoanalysis he has just completed. The legacy of that course is Greene's new interest in "ancestral fear";[10] naming H. Rider Haggard and Joseph Conrad as models, Greene announces his choice to "suffer some discomfort for the chance of finding [. . .] one's place in time, based on a knowledge not only of one's present but of the past from which one has emerged."[11] He taxonomizes Africa as a "beginning," one that affords him a glimpse into the collective past as well as an understanding of a destroyed innocence that he links to both a difficult childhood and the war.[12] He also assigns it curative value: "I couldn't help feeling [. . .] that I had got somewhere new by way of memories I hadn't known I possessed. I had taken up the thread of life from very far back, from as far back as innocence."[13] He casts his trek inland as a journey back from adulthood to childhood, and even to his unconscious mind. The journey is possible because, in his view, Africa remains connected to the distant past and offers a vision of universal childhood. "It was at their backs," he explains, making space stand for historical time, "it wasn't centuries away."[14]

Due to its perceived connection to a universal past, travel to Africa is, in Greene's view, travel into a familiar past:

But what had astonished me about Africa was that it had never been really strange. Gibraltar and Tangier—those extended just parted hands—seemed more than ever to represent an unnatural breach. The 'heart of darkness' was common to us both. Freud had made us conscious as we have never been before of those ancestral threads which still exist in our unconscious minds to lead us back. The need, of course, has always been felt, to go back and begin again. Mungo Park, Livingstone, Stanley, Rimbaud, Conrad represented only another method to Freud's, a more costly, less easy method, calling for physical as well as mental strength.[15]

Greene and Hemingway's figuration of Africa, as a land of beginnings and encounters with earlier stages of time, owes much to travel narratives and adventure writing by men of their parents' and grandparents' generations. Indeed, both writers were passionate childhood and young adult consumers of nineteenth-century and fin-de-siècle literature that dealt with sub-Saharan Africa. As argued in the last chapter, such literature typically suggested that sub-Saharan Africa could offer the European a peek at a collective past. Greene and Hemingway's travel writing shows a clear indebtedness to the Victorian travel narrative, in particular its codes of conduct for white people and its near-death plots (the two related, as I will demonstrate).[16]

Like Greene, Hemingway eagerly consumed Haggard and Conrad. Indeed, Reynolds informs us that Kipling was among the teenage Hemingway's "favorite authors," one he both read and reread, even quoting the *Jungle Book* by heart at sixteen.[17] Reynolds lists Frederick Marryat, Stuart Edward White, and Horatio Alger as authors whose works they would have read. He documents how, as a young child in Illinois, Hemingway was particularly drawn to stories about the explorer Carl Akeley and even visited his stuffed elephants at Chicago's Field Museum of Natural History. Reynolds has further demonstrated how Hemingway devoured Theodore Roosevelt's *National Geographic* essays about his post-presidential safari, just as he read the former president's 1910 book *African Game Trails*. The same year, Hemingway wore a safari hat when his grandfather took him to see Roosevelt as he sped past Oak Park on a whistle-stop tour. Less is known of Greene's adolescent reading, but his figurations do, I demonstrate, show the influence of those writers on *JWM* as well.

Greene and Hemingway's shared commitment to experiencing hardship recalls the adventurers of their childhoods, both fictional and real. Both *JWM* and *GHOA* establish an equation between ordeals and authenticity. Illness, much like war in the veteran novels contemporaneous with both books, is a guarantor of an authentic experience and also of the authority to write about it. In this way, threats to his body will allow the traveler an ideal experience of Africa. Overall, it is in this valuation of hardship that each writer unmasks his literary inheritance; it is in their perceived difficulties and their predictable dismissal of "handouts and sightseeing."[18] At a time of unprecedented travel, Greene and Hemingway mobilize hardship to both justify and give value to their narratives. In this way, the body's centrality is apparent: physical and psychological factors, even loneliness and boredom. Both traveling writers subscribe to the time-honored function in the African plot of potentially serious illness; both demonstrate the influence of Haggard's African novels and their romantic tales of adventure into territory that is as dangerous as it is unspecific. Upon his return to England from West Africa, Greene eviscerated Harry J. Greenwald and Roland Wild's *Unknown Liberia* in a review, aptly titled "Two Tall Travelers." Chastising the writers for avoiding the interior of Liberia, he caustically concludes that "they might just as well have stayed in England, where indeed, almost all their material might easily have been compiled."[19] Rather hypocritically, he mocks the writers for traveling with "twenty hammock carriers," implicitly suggesting that they have not experienced enough adversity to achieve the kind of narrative authority necessary to give an accurate account of Liberia and the many challenges travelers will face there.[20]

Both *JWM* and *GHOA* arguably function as meta-travelogues; they engage with the complexities of travel itself and, despite offering specific information that could be useful for tourists or travelers, such as directions and proper names, they at no point invite readers to undertake similar journeys. Instead both writers suggest that the possibility of an authentic experience in Africa is currently unlikely and imply that no one will be able to duplicate their experiences. Palpable in both books is the familiar ambivalence towards readers. They also forcibly, albeit potentially unintentionally, underscore one of the chief paradoxes of writing about travel more generally: only an element of sameness permits the meaningful difference that separates reader from traveler. The reader must be able to relate to the material enough to understand the extent to which the writer distinguishes himself from him by means of his presumably inimitable experiences. Tim Youngs identifies this balancing act in the works of nineteenth-century travel writers and traveling writers, the very works that so influenced both Greene and Hemingway. Such writers tread this narrative tightrope deftly, Youngs argues, by "at once establishing their cultural affinities with, and spatial, experiential difference from, their readers."[21] In like fashion, both Greene and Hemingway build their pronounced hostility towards aspiring travelers to Africa on the groundwork of a presumably shared cultural identity.

Both writers express annoyance when they encounter signs of previous travelers to Africa. There was certainly nothing particularly novel about indulging in an East African safari in the mid-1930s; nevertheless, Hemingway assiduously avoids fellow safari goers and makes clear that he chose not to settle in the camp where "the Prince of Wales had killed his kudu."[22] Greene does explicitly insert himself into a tradition of writing about travel, quoting Charles Baudelaire's "*L'invitation au voyage*" when he first sees the African coast. Although Baudelaire's poem tracks the erotic invitation of Jeanne Duval, his Haitian-born French mistress, Greene ties it to Africa. Such slippage was in great force during this period, as seen above when African masks were categorized as objects of "Negrophilia," along with African-American performing artists such as Josephine Baker.

Associating Baudelaire and the African coast, Greene allows that he is the inheritor of a tradition of writing about Africa. He also connects his quests to a number of presumably similar quests, invoking both Conrad and Céline to explain his search for answers on the continent and answer the broader question: "Why Africa?"[23] He explicitly chooses Liberia because it is both unmapped and avowedly independent (although one might ultimately dispute its actual independence from the web of colonial projects in West Africa). Indeed, he cannot pass the "seedy" coast quickly enough; the complexities of colonialism that he registers in Sierra Leone are cast as obstacles to, and distractions from, his overarching quest for authenticity.[24]

Both Greene and Hemingway frequently invoke the First World War as both explanation and justification for their travels in sub-Saharan Africa. For Greene, the horrific legacy of the war leads to, for him, the imperative to understand "at what point we went astray."[25] The war is also significant because, born in 1904, he was too young to participate in the "great test"; such belatedness informs his already robust desire to distinguish himself from idle travelers. Greene missed the crucible of the war; he hopes his travels will make up for that by offering alternative near-death experiences, presumably affording him the desired paysage of despair and mystery: "A quality of darkness is needed, of the inexplicable."[26] He states as much quite frankly in his autobiography *Ways of Escape*, indeed arguing that his peers had similar motives for traveling outside of Europe in countries that were comparatively less developed: "We were a generation who had missed the enormous disillusionment of the war so we went looking for adventure."[27] In a 1940 essay "At Home," written during the Blitz, he also suggests that arduous traveling during the interwar period helped assuage the traveler's certain, in his view, anticipatory anxiety with respect to what, at the time, seemed a both inevitable and impending war. With respect to the First World War, Hemingway and Greene's travels were compensatory; with respect to the Second World War, their travels were anticipatory. They were, in part, the consequence of an impatience for the arrival of the violence that seemed inevitable. As Greene relates, "I think it was a sense of impatience because the violence was delayed—rather than a masochistic enjoyment of discomfort—that made many writers of recent years go abroad to try to meet it half way."[28]

Hemingway echoes Greene in making a connection between war and narrative authority. He suggests that this equation is not unique to the First

World War and is instead true of war in general. Responding to a Red Cross recruitment effort, Hemingway volunteered for ambulance driving in Italy in 1918. Quickly wounded while in an observation post, he recuperated for months in a Milanese Red Cross hospital before being invalided back to the States. Even with arguably only a modicum of experience of war (compared to veterans of the war in particular), Hemingway counts himself fortunate for the part he did play, and sees himself in good company: "I thought about Tolstoi and about what a great advantage an experience of war was to a writer."[29] Although he did not fight in the war, he sees the events he witnessed and the physical suffering that he endured as an "experience of war." Scholars such as Philip Beidler have taken Hemingway to task for, they believe, falsely representing himself as a veteran. My concern here is not to adjudicate that question but rather to examine Hemingway's thesis that hardship and suffering grant authenticity and authority. We are not far here from the Conrad of his French consecrators and the masculine gravitas they praised in his work.

In Hemingway's view, the experience of war offers privileges beyond narrative authority. For him, it legitimates his killing animals as much as the East African hunting license he purchased. He creates a related moral economy out of his experience of war, whereby he is entitled to kill game due to the fact that he had been shot at himself: "I did nothing that had not been done to me. I had been shot and I had been crippled and gotten away. I expected, always, to be killed by one thing or another and I, truly, did not mind that anymore."[30] He also resolves to fight fairly and give up the hunt when he can no longer promise a swift death: "Since I loved to hunt I resolved that I would only shoot as long as I could kill cleanly and as soon as I lost that ability I would stop."[31] Fixated on the topic of war, he makes use of its vocabulary to the extent that the afternoon siesta becomes a way to "kill the hot part of the day."[32] Above all, however, the risks taken while hunting large game afford Hemingway the chance to reconnect with the drama of war, and thereby reaffirm his narrative authority.

Greene returns repeatedly in *JWM* to the riskiness and arduousness of his trek. He includes a reproduction of his copy of a "Declaration of the Alien about to depart for the Republic of Liberia" and excerpts alarmist passages from the British government's *Blue Book*. Grim statements such as "'[t]he rat population may fairly be described as swarming,'" function to telegraph Greene's hope to gain authority and authenticity through hardship.[33] "[Y]ou couldn't go deeper than that," he writes of Africa with respect to such hardship, suggesting once again that the danger that enhances his experience also guarantees authority.[34] In this way, the autonomous Republic of Liberia, noted by British authorities as a place where illness and disease were rife, serves as the ideal destination for staging self-encounters and dramatizing the resulting discoveries of that encounter.

Greene quickly concedes that Liberia's plains are barren; nevertheless, animals still serve as a form of hardship as, for instance, when he hears rats scaling his tent or discovers trails in the earth made by Siafu ants. He makes of his encounters with animal life one of the reliably recurring themes in his book and always associates it with physical ordeals and insalubrious conditions: "This, as I grew more tired and my health a little failed, seemed to be what I would chiefly remember as Africa: cockroaches eating our clothes, rats on the floor, dust in the throat, jiggers under the nails, ants fastening on the flesh."[35] He explicitly equates such hardship with authenticity, presenting the clothes-eating cockroaches as "the badge of an unconquered virginity."[36] In his aptly titled 1947 essay "The Lost Childhood," he references his Haggard-inspired fantasy about dying in Africa: "[O]ften I have wished that my hand had not moved further than King Solomon's Mines, and that the future that I had taken down from the nursery shelf had been a district office in Sierra Leone and twelve tours of malarial duty and a finishing dose of blackwater fever when the danger of retirement approaches."[37] With Greene's youthful Russian roulette games in mind, Greene biographer Michael Sheldon urges his readers to take seriously Greene's longing for an African death. It must certainly be considered when examining his valorization of what I have been calling hardship. Illness, as shown above, is one of the chief ingredients of the more general African plot.

Greene embraces opportunities to emphasize Liberia's dangers and suggest that the attendant hardship both edifies and grants narrative authority. He also emphasizes that he does not seek comfort and indeed often further endangers himself as a matter of course. Towards the end of his trek through Liberia, an ailing Greene travels on foot despite a doctor's warning that doing so might prove fatal: "I could see the doctor watching me, critically; he didn't have to tell me what he was thinking."[38] Greene casts his behavior as more heroic than foolish. Additionally, he further confabulates both the human and the ecological elements of Africa by means of an apparent interpretive susceptibility that permits him to believe in demons, in the human creation of lightning, and, finally and perhaps inevitably, in cannibals. Africa fulfills his desire for a world with looser standards for truth, one that will permit him to believe, like a child, in miracles and magic, one where he can embrace "feeling rather than thought."[39] Reflecting on his trek later in life, Greene praises Liberia for giving him the opportunity to live "continuously in the presence of the supernatural."[40]

Greene embraces the "discomfort" that he suggests will illuminate his "place in time."[41] Likewise, Hemingway embraces a severe bout of amoebic dysentery and all of "the discomforts that you paid to make it real."[42] He telegraphs the severity of his illness with meaningful understatement when he first mentions it, advising that he "was beginning to feel strong again after the dysentery."[43] He had already offered a strikingly lighthearted and jocular account of his battle with amoebic dysentery in the *Esquire* dispatch "A. D. [amoebic dysentery] in Africa: A Tanganyika Letter." The eight dispatches, or "letters," that Hemingway contributed to *Esquire* during his safari often give a more lighthearted look at the very events he describes so solemnly in the book. Indeed, the *Esquire* dispatches feature a comedic narrator, whereas *GHOA* rests on the gains and prestige of experiences of hardship, illness in particular. Like the experience of war, amoebic dysentery is a fair trade-off for the narrative authority which it bequests the author; it functions both as apology and guarantor of the authenticity of his experiences. His stoic endurance is showcased through the lighthearted yet graphic account of his illness: "Already I had had one of the diseases and I had experienced the necessity of washing a three-inch bit of my large intestine with soap and water and tucking it back where it belonged an unnumbered amount of times a day."[44] As with authenticity, he makes an explicit connection between his dysentery and his heightened knowledge of Africa: "[I]t was well worth going through for what I had seen and where I had been."[45] Going further, Hemingway deftly follows Nietzsche in the particular attention he gives to the generative power of health regained; his illness and subsequent convalescence grant him the stories, whereas his regained health affords him the necessary strength to write them down.

Barbara Greene's 1938 book *Land Benighted* was published in the United States as *Too Late to Turn Back*. It describes her decision to trek across Liberia with her cousin as the unintended result of a champagne-informed dare. In *Too Late to Turn Back*, she concentrates on humorous events and colorful trivialities. In a peppy tone, she declares that "[t]he old type of Adventure in the Wilds seems to have disappeared."[46] Barbara

Greene, like her cousin, describes indigenous peoples as pacific and child-like. However, she explicitly parts ways with Greene when it comes to the convention of hardship. Effectively ending her already taxed relationship with her cousin, Barbara Greene, in *Land Benighted*, refuses to back up his accounts of hardship and makes no claims with respect to self-discovery. She makes her position clear when she apostrophizes the readers with both caveats and disclaimers:

> Should the reader of this book lean towards the roaring lion type of adventure, let him cast this volume from him. The beasts of the forest kept away from us, the natives were friendly, our adventures were more amusing than frightening, and good luck dogged our footsteps most of the time.[47]

Recounting the same circumstances, she insinuates that her cousin exaggerated his heroics. With respect to the rats that Graham Greene mobilized to suggest peril and the danger of disease, Barbara Greene deflates his solemn account, noting that although "[the] rats were fat and well fed," they posed little nuisance: "[A]part from the noise they made they left me in peace. For two or three nights they upset me and after that I grew so used to them that I ceased to notice them, and they bothered me no more."[48] I have speculated before about a parallel tradition that might exist amongst women writers, but I have also pointed to the relative paucity of material as I have found it. Whatever the case, the same events are often cast entirely differently; Barbara Greene assiduously avoids any emphasis on suffering and self-discovery, whereas her cousin truculently foregrounds hardship. But *Land Benighted* does not necessarily offer an alternative truth, and frank joviality is, after all, but one more convention of interwar-era travel writing, as I have demonstrated in every chapter. Graham scarcely mentions Barbara in *JWM*, and, intentionally or not, creates the illusion of an all-male trek; from this one might deduce the possibility that *Land Benighted* involves some score settling. Tellingly, while Graham, like André Gide, brings Robert Burton's *Anatomy of Melancholy* to read on his trek, Barbara brings a Somerset Maugham novel. But we know this only from Barbara's book, as Graham almost entirely dismisses her from his account, perhaps missing an opportunity to cast unwelcome travel companions, just as his mocking contemporaries in Africa cast fellow passengers, as elements of hardship.

However, only one year after the publication of *Land Benighted*, Greene, in his 1939 review for *The Spectator* of Etta Donner's *Hinterland Liberia*, praises its lack of self-staging and its refusal to dramatize hardship. Lauding it as "[e]asily the best book that has been written on Liberia," Greene celebrates Donner's tendency to gloss over potential dangers:

> Miss Donner, of course, ran no risk of ordinary violence—a white skin is a passport of friendship in a country where the rulers are black—but she ran enormous risks and perhaps of poisoning. This is never brought out: for Miss Donner is not concerned with herself: there is no snapshot of the author, and she never presents herself against the background of that extraordinary land.[49]

In his 1936 review of *Journey Without Maps*, Peter Fleming took Greene to task for his tendency to draw attention to hardships, the very thing that Greene would praise Donner for not doing in 1939. In the same review, Fleming also discounts these very hardships. A traveling writer himself, Fleming, as seen in our discussion of his *Brazilian Adventure* in the third chapter, identifies and mocks the one-upmanship so dominant in travel literature overall during the interwar period. He ridicules Greene's sober enumeration of the hardships he faces, comparing the comfortable writer's tribulations to those of Mungo Park, the eighteenth-century Scottish explorer of Africa: "Mungo fared worse; but his desperation-point was lower, he had no whisky and mosquito-nets and Epsom salts, and he probably therefore minded less."[50] Although Fleming validates Greene's "brilliance," he dismisses any authority Greene claims for himself by means of what the questing writer saw as the generative nature of his trials, his loneliness, his illness, even his boredom.[51]

Miriam B. Mandel has notably argued that Hemingway's writing at large offers representations of egalitarian and engaged travel, travel that is, as she puts it, "democratic, adventurous, participatory, and exploratory."[52] This is untrue of the prohibitively expensive safari recounted in *GHOA*, one that employed dozens of East African people. It is likewise untrue of the trek represented in Greene's *JWM*. That trek brought a cook and twenty-five carriers, "only five less than the entourage of [Liberian] President Barclay," Greene notes.[53] Consumer comforts are available to both writers; hardships, for this reason and more, always unfold within an overall leisure context in which their financial and political advantages grant them a special social status. It is worth recalling again Lévi-Strauss's thesis that a Western traveler, due, to a large extent, to economic and symbolic power, typically gains social as well as economic status when he travels outside the Western world.

Neither Hemingway nor Greene dilates on this clear privilege and its ramifications for their overall comfort and security. Indeed, both, by the logic that privileges hardship over ease, are loath to describe their many comforts. Hemingway ruthlessly mocks Kandinsky, the Austrian farmer who delights in his new stature as "king" while living in a British colony entirely under direct rule.[54] Kandinsky proudly illustrates his status:

> In reality, I am a king here. It is very pleasant. Waking in the morning I extend one foot and the boy places a sock on it. When I am ready I extend the other foot and he adjusts the other sock. I step from under the mosquito bar into my drawers which are held for me. Don't you think that it is very marvelous?[55]

Kandinsky delights in his servants just as Hemingway delights in the indigenous people he has employed on his safari. Nevertheless, Kandinsky's description of luxury sits ill with Hemingway, even if he enjoys the same treatment by indigenous people during his safari. Hemingway ridicules Kandinsky, but Hemingway's safari is also undertaken in an atmosphere of luxury and he is taken care of at each stage, and, in nearly every way, by indigenous people. Hemingway, as much as Kandinsky, regularly looks at indigenous people in an instrumental fashion.

Thomas Strychacz has convincingly argued that Hemingway was well aware of his attempts to gain both authority and status by triumphing over what were often self-imposed masculine feats. As he has noted with respect to *Death in the Afternoon*, as well as other works by Hemingway, the performance of such ordeals requires an audience to ratify and affirm it; sans audience, the ordeals are meaningless: "Hemingway is always aware of manhood-making as a theatrical event played out before an audience."[56] One noteworthy audience in *GHOA* is the "white hunter," "Pop", or Philip Percival, a legendary figure who, with his virility and outsized sexual appeal, functions to approve and sanction Hemingway's safari successes as well as Hemingway himself. Having once worked for Roosevelt on his safari, Pop functions in *GHOA* as an expert audience with his sang-froid and unflappable manner. He also has a predilection for alcohol and "[d]rinks too much as a good man should."[57] Pop's overall ruggedness serves for Hemingway as a guarantor of his moral fiber; his word should be taken when he appraises Hemingway's ordeals and overall worth. Overall, Hemingway makes much of their socializing together around a bottle; he suggests that if Pop agrees to be his interlocutor, this means that Hemingway has won his approval and esteem—although Pop is technically Hemingway's employee, and, as such, possibly subject to Hemingway's whims, and obliged to act towards Hemingway in a certain fashion.

As in the third chapter, reported speech is also crucial to our study. Greene and Hemingway's verbal interaction with indigenous peoples in particular is key to understanding the vexed combination of cultural information and power each accrues on his respective journey. One of the chief ways in which Hemingway suggests the uniqueness of his African experience is through the use of the untranslated Swahili words and phrases that he strews liberally throughout the travel narrative. He begins this project on the first page of his book, quoting a guide's pidgin English and Swahili: "'No good,' he said, '*Hapana muzuri*.'"[58] In part, this inclusion of untranslated words subjects the reader to the kind of experience of incomprehension that the narrator himself might feel. In this way, Hemingway attempts to create an aura of immediacy. However, this particular dynamic changes over the course of the trek, as Hemingway's own comprehension of Swahili quickly improves. "You get your good dope always from the people," he muses to his safari mates; "and when you can't talk with people and can't overhear it's no good."[59] Hemingway's thesis here is ultimately that, without knowledge of the language spoken at a destination, "you don't get anything that's of anything but journalistic value."[60] In sum, in Hemingway's view, one can only understand a country and a culture if one speaks the language. Relatedly, as the book progresses, just as Swahili comes to signify Hemingway's expertise, so does the secret handshake his trackers offer him at the end of his safari, a physical gesture which he reports is "on the order of blood brotherhood but a little less formal."[61] The language of Africa is, for Hemingway, both physical and linguistic; two communication systems are at work.

Hemingway quickly acquires both a functional and a social vocabulary with which to command the indigenous people who satisfy his needs and desires. In *GHOA*, as in other works, Hemingway demonstrates that the relative quickness with which he learns languages—a quickness that is widely acknowledged by Hemingway scholars—allows him more effectively to communicate with indigenous people overall. Furthermore, he suggests that some knowledge of Swahili will gain him a broader understanding of African culture and permit him unique encounters with its people. Hemingway demonstrates that he knows a little Swahili when speaking to his Maasai guide: "'It's a hell of a life,' I told him in English. He grinned and said 'More beer?' in Swahili. My talking English to him was an acceptable joke."[62] Here Hemingway alerts the reader that his mastery of basic Swahili has resulted in a special connection with his Maasai guide and that this functional bilingualism even permits him to make a language-based joke.

In *GHOA*, Hemingway recalls embracing his Maasai guide after an important kill. The Maasai guide says "'Wanderloo-Masai [*sic*] good guide,'" to which Hemingway responds with a playful echo: "'Wanderobo-Masai [*sic*] wonderful Masai [*sic*].'"[63] Later that evening, he declares: "'me plenty Simba.'"[64] Occasionally Hemingway weaponizes the English or French language in order to have a laugh at indigenous people who will not understand, but must, according to tacit rules for working for Westerners, at least try to. The oft-exasperated Hemingway asserts that he speaks to his Maasai carriers in English only when he is suspicious of them. When we ask how hegemonic language is spoken in *GHOA*, to whom it is spoken, and for what end, we can clearly see elements of the colonizer in Hemingway, the traveling writer.

In the earlier stages of his trek, Greene states helplessly that he "could never understand what they said to me."[65] However, this helplessness quickly disappears, and he begins conversing with his cook and carriers in pidgin English. For the most part, he reproduces these conversations while narrating moments in which he was frustrated by misapprehensions that he cast as the fruit of Liberians' perceived cultural illegibility. True to the conventions of his era, he suggests that clock time functions only in a European context; to this he attributes the difficulties he has when negotiating the trek with his carriers: "I was still planning my journey by European time; the listlessness, the *laissez-faire* of Africa hadn't caught me."[66] Shortly after this, the reader is treated to a rare passage of pidgin English, a passage that serves as an exhibit for Greene's contention that time is a European concept. One evening, as Greene aspires to travel to a nearby village, one of the principal carriers objects: "'Too far. Better stay here. Too far.'"[67] Rather than accept his carrier's calculations, he suggests that his objection is rather proof that "a black always exaggerated, when the fact was they had so hazy an idea of time that they were just as likely to minimize."[68] But Greene shows himself surrendering easily to this new concept of time: "Later I got used to not caring a damn, just to walking and staying put when I had walked far enough, at some village of which I didn't know the name, to letting myself drift with Africa."[69] Here, as elsewhere in *JWM*, Greene performs the seemingly paradoxical task of using his agency to proceed, as he believes that he would had he surrendered or somehow given up his agency, clearly an impossible task. Throughout *JWM*, Greene rarely stops his search for another way of inhabiting consciousness.

Greene's representations of pidgin English speakers offer more examples of what—as seen in the previous chapters—Albert Memmi terms the "mark of the plural," whereby an individual, in this case, his pidgin English-speaking carrier, is used as a metonym for an entire people, as the singular is generalized into a plural.[70] Greene, however, introduces pidgin English into his narrative far less often than his fellow English traveling contemporaries examined in the third chapter. Instead of reproducing the speech of the carriers he hires for a month, he more often relates his interpretation of their behavior; the carriers are mistrustful, the carriers are lazy, the carriers are demanding more money, etc. As seen above, he reserves his representation of pidgin English to recount surprises, shocks, and annoyances. Mid-trip he grumbles: "Their complaints, the phrase 'too far,' 'too far,' had got on my nerves."[71] Shortly thereafter, he grows vexatious with his carriers and threatens to dismiss them. Greene is further annoyed by the response of one of his chief carriers: "'They no want to go.'"[72] Pidgin English is also used to represent cultural conventions that Greene seems to choose to amuse the reader. As the head servant Amedoo laments: "'England good place. You have one God and no devils. I have one God too but plenty devils.'"[73] Greene also uses pidgin English to enhance the impact of his time-worn references to cannibalism: "'This is Gio country,' Amedoo explained, 'they chop people here.'"[74] In *JWM*, indigenous speech trades in wonders. Greene represents the pidgin English of his Liberian entourage as simplistic and word poor but pregnant with meaning.

Unlike Hemingway—and, once again, unlike his peers in the third chapter—Greene does not include any reproductions of indigenous languages in *JWM*. Indeed, the longest clip of untranslated language that Greene includes in his travelogue is rather a fragment of Latin pastoral poetry he reads after casually flipping through *Anatomy of Melancholy*.

Much as his inclusion of pidgin English is oriented to support his tendentious view of African culture, so does this Latin poetry, which he associates with people he deems, unlike the indigenous people with whom he is traveling, susceptible to "flowers and dew and scent."[75] Indeed, Greene expresses a total lack of interest in indigenous languages because, as he sees it, Liberians express emotion through comportment, unlike Europeans, who express emotions in words spoken or written. He pits Western "cerebral worked-up excitement" against the "unthinking tidal urge to joy" he witnesses one evening and of which his head carrier, Mark, says only, "'Last night we were so happy.'"[76] Greene posits that Africans' primary language is a physical one, best expressed with "song and laughter and running feet."[77] Once again, he represents Liberians as a childlike people from whom he can learn how to be young and innocent again.

Both Hemingway and Greene remark their own ability to communicate with indigenous people and find a common language. For Greene, it is a matter of recalling the contours of childhood. While attending a festival in Bolahun, he is reminded of a Jack-in-the-Green from his childhood by a blacksmith rigged up as a devil: "One had the sensation of having come home, one was being scared by the same old witches."[78] But adulthood also helps Greene in his quest; having just completed analysis, he follows a psychoanalytic logic while also mirroring Victorian travel writers' tendency to register and reproduce absolute truths by means of, as Wendy Katz describes, an "escape to a remote locale, the implicit character of which recalls a time past and even an earlier stage of human development."[79] Both Greene and Hemingway champion the continent of Africa as a place that offers insights into childhood and the past as much as cultural knowledge. Both writers stage themselves as capable of negotiating this complexity and reproduce the tendency of travel writers to experience, as Mary Louise Pratt puts it, "no sense of limitation on their interpretive powers."[80]

In both *GHOA* and *JWM*, concerns about the perceived near impossibility of capturing Africa in words lead to meditations on literature. For Greene, Africa negates any belletristic urges and indeed makes them impossible. He muses on this late in the trek as he reads Burton: "It was hard to believe [. . .] that there were emotions of tenderness and regret that couldn't be expressed with a harp, a drum and a rattle, buttocks and black teats."[81] Yet, the mere prospect of Africa leads Greene to literature and to his own work. He settles a score early on in his trip; as the ship passes the Canary Islands, he registers his outrage over a recently issued "cheap banal film" based on his novel *Stamboul Train*.[82] Later it provides a forum for shop talking, such as Hemingway's fractious literary conversations with the farmer Kandinsky. The porousness of their travel narratives allowed them both to include the kind of off-the-cuff passages that were, at that time, more closely associated with the comparatively wide-ranging personal essay.

As demonstrated in previous chapters, when it comes to writing about sub-Saharan Africa from the interwar period, such meditations about literature are omnipresent. Furthermore, looking more widely, the general inclusivity of the interwar-era travel narrative meant that writers also used it as a forum to talk shop. Hemingway's adventures into metafiction in *GHOA* are exemplary; he expresses a group philosophy when he merges geography with language to grant himself the narrative authority to write about writing itself, with particular attention to both the vicissitudes and the opportunities involved in writing in and about Africa. Furthermore, in his view, his stay in East Africa grants him not only license to write about writing, but also license to comment on contemporary literature. He relishes the distance his trip offers him and suggests that this distance affords unique perspectives on writing and literature, as much as it offers interlocutors with whom to discuss them; for instance, he delivers a sermon on contemporary literature to Kandinsky.

As an interlocutor, Kandinsky functions much like the Old lady who talks to the narrator in *Death in the Afternoon*; he also poses the simple questions that permit Hemingway to expose his opinions. The presumed novelty of having a conversation about literature in East Africa with a "short, bandy-legged man with a Tyroler hat, leather shorts, and an open shirt" appears the reason for Hemingway's inclusion of this humorless character.[83] Before the first antelope is killed, *GHOA* becomes a treatise on letters. Hemingway's pointed discourses on literature and history are softened by these comical conversations with earnest Kandinsky "of the Tyroler pants" who, like the Old lady before him, is disturbed by the narrator's enthusiasm for bloody sport.[84]

Kandinsky's blunt questions win responses that situate Hemingway in the tradition of the terse traveler. The responses also serve as an ostensible statement of purpose overall:

> "And what do you want?"
> "To write as well as I can and learn as I go along.

At the same time I have my life which I enjoy and which is a damned good life."

"Hunting kudu?"

"Yes. Hunting Kudu and many other things."[85]

Hemingway's personal life is foregrounded to advance the narrative and lend it interest. But it is a certain kind of personal life that is invoked; Hemingway does not include, for example, references to his troubled marriage, although he includes details of it as subject matter in an "African" story. Overall, he suggests that his time in East Africa is transformative and that it will change his overall outlook by, in part, affording him new and pliable tropes for masculinity. "Hunting kudu" is now firmly in his lexicon and he will return with trophies.

There is a broad consensus among interwar-era traveling writers that their own brand of nonfiction is more authentic than what might be summed up as mannered writing. Hemingway declares a break with the novel in the foreword: "Unlike many novels, none of the characters or incidents in this book is imaginary. . .The writer has attempted to see whether the shape of a country and the pattern of a month's action can, if truly presented, compete with a work of the imagination."[86] GHOA is part contest. But what would this non-novel look like? Greene and Hemingway give us similar answers. Both JWM and GHOA notably include conspicuously heterogeneous material. In one of the first reviews of Hemingway's effort, Bernard de Voto quipped: "[T]he literary discussion, though it contains some precious plums, is mostly bad; the exhibitionism is unfailingly good."[87] Greene is likewise prone to amatory material. Crucially, he presents this material not as unrelated, but rather as strongly connected to his experience of Africa, to "the music and the heat and the strangeness."[88] Recalling the louche vagaries of his early adulthood, he writes: "I was twenty-one, and you couldn't talk of darkest Africa with any conviction when you had known Nottingham well."[89] Greene's interest in "seediness," mirrored by Hemingway's boastful anecdotes, signals a rhetorical move that we must now be familiar with, namely, the creation of a metonym that makes Africa stand for the European underworld.

Greene stages the continent of Africa as a repository for both personal and collective memories, linking it to suggestive material. Long before he has left England, the word Africa calls up in him a miserable tableau: "a crowd of words and images, witches and death, unhappiness and the Gare

St Lazare, the huge smoky viaduct over a Paris slum."[90] In "The Shape of Africa," an early chapter in which he narrates his ship journey to Africa, he includes a number of bleak or bleakly sexual personal memories, including "a dead dog at the bottom of my pram" and "a girl lodging close by I wanted to do things to."[91]

Greene's detailed account of his memories of street prostitution in Riga, Latvia, comprises an entire subsection of *JWM*. He recasts his personal memories as collective memories by linking them qualitatively to Africa. He connects these memories with Africa insofar as they appear to him to reflect a similar kind of seediness. In all, his image of Africa is one of aspirational curiosity: "not a particular place, but a shape, a strangeness, a wanting to know."[92] Like the psychoanalytic course that guides "the patient back to the idea that he is repressing," Greene casts his trek as a quest to a collective past and a collective repression. His task then is to read his environment for cues, "catching a clue here and a clue there, as I caught the names of villages from this man and that, until one has to face the general idea, the pain or the memory."[93]

In a similar meditation in *GHOA*, Hemingway recalls the sight of offshore garbage in Cuba with particular attention to sex-related goods: "[T]he flotsam of palm fronds, corks, bottles, and used electric light globes, seasoned with an occasional condom or a deep floating corset."[94] Like Greene, Hemingway associates Africa with eros. Hemingway elides his sexual life, although it does manifest as subject material in his "African" short stories. When it comes to subject material, both Greene and Hemingway turn instead to individual concerns that they then project onto the environment. Jacques Rancière offers useful accounts of "the way in which a thought comes to incarnate itself, in a landscape or a living scene, in order to make a concept present."[95] Sub-Saharan Africa functions in both books as one such incarnation, just as authenticity functions as the concept.

Greene's Latvian prostitutes and Hemingway's flotsam, with its corset and its condom, introduce sexuality-themed subject matter that is otherwise missing from both of their books. Through such digressions, both writers offer readers the kind of treatment of such subject material for which each was so roundly praised. Hemingway's digressions bring sexuality into *GHOA* and presumably function as compensation for the lack of amatory material, a choice he defends in the preface while also challenging the disappointed reader: "Any one not finding sufficient love interest is at liberty, while reading it, to insert whatever love interest he or she may have at the time.[96] Just as he parried with the reader in *Death in the Afternoon*, so does he in *GHOA*.

Trading among memories, such digressions contribute to the nostalgic tone that dominates both books. Anticipatory nostalgia plays a crucial role in both *JWM* and *GHOA*, but it does so with a twist. Both writers write of experiencing nostalgia before returning and, in Greene's case, even departure. While still mid-safari, Hemingway muses: "All I wanted to do now was to get back to Africa. We had not left it, yet, but when I would wake in the night I would lie, listening, homesick for it already."[97] The prospect of returning is no comfort, and both writers note the finality of their respective stays. "You could always come back," Hemingway muses, "but really you couldn't."[98]

On the final page of *GHOA*, Hemingway announces that his book is his way of making good on a promise to his wife. When her image of Pop begins to blur only one month post-safari, he suggests that he will restore both it and the safari. But a return is impossible; both Greene and Hemingway made clear that their travels were unrepeatable. As seen above, such insistence is a crucial component of the robust practice of one-upmanship that characterizes both of their works, in which they offer detailed information such as maps and directions but in no way suggest that the reader attempt a similar trip. Likewise, expressions of nostalgia, by affording the writer the option to reminisce at the same time that he emphasizes the uniqueness of his account, reveal the tension in both books between revealing and concealing, between sharing a personal history and suggesting its uniqueness. For instance, the trope of nostalgia permits Hemingway to indulge in "evening braggies," just as he notes his prevailing reluctance to "share this life with any one [sic] who was not there."[99]

Jed Esty argues that interwar-era writers shared a sense of gloom and pessimism insofar as they had "inherited the cultural detritus and political guilt of empire without the corresponding advantages of metropolitan perception."[100] Much as they eulogize a rapidly industrializing Africa, they also reflect on a home culture that they describe as both uncanny and unappealing. In *GHOA*, Hemingway suggests that writing about Africa is necessarily also writing about home and the desire to leave it, if only temporarily. He draws a distinction between "finished" places and "unfinished" places; in his view, the experience of nostalgia indicates that a place's time is over. This can happen over the course of a visit; Africa will be finished by the time the book is published. He notes this alarming celerity in frank terms: "A continent ages quickly once we come."[101] In *Death in the Afternoon,* the pronoun "we" does not include the reader. Instead, as Mark Spilka has argued, it includes his "pioneering ancestors whom he will now emulate by finding a new frontier."[102] Hemingway argues for his own manifest destiny, defending his elaborate safari by sketching his perpetual need to emigrate: "I loved this country and I felt at home and where a man feels at home, outside of where he's born, is where he's meant to go."[103] He feels at home in Africa; it is one of his "good places."[104] While elaborating this theory of personal migration, Hemingway, like Greene, appears to take for granted the enormous privilege that permits him to change locations. Contra Greene, Hemingway makes scant connections between the political and the aesthetic, just as he makes no connection between colonialism and the "aging" continent referenced above. He does, however, explicitly recognize his role in creating the economic and social vicissitudes that characterize an aging country: "A country was made to be as we found it. We are the intruders and after we are dead we may have ruined it but it will still be there and we don't know what the next changes are."[105]

Greene and Hemingway emphasize the uniqueness of their respective journeys. Neither writer offers readers a reliable blueprint for future visits; instead, they express a shared yearning for precolonial purity and a shared disappointment in the ways in which Africa continues to modernize. When Greene describes his breed of anticipatory nostalgia, he nods to this different sense of time and associates it with freedom. He is nostalgic for "the timelessness, the irresponsibility, the freedom" that he claims to have found in Africa.[106] Greene describes experiencing nostalgia that is as much for "the simple and uncorrupted past" as it is for "the end of something that was unlikely to happen again."[107] By Greene's logic, he will only experience to the fullest Africa's salvific power if he bridges the gap between the present and the collective past. He is at times optimistic, at other times pessimistic. Such intermittent anxieties about failure complicate his overall nostalgia for something he has never experienced, i.e. different (and, in his view, earlier) paradigms of social organization.

Greene describes encountering both welcome and unwelcome memories on his trek. He attributes both to the collective past he believes that he is confronting. Ultimately, in his view, it is only uncolonized people who will provide the answers to the questions that subtend his trek; only through contact with such people can he satisfy his quest for a Rousseauian state of nature. He lovingly recollects a festive yet calm night in an isolated Liberian village:

> I remember wandering round the village listening to the laughter and the music among the little glowing fires and thinking that, after all, the whole journey was worthwhile: it did reawaken a kind of hope in human nature. If one could get back to this bareness and simplicity, instinctive friendliness, feeling rather than thought, and start again.[108]

Greene is characteristically solo in this sentimental recollection; fellow Englishmen or Europeans would no doubt damage the episode's power from his perspective. As for the indigenous people, they are described as magical in their simplicity; predictably, he describes them as guided more by intuition than by reason.

Greene's fond recollection of the village further suggests his belief that he has successfully communicated with Liberians. Hemingway, as noted above, also believes that he truly communicated with the Maasai. However, both, despite their professed success with communication, continue to suggest that Africans and non-Africans are different in significant and essential ways. In particular, they seize on events and encounters that they presume will demonstrate the African's inability to conceptualize aspects of Western modernity. Furthermore, both include numerous accounts of cultural misunderstandings that they marshal as evidence that Africans have a different manner of cerebration. For instance, Greene recalls a young boy who cut off his arm: "[He] knelt below a hideous varnished picture. (He had fallen from a palm-tree gathering nuts, had broken his arm, and feeling its limp uselessness had taken a knife and cut it off at the elbow."[109] At times, such anecdotes might appear to give indigenous people the advantage. At the beginning of his trip, just as the ship touches Dakar, Greene sees two men walk by, affectionately holding hands. He muses: "It wasn't love; it didn't mean anything we could understand."[110] Nevertheless, such musings are not neutral. Both Greene and Hemingway conform to the wider trend of searching for a counterpoint to their own lives among indigenous cultures. Such searches, as Simon Gikandi has noted, typically entrench dominant narratives about race, in particular, he argues, "the belief that the primitive constituted a different subject, with a different body, and a different system of cognition."[111] Greene and Hemingway reproduce dominant narratives about race when they describe Africans' encounters with Western products and attitudes as alternately comic and grotesque. Describing a drive through the Kenyan interior, Hemingway reasons that, due to the "utter rapture and ecstasy" the klaxon occasions among the Maasai, his driver "could have had any woman in the tribe."[112] Greene paints his encounters with Africans overall as "almost as intimate as a love affair."[113] Nevertheless he doubts the capacity for rational politics amongst people whose "minds do not move on the level of reason" and he discounts his debates with them.[114] In both *JWM* and *GHOA* then, we can observe both claims of success and disavowals when it comes to the question of communicating with indigenous peoples.

Both Greene and Hemingway attempt to back up such cultural speculation with anecdotes that appear to suggest that the indigenous people they encounter can be associated with an idyllic collective past. Holland and Huggan's study of Bruce Chatwin demonstrates the persistence of this kind of cultural nostalgia, one that "often co-exists with a kind of mysticism, a sentimental belief that the world, for all its eye-catching diversity, is somehow united, or was once united, in the spiritual kinship of different things."[115] To the extent that Greene and Hemingway cast their cultural encounters as sources of insight, they share a contradictory logic; both seek to demonstrate cultural connections whether, like Greene, through the language of childhood, or else, like Hemingway, with virile intuition, at the very moment that they suggest incompatibility between the two races. Their accounts of intercultural misunderstandings make one-dimensional characters of indigenous Africans who become "vivid grotesques," as Greene, self-aware, terms them, making of them "people so simple that they always have the same side turned to one."[116] Both Greene and Hemingway use anecdotes, often presented as comic, to back up cultural speculation; such anecdotes lead to meditations on Africans as a unified group. In these meditations, the unified group is characterized, to a large extent, by what both writers describe as a childlike outlook; the singular is quickly made plural, one person and one circumstance come to stand for Africans and their experience overall. Although both Greene and Hemingway avowedly despise tourists, their generalizations conform to Jonathan Culler's definition of a tourist as one who is "interested in everything as a sign of itself, an instance of a typical cultural practice."[117]

Both writers lament the Westernization of Africa and cast it as monstrous. Their shared disapproval of signs of Westernization—even aspects of it that might improve the lives of the people they encounter—must make us reconsider the more tendentious side of the notion of authenticity, as well as the casual racism manifest in their primitivist aesthetic. For Greene, for instance, an indigenous African in a suit is an instance of the "Creole's painful attempt at playing the white man."[118] Ultimately, both writers must resolve the tension between a dogged search for authenticity—read here as the search to experience Africa without colonialism (Greene) and commercialism (Hemingway)—and the goal of publication, with publication necessarily involving the marketing of those desiderata. To the degree that they quest for an untainted authenticity, they are participating in a tradition of similar quests with similar outcomes and claims. As they privilege the perceived primitive, both writers are continuing the tradition of their Victorian precursors, who were, as Marianna Torgovnick has put it, "informed by desires of known beginnings and, by extension, for predictable ends" in their shared search to "reinhabit core experiences."[119] Both Greene and Hemingway seek a pristine landscape and access to a collective past; both seek answers in Africa for questions that have very little to do with Africa.

In this way, both Greene and Hemingway neglect the combustible politics of the interwar period in favor of personal matters and aesthetic recompense. In doing so they clearly, if unwittingly, echo the solipsism that haunts interwar-era quests for authenticity overall. They share a commitment to offering readers a "true" story, but this commitment is complicated by assumptions about the nature of a true story, and also about the kind of authority necessary to narrate it. Furthermore, their shared rejection of tradition is itself a tradition, a predetermined plot geared to seize authority by means of experiences that they present as both authentic and unique. Both dance between portraying Africa and showcasing the fascination of their person. "The Way to Africa," as Greene titles his first chapter, is, for both writers, routed through the self as much as the continent. The blend of solemnity, speculation, bragging, and self-revelation that sets both books apart ultimately unites them.

Terminus: Inward Travel Narratives of the War Years

This book began with the mobilized Jean-Paul Sartre's epiphanic realization that, although he thought himself a transgressive traveler by visiting seedy neighborhoods and exploring the underworld during his travels abroad, he was ultimately following a pattern; his travels were still "grand tourism," his quest for authenticity always already foiled.[1] What else happens to travel writing and quests for authenticity during World War Two? Who joins the questers, expands their ranks, redirects their concerns? From my survey of literature of the war years, I find the most relevant quests for authenticity and questions about existential issues to be the purview of what might be called "inward travel narratives." These wartime narratives lack movement and displacement but can nevertheless be considered travel narratives because the guiding impulses behind travel have not been abandoned; instead, they have, of necessity, been redirected inward. Even confrontations with alterity persist, now redirected towards the self-as-other and, at times, one's own culture.

I identify three such wartime inward travel narratives (perhaps someday to be productively compared to work written during a quarantine), including Sartre's *War Diaries* (English translation: 1983), Gertrude Stein's *Wars I Have Seen* (1945), and Virginia Woolf's "A Sketch of the Past" (published posthumously in 1976 in the collection *Moments of Being*). I will briefly explore them as inheritors of a tradition and creators of a new one and speculate as to what a comparative study of them might find. One of their chief characteristics is that they are written under enforced non-mobility, which is not the same situation, of course, as that of a writer who simply happens to be in one place while writing. Our World War Two questers pointedly cannot go anywhere, and, to a large extent, explicitly reorient the focus of their writing toward self-scrutiny, even as they move away from the pronounced individualism of the interwar-era traveling writers examined in this book.

I will begin with Sartre's *War Diaries*, which I quoted and referenced above, written while Sartre was mobilized and billeted in Alsace, in northeastern France. Sartre was one of thousands of reservists who had been mobilized on September 1, 1939. Stuck in a classroom in a small town, he worked out, in a series of notebooks, the terms and topics of his magnum opus *Being and Nothingness* (1943). In his notebooks, he notably subjects himself to a thorough self-study by undertaking a quest to understand the status of what he calls authenticity, here cast as authenticity of self. He is ultimately pessimistic on this front. There may be authenticity in theory, but from the point of view of the ontology he sketches, we can never experience it as such: "It must be said, there are just two alternatives: either the desire for authenticity torments us in the midst of inauthenticity, and then it's itself inauthentic; or else it's already full authenticity, though it's unaware of itself and hasn't yet taken stock of itself. There's no room for a third state."[2] Plenitude, from this perspective, is in bad faith. Authenticity is a problematic desideratum, always already out of reach, but always struggled for.

As I outlined above, Sartre, in his inventory of himself, does address travel. But in this wartime writing, the anticipatory nostalgia of our questers is shifted to what might be called "subjunctive nostalgia," as Sartre is nostalgic for the places that he would like to visit, but cannot for the foreseeable future, if ever.[3] He is nostalgic for the places he knows, but also the places he has never been, and to which he could never travel in his current situation: "Since my call-up, I have often missed the cities and landscapes of the world I know—and sometimes that's bitter. But this evening I miss Argentina, the Sahara, all the parts of the world I don't know, the whole earth—and that's much milder, more resigned and hopeless."[4] And yet he is both amused and touched by the homosocial kinship enlistment entails. As he wrote in a related letter written in Alsace exactly three weeks after his call-up: "[H]ow odd it is to live with men."[5] In the same letter, he talks about the reorientation I posited above: "I am no longer the same: my personality hasn't changed, but certainly my being-in-the-world has. It is a being-for-the-war."[6] Backed up to a wall of stasis while the war has not yet come, although the war is coming, Sartre dives into the story of himself, believing that the time had come for an investigation:

Yet I went more than fifteen years without looking at myself living. I didn't
interest myself at all, I was curious about ideas and the world and other
people's hearts. [. . .] Furthermore, pride deflected me from it: it seemed
to me that by prying into trifling acts of meanness, one inflated and re-
inforced them. It has taken the war, and also the assistance of several new
disciplines [. . .] as well as a reading of *L'Age d'homme* [*Manhood*, Michel
Leiris, French original: 1939.—to prompt me to draw up a full-length portrait of myself.[7]

The enforced interlude far away from the normal course of his life has
made his study of himself both possible and urgent. He expects the study
to yield much and links his project to the war.

As Sartre indicates, Michel Leiris's recently published *Manhood*, a self-
ethnography, is one of the templates for Sartre's self-scrutinizing in *War
Diaries*. Understanding Michel Leiris's quest for authenticity has been one
of this book's chief concerns. My hunch is that Leiris's expatiating and
self-flagellating work becomes particularly relevant for Sartre's discussion of his relationship with women in the diaries as the "being-for-war"
comes to stand in for what he describes in other words as a kind of being-
for-women. I also believe that *Manhood*, in one sense, authorized his *War
Diaries* by standing as an example of the philosophical possibilities offered
by writing embarrassing material, and sharing highly personal and not
necessarily flattering revelations. Although Sartre shares these tendencies
with Leiris, his wartime diaries extend the domain of the struggle for self-
knowledge almost beyond recognition.

Sartre describes his archaeology of the self as a wartime product; the
war is a "grand circonstance" [great event], even as a wartime self-study is
necessarily a study of a self that is changing in profound ways:

I used to have a horror of private diaries and think that man isn't made
to see himself, but must always keep his eyes fixed before him. I haven't
changed. It simply seems to me that on the occasion of some great event,
when one is in the process of changing one's life like a snake sloughing its
skin, one can look at that dead skin—that brittle snake image one is leaving behind—and take one's bearings. After the war I shall no longer keep
this diary, or if I do I shall no longer speak about myself in it. I don't want
to be haunted by myself till the end of my days."[8]

These diaries, which ultimately conclude that authenticity of self is impossible, thus comprise a wartime inward travel narrative. Sartre's enforced physical stasis results in a refocusing of questions and possibilities, moving from a concern with authenticity of place and experience to a concern with authenticity of self, from the study of the quick encounter abroad to the microanalysis of personal relationships.

Sartre's inward turn is time-stamped in other ways as well; it is the fruit of vast amounts of free time, the absence of loved ones, and voracious reading. He recognizes the connection between confinement and self-study, between staying in place and searching for authenticity. He sets an enormous task for himself, knowing that his project will end with the war: "Once launched upon this undertaking, I go at it with a will, out of systematic spirit and a taste for totality; I yield myself up to it entirely, out of obsession. [. . .] But I don't think there's any advantage in spending one's whole life delousing oneself. Far from it."[9] Fully motivated and in a surprisingly propitious environment for writing, Sartre was highly productive before he was captured by advancing German forces in late June of 1940. He experienced the negation of [his own] freedom while mobilized. This served to shape the infrastructure of his self-study but also his study of his relationships with other people.[10] Sartre's inward travel narrative, like our questers' travel narratives, is concerned with alterity and the status of the self in the face of it. Alterity here indicates familiar people but people who have become both defamiliarized and crystallized from Sartre's vantage point.

Like Sartre, Virginia Woolf also used the war for self-study. Her memoir of childhood and adulthood, "A Sketch of the Past," was written during 1939–1940, when Woolf was nearly sixty. She had tried her hand at the genre once long before with the short and posthumously published memoir "Reminiscences." Writing about the past did not come easily to her and, conceivably under the spell of the major depression she experienced at this time, she at times seems unconvinced of the essay's value, and throws it away at least once, only to rescue it out of the trash. "A Sketch of the Past" is an account of the world she lived in from childhood to adulthood. However, in addition to painting a portrait of Edwardian family life, Woolf uses the form to offer an investigation into her sources of creativity and also her illness. She uses the practice of writing in a way that recalls Martin Heidegger's notion of the existential; writing serves as a way to give form to the present, even to stay sane:

The battle is at its crisis; every night the Germans fly over England; it comes closer to this house daily. If we are beaten then—however we solve that problem, and one solution is apparently suicide (so it was decided three nights ago in London among us)—book writing becomes doubtful. But I wish to go on not to settle down in that dismal puddle.[11]

At other points, Woolf paints her forays into the past as a wartime product and perhaps, also, as a kind of analgesic: "Today the dictators dictate their terms to France. Meanwhile, on this very hot morning, with a blue bottle buzzing and a toothless organ grinding and the men calling strawberries in the Square, I sit in my room at 37 M[ecklenburgh] S[quare] and turn to my father."[12] Although Woolf does not use the word authenticity in "A Sketch of the Past," I find the self-scrutiny involved in quests for authenticity to be present in this work, as well as an imperative to, in whatever way possible, have access to the meaningful part of the past. Finally, I find the quest for authenticity echoed in the probing questions that Woolf poses about art, life, spirituality, and insight, which she attributes to a keen mode of experience that she terms "moments of being."[13] Only such moments of being are authentic and worthwhile. Authenticity, in Woolf's inward travel narrative, is thus a kind of experience, one that leads to insight.

For Woolf, there is an ideal mode that allows her to undertake her investigations of the past. A kind of peace is needed. Ironically, it is precisely the war that proffers that peace, however catastrophic and traumatic, with its moving indoors, its pausing of regular socializing, its induction of people into often tiresome but necessary daily habits. Woolf describes the conditions that must be in place for the past to return and for it to make meaning for the present:

The past only comes back when the present runs so smoothly that it is like the sliding surface of a deep river. Then one sees through the surface to the depths. In those moments I find one of my greatest satisfactions, not that I am thinking of the past; but that it is then that I am living most fully in the present. For the present when backed by the past is a thousand times deeper than the present when it presses so close that you can feel nothing else, when the film on the camera reaches only the eye. But to feel the present sliding over the depths of the past, peace is necessary. The present must be smooth, habitual.[14]

Overall, states, or moods, are central to her attempt to understand her own aesthetics. From her examples, we see that such moments of being are on a spectrum between engaging and rapturous but always involving insight, whereas a state of nonbeing is not exceptional, but is more common: "A great part of every day is not lived consciously."[15] Her fundamental project then becomes finding a way to experience life as moments of being, full of insight and cosmic feelings. She associates this with writing; her thesis about being is borne out by her writing. It is tied up with the notion of a normative "shock" that she has experienced at several key moments in her life:

> It is only by putting it into words that I make it whole [. . .] Perhaps this is the strongest pleasure known to me. It is the rapture I get when in writing I seem to be discovering what belongs to what; making a scene come right; making a character come together. From this I reach what I might call a philosophy; at any rate it is a constant idea of mine; that behind the cotton wool is hidden a pattern; that we—I mean all human beings—are connected with this; that the whole world is a work of art; that we are parts of the work of art. *Hamlet* or a Beethoven quartet is the truth about this vast mass that we call the world. But there is no Shakespeare, there is no Beethoven; certainly and emphatically there is no God; we are the words; we are the music; we are the thing itself. And I see this when I have a shock.[16]

With her move from the personal to the universal, Woolf traces the contours of her cosmic vision of human collectivity. Moments of being are filled with insight into herself and other people. Woof's journey inward is productive and salvific.

As with Sartre and Woolf, the war years were particularly prolific for Gertrude Stein, who writes another kind of inward travel narrative during the war. *Wars I Have Seen* (1945) charts the gloomy but solidarity-filled years before the Allied victory, which Stein and her partner, Alice B. Toklas, spent in the idyllic village Culoz in southeastern France. But just as she looks outward to understand and celebrate America and Americans while reflecting on specific wars and war in general, she also looks inward to understand and test her own Americanness, explaining the ways in which her identity is soldered to American discourses. The book is self-questioning, and Stein's search to understand herself within the context of a geopolitical disaster thus becomes, in effect, a search to understand questions about national identity. The interwar years saw literary travel writing about foreign places and nationalities, but during the war years, it seems to me, questions about the other are rotated so that the "I" in search of alterity will look to itself but also to its own culture at a time when one's nationality was of significant importance. Stein, seeking her place in the universe, echoes our questers for authenticity in her search to make tangible something that is always in flux, but nevertheless rejects the kind of essentializing implicit and explicit claims to mastery that this book has understood as part of a masculinist discourse. Indeed, her book begins with the question of herself and her own memory with the ludic first sentence, playing with the notion of authorial credibility: "I do not know whether to put in the things I do not remember as well as the things I do remember."[17] This is a different kind of narrative authority from that claimed by Graham Greene or Ernest Hemingway.

Wars I Have Seen affords readers the perspective of an American insider/outsider as cultural translator, a person seemingly attached to an American identity, an identity that only grows stronger during the war. This is an interesting perspective from which to adjudicate questions about nationality because of the defamiliarization and reterritorialization it entails, one propitious for a unique kind of knowledge, a perspective shared in very different ways by both privileged and, in a more brutal fashion, highly underprivileged people during this time.

Stein, the wealthy expatriate, for many, got far too close to Marshal Philippe Pétain's Vichy regime, in particular by translating into English in 1941—for an unfinished manuscript brought to scholars' attention in 1996 by then-graduate student Wanda van Dusen—nearly two hundred of his anti-Semitic speeches. Stein hoped to publish her translations in the United States, including a preface that compared Pétain to George Washington. Pétain was the chief architect of the deportation and death of almost eighty thousand French Jews. As Barbara Will has demonstrated in *Unlikely Collaboration* (2013), Stein was affiliated and on extremely friendly terms with Bernard Fäy, the director of France's national library, the Bibliothèque nationale de France, under the collaborationist Vichy government. Bernard Fäy kept Stein and Toklas from persecution during the war, just as he earlier arranged for the Pétain translations as propaganda. In her book, Will demonstrates that the unfinished manuscript is "evidence of a propaganda project in support of Vichy France that Stein began in 1941, one she hoped to sell to and influence a skeptical American public."[18] Some have suggested that Gertrude's and Fäy's friendship was a strategic one, but Toklas later referred to Fäy as Stein's "dearest friend during her life."[19] Such connections allowed them to live, to a large extent, without the fear and tragedy shared by many in France, including, most relevantly for them, other coreligionists.

Stein and Toklas thus had a vastly different war experience than they might have had without personal connections, and a related tranquility marks the book that, along with its stark musicality, expresses strikingly less anguish than those of her contemporaries. Indeed, she rather expresses frustration and ennui; as she notes: "A vegetable garden in the beginning looks so promising and then after all little by little it grows nothing but vegetables, nothing, nothing but vegetables."[20] With *kairos* slowly sliding into *chronos*, she is more impatient than alarmed. She recounts a man telling her the war will be over soon, as his wife can no longer stand it. Stein riffs on this: "Yes everybody has had enough of it everybody's wife and everybody's husband and everybody's mother and everybody's father and everybody's daughter and everybody's son, they all have had enough."[21] This is the doxa in her world.

But there is also travel in this inward travel narrative. Travel, in *Wars I Have Seen*, indicates a different kind of mobility; the American soldiers billeted to Stein's home are also, in one sense, traveling through France just as war and famine displace millions of people. Stein tells the story of these young soldiers with extreme fondness and wonder. Long awaited, they are traveling through her inward travel narrative. But hers, like those of Sartre and Woolf, is nevertheless a narrative of nonmobility: "Life has completely changed since I have been here, I never stop thinking of my former life, in those days when I wanted to go out, I went out, I remained out as long as I wanted to stay out, I came in when I wanted to, but alas that life is over [. . .]."[22] Like Sartre's, her inward travel narrative is also characterized by subjunctive nostalgia: "We live the life of trains, so much more now that there are none."[23] Jammed up against herself, Stein, like Sartre and Woolf, turns to the story of herself, but, like them, does not will a return, claims no authority from it.

*

Overall, certain aspects of the concept of authenticity have been taken to task on a number of fronts, most of them too familiar to rehearse here, even as it continues to be reproduced in a vast variety of realms. We can think, for instance, of the notion of authenticity both as it has been reterritorialized by the self-help industry but also, critically, as it finds itself in current debates about cultural appropriation. Indeed, an Internet search for the combined terms "authenticity" and "cultural appropriation" yields half a million results today. The meaning of the word has been broadened, the concept has been significantly renewed and redirected, and we must remember the specificity of the quest during the interwar years. Masculine authority and European privilege have certainly been challenged for a good while now on a variety of fronts, however much both continue to code fields of knowledge and determine power structures. The same is true of antiblackness and other forms of racism and prejudice. Nevertheless, many are still in conversation with the questers with whom I engaged. Some sketch its discipline into their own romances with the past. Some still travel with self-transformation in mind. The "mark of the plural" unfortunately persists into the third decade of this century. Others continue, often despite themselves, to share in the ongoing practice of spatializing time, and taking a hierarchical approach to development. All of us enter into relationships of power every time we leave our homes. And a quick Girardian look at contemporary advertisement suggests that felicity and exaltation are still associated with faraway places, typically those seen to promise respite from the confusions of contemporary life, both urban and suburban. The questers for authenticity are belated, Conrad-envious, and awash with anticipatory nostalgia. At the same time, they see their way through to us, a century later.

NOTES

Introduction

1. Sartre, Jean-Paul, *War Diaries: Notebooks from a Phony War 1939–1940* (London: Verso, 2011), 143. "Nous avons tous été formés à cette façon-*là* de voyager. Nous avons tous mis autant de scrupules à visiter le Barrio Chino de Barcelone, le quartier réservé de Hambourg ou tout simplement les quartiers ouvriers du Trastevere, que les Allemands vingt ans plus tôt à recenser les collections d'estampes, Baedeker en main. Nous avions aussi nos Baedeker mais ils ne se voyaient pas. Et ce bout de soirée que j'ai passé dans un bordel de Naples où des marins m'avaient conduit, c'était encore du grand tourisme." [Sartre, Jean-Paul *Carnets de la drôle de guerre* (Paris: Gallimard, 1995), 357.]

2. Cioran, E. M., *Anathemas and Admirations*, trans. Howard, Richard (New York: Skyhorse Publishing, 2012), n.p.

3. Mikkonen, Kai, *Narrative Paths: African Travel in Modern Fiction and Nonfiction* (Columbus: The Ohio State University Press, 2015), 4.

4. Scholars have long argued for the influence of French writing on Conrad's work. Paul Kirschner arguably began this discussion in 1968 in his monograph *Conrad: The Psychologist as Artist*. Yves Hervouet, in *The French Face of Joseph Conrad* (1990), for instance, has demonstrated the influence that nineteenth-century French writers such as Gustave Flaubert, Anatole France, and Guy de Maupassant had on Conrad. We can thus extend the metaphor of the traveling text.

5. Warren, Calvin, ed., "Introduction," *Ontological Terror: Blackness, Nihilism, and Emancipation* (Durham and London: Duke University Press, 2018), n.p., e-book.

6. Pratt, Mary Louise, *Imperial Eyes: Travel Writing and Transculturation* (London: Routledge, 1992), 3.

7. Das, Nandini and Youngs, Tim, "Introduction," *The Cambridge History of Travel Writing* (Cambridge: Cambridge University Press, 2019), 1–16: 9.

8. Baucom, Ian, "Mournful Histories: Narratives of Postimperial Melancholy," *MFS Modern Fiction Studies* 42:2 (1996), 259–288: 281, 280.

9. Baucom, Ian, *Out of Place: Englishness, Empire, and the Locations of Identity* (Princeton: Princeton University Press, 1999), 51.

10. Although my work does not overlap with his, I note that Aaron DeRosa (2014) has notably used the term "proleptic nostalgia" to designate a new genre in fiction, one characterized by protagonists who, post 9/11, undertake lives very differently from those they had imagined before the attacks. He casts proleptic nostalgia as thus nostalgia for a life never had, but for which one had wished. In what follows, I will refer to such nostalgia as "subjunctive nostalgia" and bring it into the terminus in my discussion of Sartre.

11. Rae, Patricia, "'There'll be no more fishing this side of the grave': Radical Nostalgia in George Orwell's *Coming up for Air*," in *Modernism and Nostalgia: Bodies, Locations, Aesthetics*, ed. Clewell, Tammy (New York: Palgrave, 2013), 149–165: 152.

12. Rae, Patricia, "Double Sorrow: Proleptic Elegy and the End of Arcadianism in 1930s Britain," *Twentieth-Century Literature* 49:2, 246–275: 247.

13. Orwell, George, *The Road to Wigan Pier* (New York: Houghton Mifflin Harcourt, 1958), 200.

14. Vincent Sherry, "T. S. Eliot, Late Empire, and Decadence," in *Modernism and Colonialism*, eds. Begam, Richard and Valdez Moses, Michael (Durham: Duke University Press, 2007), 111–135: 112.

15. Porter, Dennis, *Haunted Journeys: Desire and Transgression in European Travel Writing* (Princeton: Princeton University Press, 1991), 3.

16. Burton, Stacy, *Travel Narrative and the Ends of Modernity* (Cambridge: Cambridge University Press, 2013), 30.

17. André Lefevere, *Translation, Rewriting and the Manipulation of Literary Fame* (London: Routledge, 1992), ix.

18. Polezzi, Loredana, *Translating Travel: Contemporary Italian Travel Writing in English Translation* (New York: Ashgate, 2001), 82–83.

19. Pratt, Mary Louise, *Imperial Eyes: Travel Writing and Transculturation* (London: Routledge, 1992), 8.

20. Bassnett, Susan, "Translation and Travel Writing," *The Cambridge History of Travel Writing* (Cambridge: Cambridge University Press, 2019), 550–564: 550.

Chapter One

1. Conrad, Joseph, "Ocean Travel," in *Last Essays*, eds. Stevens, Harold Ray and Stape, J. H. (Cambridge: Cambridge University Press, 2010), 27–29: 27.

2. For a look at Conrad's own commitment to authenticity, see: Erdinast-Vulcan, Daphna, *The Strange Short Fiction of Joseph Conrad: Writing, Culture, and Subjectivity* (Oxford: Oxford University Press, 1999).

3. Leander, Niels Buch, "The Colonial Metropolis and its Artistic Adventure: Conrad, Congo, and the *Nouvelle Revue française*," *Romanic Review* 99:1/2 (2008), 87–102: 88.

4. Casanova, Pascale, *The World Republic of Letters* (Cambridge: Harvard University Press, 2004), 20.

5. Casanova, *World*, 12.

6. Conrad, Joseph, *The Mirror of the Sea and a Personal Record* (Oxford: Oxford University Press, 1980), vii.

7. Hervouet, Yves, *The French Face of Conrad* (Cambridge: Cambridge University Press, 1990), 263.

8. Qtd. in Nadjer, Zdzislaw, ed., *Conrad's Polish Background: Letters to and from Polish Friends*, trans. Halina Carroll (Oxford: Oxford University Press, 1964), 234.

9. Conrad, Joseph, *The Collected Letters of Joseph Conrad*, 9 vols, eds. Karl, Frederick R., et al. (Cambridge: Cambridge University Press, 1983–2008), 1:165.

10. Conrad, *Collected*, 2:69.

11. Rivière, Jacques, "The Adventure Novel," in *The Ideal Reader: Selected Essays by Jacques Rivière*, trans. Price, Blanche A. (New York: Meridian Books, 1960), 84–124: 123. "Le moment me semble venu où la littérature française, qui tant de fois déjà a su se rajeunir par des emprunts, va s'emparer, pour le fonder dans son sang, du roman étranger." [Rivière, Jacques, "Le roman d'aventure," *La Nouvelle Revue française* 55 (1913), 56–77: 76.]

12. Rivière, "Adventure," 94. "Nous sommes des gens pour qui s'est réveillée la nouveauté de vivre." [Rivière, "aventure" 53, 761–762.]

13. Rivière, "Adventure," 94 "C'est le matin, encore une fois. Tout recommence; nous avons été mystérieusement rajeunis; ce n'est plus avec nos habitudes que nous touchons le monde; les choses autour de nous n'offrent plus à nos mains cette surface lisse et usée, qui faisait que nous glissions le long d'elles sans même les remarquer. Au centre de nous-mêmes, une âme, vive aiguë et susceptible s'est remise à brûler et c'est avec elle que nous nous approchons des objets, c'est elle qui les rencontre, qui les reçoit, qui les éprouve." [Rivière, "aventure" 53, 762.]

14. Rivière, "Adventure," 94. "[L]a moindre aventure leur paraissait un déshonneur; ils se croyaient compromis s'ils se trouvaient pris dans quelque incident de la rue." [Rivière, "aventure" 53, 762.]

15. Rivière, "Adventure," 111. "Elle est dans une atmosphère de multiplication, d'exagération et de débordement, elle est travaillée par l'énormité. A la fin, c'est un monstre; elle apparaît couverte d'excroissances: récits interminables venant interrompre l'histoire principale, confessions, pages de journal, exposé des doctrines professées par l'un des personnages. Elle forme une sorte de conglomérat naturel, un gâteau de terre et de pierres, dont les éléments tiennent ensemble on ne sait pas comment." [Rivière, "aventure" 55, 59.]

16. Rivière, "Adventure," 119, 120. "L'émotion qu'il nous faut demander au roman d'aventure, c'est, au contraire de l'émotion poétique, celle d'attendre quelque chose, de ne pas tout savoir encore, c'est celle d'être amené aussi près que possible sur le bord de ce qui n'existe pas encore. [. . .] en lisant un roman d'aventure, nous nous livrons sans réserve au mouvement du temps et de la vie, nous acceptons d'éprouver jusqu'au fond de nos moelles cette question obscure et infatigable qui pousse et travaille tous les êtres vivants." [Rivière, "aventure," 55, 71.]

17. Putnam, Walter, *L'aventure littéraire de Joseph Conrad et d'André Gide* (Saratoga: ANMA Libri, 1990), 187.

18. Chevrillon, André, "Conrad," *Hommage à Joseph Conrad, La Nouvelle Revue française* 12:135 (December 1924), 62–65: 62, *my translation.* ["Ses tableaux de mer sont d'un artiste de génie mais c'est l'expérience d'un marin professionnel qu'il interprète."]

19. Lefevere, André, *Translation, Rewriting and the Manipulation of Literary Fame* (London: Routledge, 1992).

20. May, Georges, "Valery Larbaud: Translator and Scholar," *Yale French Studies* 6, 83–90: 83.

21. Cazantre, Thomas, *Gide lecteur: La littérature au miroir de la lecture* (Paris: Kimé, 2003), 52, *my translation.* "[C]'est en partie à ce désir de découverte que l'on peut attribuer le soin que prenait Gide d'avoir, dans chaque pays étranger, un correspondant littéraire qui pût l'informer, le conseiller."

22. Casanova, *World*, 21.

23. Casanova, *World*, 115.

24. Casanova, *World*, 115.

25. Lefevere, *Translation*, 2.

26. Conrad, *Collected*, 4: 195.

27. Lefevere, *Translation*, 2.

28. Gide, André, *The Journals of André Gide 1889–1946* 6 vols., ed. and trans. O'Brien, Justin (Chicago: University of Illinois Press, 2000), 2: 211. "des traducteurs nouveaux qui se proposent pour Conrad." [Gide, André, *Journal 1 1887–1925* (Paris: Gallimard, 1996), 1039.]

29. Gide, *Journals* [English], 1: 332. "Ce matin, au travail dès 6 heures. Spenser et Skeat, puis Conrad. J'écris à mon teacher pour reprendre des leçons." [Gide, André, *Journal 1*, 733.]

30. Stape, J. H., "The Art of Fidelity: Conrad, Gide, and the Translation of *Victory*," *Journal of Modern Literature* 27:1 (1990), 155–165: 156.

31. Gide, *Journals* [English], 2: 191–192. "Traduction. Si éreintant qu'il soit, ce travail m'amuse. Mais que de temps il y faut! Je compte, en moyenne, et quand tout va bien, une heure par demi-page (de l'édition Heinemann—c'est du *Typhon* qu'il s'agit). Je crois que le résultat sera très bon; mais qui s'en apercevra?. . . Peu importe." [Gide, *Journal 1*, 1016.]

32. Gide, André, *Œuvres complètes*, 15 vols., ed. Martin-Chaufier (Paris: Gallimard Bibliothèque de la Pléiade, 1934), 15: 541, *my translation.* "une de celles [questions] sur lesquelles j'ai le plus, et depuis longtemps, réfléchi."

33. West, Russell, "Gide traduit (par) Conrad," *Bulletin des amis d'André Gide* 21:100 (October 1993), 593–611: 601, *my translation.* "désir d'échapper à l'angoisse et au déchirement causé par la guerre."

34. Monod, Sylvère, "Deux traductions du *Typhoon* de Conrad," *Bulletin des amis d'André Gide* 21:100 (October 1993), 577–92: 578, *my translation.* "[R]ien ne ressemblait moins que *Typhoon* au genre de récits que Gide avait lui-même écrit ou pouvait envisager de produire encore."

35. Gide, *Œuvres complètes d'André Gide,* 15: 545, *my translation.* "Je crois absurde de se cramponner au texte de trop près; je le répète, ce n'est pas seulement le sens qu'il s'agit de rendre, il importe de ne pas traduire des mots, mais des phrases et d'exprimer, sans en rien perdre, pensée et émotion, comme l'auteur les eût exprimées s'il eût écrit directement en français, ce qui ne se peut que par une tricherie perpétuelle, par d'incessants détours et souvent en s'éloignant beaucoup de la simple littéralité."

36. Conrad, Joseph, *Typhoon and Other Stories* (New York: Doubleday, 1921), 119.

37. Conrad, Joseph, *Typhon,* translated by André Gide (Paris: Gallimard, 1923), 226.

38. Conrad, *Typhon,* 226.

39. Gide, *Journals* [English] 1: 193, "mais là, du moins c'est œuvre mienne, à mon gré, et que je signerai joyeusement." [Gide, André, *Journal 1,* 1018.]

40. Gide, *Journals* [English] 1: 191. "enfantines théories sur la fidélité que doit respirer une traduction" [Gide, André, *Journal 1,* 1015.]

41. Gide, *Journals* [English], 1: 91. "hérissée d'impropriétés, de gaucheries, de cacophonies, de hideurs." [Gide, André, *Journal 1,* 1015.]

42. Gide, *Journals* [English] 1: 91. "me vieillit de quinze jours." [Gide, André, *Journal 1,* 1015.]

43. Putnam, Walter, *L'aventure,* 21, *my translation.* "au rang d'un art noble."

44. _____, "De *Typhoon* à *Typhon*: Gide et sa traduction de Conrad," *Bulletin des amis d'André Gide,* 24:89 (1991), 77–90: 81, *my translation.* "Ce fut justement la question de la littéralité qui oppose Gide à d'autres traducteurs de Conrad, notamment Isabelle Rivière et André Ruyters."

45. Cigoj-Leben, Breda, "Les idées d'André Gide sur l'art de traduction," *Bulletin des amis d'André Gide* 12 (January 1984), 31–46: 43, *my translation.*

46. Venuti, Lawrence, "Translation, Community, Utopia" in *The Translation Studies Reader,* ed. Venuti, Lawrence (New York: Routledge, 2004), 482–50: 482.

47. Venuti, "Translation," 482.

48. Lefevere, *Translation, Rewriting,* 7.

49. Conrad, *Collected Letters,* 4: 592. "le plus grand trésor que j'aie conquis à la pointe de ma plume." [Conrad, *Collected Letters,* 4: 590]

50. Karl, Frederick R., "Conrad and Gide: A Relationship and a Correspondence," *Comparative Literature* 29:2, 148–171: 163.

51. Vidan, Gabriejela and Vidan, Ivo, eds., "Further Correspondence Between Joseph Conrad and André Gide" *Studia Romanica et Anglica Zagrabiensia* 29 (1970), 523–536: 532, *my translation.* "quelle qu'elle soit, est incapable, par nature, de comprendre Conrad. [. . .] Conrad est un auteur essentiellement masculin: quand une femme le traduit, elle l'émascule."

52. Vidan and Vidan, "Further," 532, *my translation.* "D'ailleurs c'était également le sentiment de Conrad lui-même."

53. Conrad, *Collected,* 6: 470.

54. Conrad, *Collected*, 6: 16. "Si mes écritures ont un caractère prononcé, c'est leur virilité—esprit, allure, expression. Personne ne m'a dénié ça. Et vous me jetez aux femmes! Vous dites Vous-même dans Votre lettre qu'au bout du compte une traduction est une interprétation. Eh bien, j'ai le désir d'être interprété par des esprits masculins. C'est tout naturel. [Vidan and Vidan,"Further," 527.]

55. Conrad, *Collected*, 4: 532.

56. Conrad, *Collected*, 4: 532. "comme ça se doit entre hommes" [Vidan and Vidan,"Further," 527.]

57. Conrad, *Collected*, 6: 503. "Je viens de recevoir une lettre de Gide où il me dit qu'une femme vient de s'emparer de *Arrow* pour le traduire. Je vais protester de toutes mes forces. Il me jette en pâture à un tas de femmes qui lui font des histoire [*sic*] (il le dit lui-même). Tout ça m'ennuie." [Vidan, Ivo, "Thirteen Letters of André Gide to Joseph Conrad," *Studia Romanica et Anglica Zagrabiensia* 24 (December 1967), 145–168: 157.]

58. Vidan and Vidan, "Further," 530, *my translation*. "Etes-vous [*sic*] sûr que cela qu'une traduction masculine sera forcément meilleure qu'une féminine?"

59. Conrad, *Collected*, 6: 88–89.

60. Conrad, *Collected*, 4: 592.

61. Conrad, *Collected*, 4: 29. "un écrivain Anglais se prétend peu à la traduction." [Conrad, *Collected*, 4: 28.]

62. Larbaud, Valery, *Sous l'invocation de saint Jérôme* (Paris: Gallimard, 1946), 329, *my translation*. "hautement classés dans l'estime de lettrés."

63. Gide, André, "Joseph Conrad," *La Nouvelle Revue française* 12:135 (December 1924), 17–20: 18, *my translation*. "Ne regardez pas cela, me dit-il en m'entraînant dans le salon [. . .] Parlons de littérature."

64. Conrad, *Collected,* 8: 130.

65. Curle, Richard, *Joseph Conrad: A Study* (London: K. Paul, Trench, Trüber & Co., 1914), 13.

66. Conrad, *Collected*, 4: 442.

67. Conrad, *Collected*, 4: 441.

68. Conrad, Joseph, *The Mirror of the Sea and a Personal Record*, 191.

69. Gide, *Journals* [English], 2: 426. "Et quant aux bateaux mêmes, étant donné que le Congo ne redevient navigable qu'à une très grande distance de son embouchure, il faut—il a fallu longtemps de moins (voir *Cœur des Ténèbres*) faire transporter à travers la brousse, à dos d'hommes, les lourdes pièces démontées de n'importe quelle embarcation." [Gide, André, *Journal 2* (Paris: Gallimard, 1997), 65.]

70. Gide, André, *Travels in the Congo* (Berkeley: University of California Press, 1962), 13–14. "On a blâmé Conrad, dans le *Typhon*, d'avoir escamoté le plus fort de la tempête. Je l'admire au contraire d'arrêter son récit précisément au seuil de l'affreux, et de laisser à l'imagination du lecteur libre jeu, après l'avoir mené, dans l'horrible, jusqu'à tel point qui ne parût pas dépassable." [Gide, André, *Voyage au Congo* (Paris: Gallimard, 1927), 32.]

71. Gide, *Journals* [English], 3: 94. "L'on ne sait ce qu'il sied d'admirer le plus: le prodigieux sujet, l'agencement, la hardiesse d'une si difficile entreprise, la patience dans la conduite du récit, l'intelligence et l'épuisement du sujet; et, lorsqu'on ferme le livre, le lecteur voudrait dire à l'auteur: Et maintenant, reposons-nous." [Gide, André, *Journal 2*, 186.]

72. See West, Russell, "Conrad, Gide and Dostoyevsky: Critical Intertextualities," *The Conradian* 20:100 (1995), 109–130, and West, Russell, *Conrad and Gide: Translation, Transference and Intertextuality* (Amsterdam: Rodopi, 1996).

73. Gide, *Journals* [English], 3: 94–95. Fort intéressé par la parenté que je découvre entre *Sous les yeux d'Occident* et *Lord Jim* (Regrets de n'en avoir point parlé à Conrad). Cette *inconséquence du héros*, pour le rachat de laquelle toute une vie, ensuite mise en gage. Car ce qui tire le plus à conséquence, ce sont précisément les inconséquences d'une vie. Comment effacer cela? Il n'y a pas sujet de roman plus pathétique et qu'ait plus empêché, dans notre littérature, la croyance en la règle de Boileau, que le héros doive demeurer, d'un bout à l'autre d'un drame ou d'un roman "tel qu'on l'a vu d'abord." [Gide, André, *Journal 2*, 186–187.]

74. Gide, *Journals* [English], 3 :123. "A remarquer que les fatales inconséquences des héros de Conrad (je songe en particulier à *Lord Jim* et à *Under Western Eyes* sont involontaires et gênent aussitôt grandement l'être qui les commet. Toute la vie, par la suite, ne suffit pas à les démentir et à en effacer les traces." [Gide, *Journal 2*, 326.]

75. Gide, *Journals* [English], 2: 368. "N'ai pu achever *L'Agent secret*" [Gide, *Journal 1*, 1280.]

76. See West, "Conrad, Gide and Dostoyevsky" and West, Russell, *Conrad and Gide*.

77. See Cazantre, Thomas, *Gide lecteur: La littérature au miroir de la lecture*.

78. Larbaud, devoted to Joyce, distanced himself from the *NRF* after the disagreement. Larbaud's role as *passeur* was cemented through his critical celebration of Joyce's writing. He also oversaw the translation of *Ulysses* in the years following Joyce's death.

79. Larbaud, Valery, "*Chance* par Joseph Conrad," *Nouvelle Revue française* 6:1 (1914), 527–529: 527, *my translation*. "en Angleterre, comme chez nous, de division bien nette entre le grand public et *the happy few*."

80. Larbaud, "*Chance*," 527, *my translation*.

81. Larbaud, "*Chance*," 527, *my translation*. "vieille carcasse rouillée de l'intrigue."

82. Larbaud, "*Chance*," 529, *my translation*. "Joseph Conrad et son œuvre attendent encore l'étude complète et détaillée qui la fera connaître des nombreux lecteurs que des romans comme *Nostromo* et *Chance* peuvent trouver en France; et nous souhaiterons qu'une telle étude fût offerte d'abord aux lecteurs de cette revue."

83. Mac Orlan, Pierre, "*La Folie-Almayer* et les aventuriers dans la littérature," *Nouvelle Revue française* 81 (June, 1920), 930–933: 931, *my translation*. "Joseph

Conrad, Anglais d'origine polonaise, et qui fut long-courrier, se place en tête de cette série d'écrivains, modelés par une existence dure et farouche et dont le génie littéraire sut retenir les images pour faire un livre dur et farouche."

84. Mac Orlan, "*Folie*," 931, *my translation*.

85. Mac Orlan, "*Folie*," 931, *my translation*.

86. Mac Orlan, "*Folie*," 931, *my translation*. "offrant aux personnages un champ d'action illimité."

87. Jean-Aubry, G., "Souvenirs," *La Nouvelle Revue française* 12:135 (December 1924), 30–39: 37, *my translation*. "[J]amais une erreur de genre ni une faute de grammaire."

88. Gide, André, "Joseph Conrad," *La Nouvelle Revue française* 12:135 (December 1924), 17–20: 18, *my translation*. "Comme il connaissait bien nos auteurs!"

89. Valéry, Paul, "Sujet d'une conversation avec Conrad," *La Nouvelle Revue française* 12:135 (December 1924), 17–20: 21, *my translation*. "Être un grand écrivain dans une langue que l'on parle si mal est chose rare et éminemment originale."

90. Jean-Aubry, "Souvenirs," 38, *my translation*. "[S]i grand écrivain anglais qu'il fut, il était un des nôtres."

91. Jean-Aubry, "Souvenirs," 35–36, *my translation*. "sentiment de la langue, des ressources, du vocabulaire, du style français."

92. Conrad, *Collected*, 6: 227.

93. Gide, "Joseph Conrad," 20, *my translation*. "Et je crois que ce que j'aimais le plus en lui, c'était une sorte de native noblesse, âpre, dédaigneuse, et quelque peu désespérée, celle même qu'il prête à Lord Jim et qui fait de ce livre un des plus beaux que je connaisse, un des plus tristes aussi, encore qu'un des plus exaltants."

94. Chevrillon, "Conrad," 62, *my translation*. "Il ne procède pas des écoles, des cénacles, il n'a pas cherché une nouvelle façon d'écrire."

95. Francillon, Robert, "Conrad psychologue de l'imagination," *La Nouvelle Revue française* 12:135 (December 1924), 82–87: 87, *my translation*. "L'unité de la vie de Conrad navigateur et romancier réside en un acte d'abandon toujours renouvelé au pouvoir de l'imagination."

96. Jaloux, Edmond, "Joseph Conrad et le roman d'aventures anglaise," *La Nouvelle Revue française* 12:135 (December 1924), 71–77: 75, *my translation*. "en face de circonstances anormales."

97. Gide, "Joseph Conrad," 20, *my translation*. "Nul n'avait plus sauvagement vécu que Conrad; nul ensuite n'avait soumis la vie à une aussi patiente, consciente et savante transmutation d'art."

98. Chevrillon, "Conrad," 64–65, *my translation*. "On peut discuter certains livres de Conrad, lui reprocher des longueurs, une composition compliquée, parfois déconcertante. Mais, quand il n'a dit que la mer et les marins, quelle sûreté de la conception, quelle directe, rapide venue du récit, quelle grandeur croissante des évocations!"

99. Maurois, André, "En marge des marées," *La Nouvelle Revue française* 12:135 (December 1924), 66–67: 1 69, *my translation*. "Le Conrad d'*Une Victoire*

ne peut pas avoir cru à ses personnages romantiques et monstrueux comme le Conrad de *Typhon* croyait aux marins ses amis."

100. Jean-Aubry, G. *Joseph Conrad: Life and Letters,* 2 vols. (New York: Doubleday, 1927), 1: 28–29.

101. Jean-Aubry, "Conrad," 1: 28–29.

102. Conrad, Joseph, *Typhoon and Other Stories* (New York: Doubleday, 1921), xiii.

103. Jean-Aubry, "Conrad," 1: 156.

104. Venuti, Lawrence, *The Translator's Invisibility: A History of Translation* (New York: Routledge, 1995), 18.

105. Forsdick, Charles, "Sa(l)vaging Exoticism: New Approaches to 1930s Travel Literature in French," in *Cultural Encounters: European Travel Writing in the 1930s,* eds. Burdett, Charles and Duncan, Derek (New York: Berghahn Books, 2002), 29–45: 29.

106. Guillame, Isabelle, "*La voie royale* et *Voyage au bout de la nuit*: deux réécritures françaises de *Heart of Darkness*," *Cahier de narratologie* 13 (2006), n.p.

107. Kessel, Joseph, *Marchés d'esclaves* (Paris: Union Général d'Éditions, 1984), 125, *my translation*. "Je me souviens qu'en achevant de lire ce récit une profonde mélancolie se mêla à mon admiration. Je pensais que jamais je ne connaîtrais la belle et pure joie qu'avait éprouvée Conrad, marin du siècle passé."

108. Kessel, *Marchés,* 125, *my translation*. "Les paquebots sont devenus les autobus de l'océan, me disais-je, et comment imaginer que je pourrais me trouver un jour sur des vagues lointaines à bord d'un fragile bâtiment et découvrir des rivages inconnus et prestigieux comme ceux où l'on aborde parfois au cours des rêves."

109. Kessell, *Marchés,* 125, *my translation*. "Et tandis que défilait la côte, la nouvelle de Conrad, *Jeunesse,* me revint à la mémoire."

110. Hand, Séan, *Michel Leiris: Writing the Self* (Cambridge: Cambridge University Press, 1991), 2.

111. Leiris, Michel, *Phantom Africa,* trans. Edwards, Brent Hayes (York, PA: Seagull Books, 2017), 671. "Cafard effroyable. Le vrai cafard: le cafard colonial." [Leiris, Michel, *Miroir de l'Afrique* (Paris: Gallimard, 1996), 852.]

112. Leiris, *Miroir,* 832.

113. Leiris, *Phantom,* 671.

114. Leiris, *Phantom,* 671. "Rétrospective de tous mes ratages: actes manqués, aventures manquées, coïts manqués." [Leiris, *Miroir,* 832.]

115. Leiris, *Phantom,* 672. "Certains disent que ce n'est pas "un homme": il ne bouge pas, il ne chasse pas, il est très mou avec les indigènes, il se trouble très facilement." [Leiris, *Miroir,* 833.]

116. Leiris, *Phantom,* 675.

117. Leiris, *Phantom,* 675. "La plupart le considèrent comme un poseur; les moins incultes le traitent d'esthète. On trouve étrange qu'il ne monte pas à cheval et qu'il n'aime pas chasser." [Leiris, *Miroir,* 836.]

118. Leiris *Phantom*, 657. "Je suis chaste depuis bientôt deux ans. D'aucuns me traiteront d'impuissant, diront que je n'ai pas de coquilles." [Leiris, *Miroir*, 836.]

119. Leiris, *Phantom*, 676. "Qu'on ne dise pas qu'Axel Heyst est un esthète, un fou ou un original. Il n'est qu'un homme demi-lucide dans un monde d'aveugles." [Leiris, *Miroir*, 838.]

120. Edward Said, "Conrad and Nietzsche," in *Reflections on Exile and Other Essays* (Cambridge: Harvard University Press, 2000), 70.

121. Leiris, *Phantom*, 675. "crudité et netteté écrasantes." [Leiris, *Miroir*, 836.]

122. Leiris, *Phantom*, 673. "bloc assez gros de feuillets séparés, constituent une sorte de journal intime assez confus, écrit le plus souvent sans date." [Leiris, *Miroir*, 834.]

123. Leiris, *Phantom*, 673. "'montrer que lui aussi était 'un homme.'" [Leiris, *Miroir*, 835.]

124. Leiris, *Phantom*, 676. "l'éducation que j'ai reçue [. . .] règles qui n'ont abouti qu'à me lier, à faire de moi l'espèce de paria sentimental que je suis, incapable de vivre sainement, en copulant sainement." [Leiris, *Miroir*, 838.]

125. Leiris, "Préface 1951," *Miroir de l'Afrique* (Paris: Gallimard, 1996) 93–94: 94, *my translation*. "cessant d'aspirer au rôle romantique du Blanc [. . .] tel Lord Jim.[. . .] ça signifiait pour lui, en même temps qu'une épreuve, une poésie vécue et un dépaysement."

126. Leiris, *Phantom*, 674–675. "Si le docteur avait un peu réfléchi, sans doute aurait-il épilogué sur l'affaire du coup donné au "manœuvre indigène célèbre dans le pays pour le grand développement de son organe viril." Il aurait remarqué combien la réaction d'Axel Heyst—ce mouvement de fureur puritaine à l'égard d'un homme de couleur—le montrait obscurément contaminé, malgré l'ouverture d'esprit qu'on peut lui supposer, par un des pires préjugés racistes: celui qui, aux yeux de nombreux Blancs, change les Noirs en rivaux sexuels dangereux qu'il est urgent de tenir à distance. Et peut-être aurait-il soupçonné que si Heyst n'était pas parvenu à éviter le suicide, c'est que la crainte dont il souffrait de s'avérer inférieur –marquant le prix élevé qu'il attachait à son prestige et le souci trop grand qu'il avait de lui-même ne pouvait pas se liquider sans une conversion radicale, telle qu'en une femme, par exemple, il aurait su ne plus voir que cette femme au lieu de la réduire à l'état d'instrument lui permettant de tenter une expérience ou de faire ses preuves; telle qu'en somme que, d'une manière tout à fait générale, inquiet de *virilité* à un moindre degré il se fût révélé plus prodigue de pure et simple *humanité*." [Leiris, Préface 1951, 835.]

127. Said, "Conrad and Nietzsche," 287.

128. Lefevere, *Translation*, 7.

129. Mongia, Padimi, "Between Men: Conrad in the Fiction of Two Contemporary Indian Writers," in *Conrad in the Twenty-First Century: Contemporary Approaches and Perspectives*, eds. Kaplan, Carola, Mallios, Peter, and White, Andrea (London: Routledge, 2005), 85–100: 90.

130. Said, Edward, *Freud and the Non-European* (London: Verso, 2004), 24.

131. Said, *Freud*, 24.

132. Casanova, *World*, 351.

133. Said, *Freud*, 25.

134. Said, *Freud*, 27.

135. Said, *Freud*, 27.

136. Tadié, Jean-Yves, *Le roman d'aventures* (Vendôme: Presses Universitaires de France, 1982), 182, *my translation*. "[S]on mouvement est celui d'interrogation, non du réalisme, ni de la certitude."

137. Conrad's reputation in France continued to grow, and he was a formative force for many writers. By 1940 Conrad had influenced so many young writers that three successive editions of the journal *Les nouvelles littéraires* devoted space to an extended study by George Higgins entitled "Les Conrads français" ["The French Conrads"].

Chapter Two

1. Thurston, Michael, "Genre, Gender and Truth in *Death in the Afternoon*," *Hemingway Review* 17:2 (1998), 47–63: 47.

2. Anthony Brand has convincingly argued that Hemingway's extensive use of photographs made good sense at the time: "he [Hemingway] recognized that recent advances in photography would enable him to present his subject more vividly than had previously been possible." "'Far from Simple': The Published Photographs in *Death in the Afternoon*," *A Companion to Hemingway's* Death in the Afternoon, ed. Mandel, Miriam B. (Rochester, NY: Camden House, 2004), 165–187: 165.

3. Collins, Steward, "Bull-Fights and Politics," *Ernest Hemingway: The Critical Reception*, ed. Stephens, Robert C. (New York: Burt Franklin, 1977), 113–115: 115

4. Hemingway, Ernest, *Death in the Afternoon* (New York: Charles Scribner's Sons, 1932), 144.

5. Hemingway had already explored the Spanish bullfight in a variety of genres before *Death in the Afternoon*. In 1923, he published three essays on the bullfight ("Tancredo is Dead," "Bull Fighting is Not a Sport—It Is a Tragedy," and "World's Series of Bullfighting a Mad, Whirling Carnival"). In 1924, he published "Pamplona Letter" and, in 1930, the much longer "Bullfighting, Sport and Industry." He also wrote poems about the *corrida*, five of which were published prior to *Death in the Afternoon*. In addition, a 1923 fictional piece entitled "Maera Lay Still" described the death-by-goring of the famous matador, although—in truth—Maera would die of tuberculosis in 1924. Earlier stories offering a fictional treatment of the bullfight include "The Mother of a Queen," "Banal Story," and "The Undefeated." When *Death in the Afternoon* was published in 1932, Hemingway had thus already treated the bullfight in a variety of different styles and with a number of different techniques. We arguably see all of these genres at play in *Death in the Afternoon*, which notably mixes fact and fiction as it circulates various styles and techniques.

6. Cowley, Malcolm, "A Farewell to Spain," in *Ernest Hemingway: The Critical Reception*, ed. Stephens, Robert O. (New York: Burt Franklin, 1977), 120–123: 123.

7. Hemingway, *Death*, 33.

8. Cowley, Malcolm, "A Farewell to Spain," 123.

9. Hemingway, *Death*, 40.

10. Hemingway, *Death*, 63.

11. Hemingway, *Death*, 63.

12. Said, Edward, "How Not to Get Gored," in *Reflections on Exile and Other Essays* (Cambridge, MA: Harvard University Press, 2000), 230–238: 238.

13. Hemingway, *Death*, 272.

14. Hemingway, *Death*, 380.

15. Hemingway, Ernest, *The Sun Also Rises* (New York: Scribner's Sons, 1954), 132.

16. Peat, Alexandra, *Travel and Modernist Literature: Sacred and Ethical Journeys*
(New York: Routledge, 2011), 97.

17. Hemingway, Ernest, *Selected Letters; 1917–1961*, ed. Baker, Carlos (New York: Scribner's, 1960), 131.

18. Hemingway, *Selected*, 131.

19. Reynolds, Michael, "*The Sun* in its Time: Recovering the Historical Context," *New Essays on* The Sun Also Rises, ed. Wagner-Martin, Linda (Cambridge: Cambridge University Press, 1987), 43–64: 47.

20. Rosaldo, Renato, *Culture and Truth: The Remaking of Social Analysis* (Boston: Beacon Press, 1989), 68.

21. Rosaldo, *Culture*, 70.

22. Hemingway, *Death*, 2.

23. Hemingway, *Death*, 3.

24. Hemingway, *Death*, 91.

25. Hemingway, *Selected*, 88.

26. Hemingway, *Death*, 380.

27. Hemingway, *Death*, 232.

28. Douglas, Ann, *Terrible Honesty: Mongrel Manhattan in the 1920s* (New York: Farrer, Straus, and Giroux: 1996), 224.

29. Hemingway, *Death*, 232.

30. Comley, Nancy R. and Scholes, Robert, *Hemingway's Genders* (New Haven, CT: Yale University Press, 1994), 4.

31. Coates, Robert M., "Bullfighters," in Stephens, 116

32. Qtd. in Irmscher, Christoph, *Max Eastman: A Life* (New Haven: Yale University Press, 2017), 250.

33. Hemingway, *Selected*, 191.

34. Hemingway, *Selected*, 156.

35. Hemingway, *Selected*, 158.

36. Hemingway, *Selected*, 148.

37. Strychacz, Thomas, *Hemingway's Theaters of Masculinity* (Baton Rouge: Louisiana State University Press, 2003), 11.

38. Hemingway, *Selected*, 148.

39. Hemingway, *Death*, 34.

40. Hemingway, *Death*, 34.

41. Hemingway, *Death*, 277.

42. Hemingway, *Death*, 42.

43. Hemingway, *Death*, 487.

44. Hemingway, *Death*, 8.

45. Hemingway, *Death*, 487.

46. Hemingway, *Selected*, 236.

47. Hemingway, *Death*, 4.

48. Hemingway, *Death*, 1.

49. Hemingway, *Death*, 8.

50. Hemingway, *Death*, 11.

51. Hemingway, *Death*, 41.

52. Hemingway, *Death*, 373, 393.

53. Hemingway, Ernest, *For Whom the Bell Tolls* (New York: Scribner, 1995), 166.

54. Hemingway, *Death*, 96.

55. Hemingway, *Death*, 452.

56. Hemingway, *Death*, 204.

57. Hemingway, *Death*, 205.

58. Hemingway, *Death*, 417–418.

59. "*maricón*" and "*maricones*" (the plural) are also used in Hemingway's "Spanish" novel, *For Whom the Bell Tolls* (1940), albeit more in passing.

60. Hemingway, *Death*, 393.

61. Venuti, Lawrence, *The Translator's Invisibility: A History of Translation* (New York: Routledge, 1995) 20.

62. Hemingway, *Death*, 157.

63. Gayle Rogers, *Incomparable Empires: Modernism and the Translation of Spanish and American Literature* (New York, Columbia University Press, 2016), 535.

64. Lonsdale, Laura, *Multilingualism and Modernity: Barbarisms in Spanish and American Literature* (New York: Palgrave Macmillan, 2017).

65. Rogers, *Incomparable*, 551.

66. Lonsdale, *Multilingualism*, 235.

67. Taylor-Batty, *Multilingualism*, 81.

68. Hemingway, *Death*, 64.

69. Hemingway, *Death*, 64.

70. Hemingway, *Death*, 101.

71. Hemingway, *Death*, 103.

72. Weber, Robert, *Hemingway's Art of Non-Fiction* (Basingstoke, UK: Macmillan, 1989), 87.

73. Hemingway, *Death*, 121.

74. Hemingway, *Death*, 190.

75. Hemingway, *Death*, 133.

76. Hemingway, *Death*, 138.

77. Hemingway, *Death*, 134.

78. Hemingway, *Death*, 134.

79. Hemingway, *Death*, 137.

80. Hemingway, *Death*, 136.

81. Hemingway, *Death*, 135.

82. Hemingway, *Sun*, 167.

83. Hemingway, *Sun*, 168.

84. Hemingway, *Sun*, 167.

85. Hemingway, *Sun*, 131.

86. Hemingway, *Death*, 65.

87. Hemingway, *Death*, 191.

88. Hemingway, *Death*, 192.

89. Hemingway, *Death*, 191.

90. Hemingway, *Death*, 270.

91. Hemingway, *Death*, 278.

92. Hemingway, *Death*, 278.

93. Hemingway, *Death*, 273.

94. Hemingway, *Death*, 48.

95. Hemingway, *Death*, 8.

96. Boym, Svetlana, *The Future of Nostalgia* (New York: Basic Books, 2001), 41.

97. Hemingway, *Death*, 240.

98. Hemingway, *Death*, 465.

99. Boym, *Nostalgia*, 11.

100. Young, Philip, *Ernest Hemingway: A Reconsideration* (University Park: Pennsylvania State University Press, 1966), 205.

101. Boym, *Nostalgia*, 49.

102. Josephs, Allen, "*Death in the Afternoon*, A Reconsideration," *Hemingway Review* 2:1 (1982), 2–16: 6.

103. Rosaldo, *Culture*, 71.

104. Starobinksi, Jean, "The Idea of Nostalgia," *Diogenes* 54 (1966), 81–103: 103.

105. Hemingway, *Death*, 100.

Chapter Three

1. Esty, Jed, *A Shrinking Island: Modernism and National Culture in England* (Princeton: Princeton University Press, 2003), 8.

2. Brantlinger, Patrick, "Victorians and Africans: The Genealogy of the Myth of the Dark Continent," *Critical Inquiry* 12:1 (1985), 166–203: 176.

3. Lawrence, D. H., *Mornings in Mexico* (Amsterdam: Fredonia Books, 2003), 95.

4. Lawrence, D. H., Roberts, Warren, Boulton, James and Mansfield, Elizabeth, eds. *The Letters of D. H. Lawrence Vol. 4* (Cambridge: Cambridge University Press, 2000), 154.

5. Lawrence, *Mornings in Mexico*, 58.

6. Lawrence, *Mornings*, 22.

7. Lawrence, *Mornings*, 24.

8. Lawrence, *Mornings*, 24.

9. Lawrence, *Mornings*, 24.

10. Lawrence, *Mornings*, 38.

11. Lawrence, *Mornings*, 40.

12. Lawrence, *Mornings*, 49.

13. Lawrence, *Mornings*, 57.

14. Lawrence, *Mornings*, 59.

15. Lawrence, *Mornings*, 105.

16. Fussell, Paul, *Abroad: British Literary Traveling Between the Wars* (Oxford: Oxford University Press, 1982), 147.

17. Lawrence, *Mornings*, 105.

18. Waugh, Alec, *Hot Countries* (New York: Paragon House, 1989), 37–38.

19. Waugh, *Hot*, 61.

20. Waugh, *Hot*, 66.

21. Waugh, *Hot*, 64.

22. Waugh, *Hot*, 72.

23. Waugh, *Hot*, 19.

24. Waugh, *Hot*, 25.

25. Waugh, *Hot*, 54.

26. Waugh, *Hot*, 129–130.

27. Waugh, *Hot*, 140.

28. Waugh, Evelyn, *Waugh Abroad: Collected Travel Writing* (New York: Alfred A. Knopf, 2003), 49.

29. Waugh, *Waugh Abroad*, 93.

30. Greenberg, Jonathan, "Travel Writing as Modernist Autobiography," in *Modernism and Autobiography*, eds. DiBattista, Maria and Wittman, Emily O. (Cambridge: Cambridge University Press, 2014), 69–83: 81.

31. Kaplan, Caren, *Questions of Travel: Postmodern Discourses of Displacement* (Durham, NC: Duke University Press, 1996), 36.

32. Orwell, George, *Down and Out in Paris and London* (New York: Shocken Books, 1961), 213.

33. Schweizer, Bernard, *Radicals on the Road: The Politics of English Travel Writing in the 1930s* (Charlottesville, VA: The University of Virginia Press, 2001).

34. Porter, Dennis, *Haunted Journeys: Desire and Transgression in European Travel Writing* (Princeton: Princeton University Press, 1991), 12.

35. Orwell, *Down*, 9.

36. Orwell, *Down*, 7.

37. Orwell, *Down*, 13.

38. Orwell, *Down*, 15.

39. Orwell, *Down*, 78.

40. Qtd. in Williams, Ian, *Political and Cultural Perceptions of George Orwell: British and American Views* (New York: Palgrave, 2017), 88.

41. Fussell, *Abroad*, 13–14.

42. Fleming, Peter, *Brazilian Adventure* (Evanston, IL: The Marlboro Press/ Northwestern Press, 1999), 9.

43. Fleming, *Brazilian*, 121.

44. Fleming, *Brazilian*, 122.

45. Fleming, *Brazilian*, 132.

46. Fleming, *Brazilian*, 132.

47. Fleming, *Brazilian*, 132.

48. Fleming, *Brazilian*, 133.

49. Fleming, *Brazilian*, 133.

50. Fleming, *Brazilian*, 133.

51. Fleming, *Brazilian*, 133.

52. Fleming, *Brazilian*, 133.

53. Fleming, *Brazilian*, 375.

54. Fleming, *Brazilian*, 375.

55. Fleming, *Brazilian*, 376.

56. Fleming, *Brazilian*, 9.

57. Youngs, Tim, "Travel Writing after 1900," in *The Cambridge History of Travel Writing*, eds. Das, Nandini and Youngs, Tim (Cambridge: Cambridge University Press, 2019), 125–139: 127

58. Booth, Howard J., "Making the Case for Cross-Cultural Exchange: Robert Byron's *The Road to Oxiana*," in *Cultural Encounters: European Travel Writing in the 1930s*, eds. Burdett, Charles and Duncan, Derek (New York: Berghahn Books, 2002), 159–172: 167.

59. Byron, Robert, *The Road to Oxiana* (New York: Oxford University Press, 1966), 128.

60. Byron, *Road*, 128.

61. Maher, Brigid, "Pseudotranslation," in *The Routledge Handbook of Literary Translation*, eds. Van Wyke, Ben and Washbourne, Kelley (New York: Routledge, 2018) 382–393: 387.

62. Fussell, *Abroad*, xi.

Chapter Four

1. Gikandi, Simon, *Maps of Englishness: Writing Identity in the Culture of Colonialism* (New York: Columbia University Press, 1996), 179.

2. Torgovnick, Marianna, *Primitive Passions: Men, Women, and the Quest for Ecstasy* (New York: Knopf, 1996), 23.

3. Torgovnick, *Primitive*, 23.

4. Leiris, Michel to Olga and Pablo Picasso, May 20, 1932, Archives Picasso, Paris, France, *my translation*. "Ce sera une grande joie pour moi, vers cet hiver, quand nous serons rentrés, de jouer avec lui à l'Afrique, et de remplir, auprès de vous, le rôle de l'explorateur bavard qui débite, sans que rien puisse l'arrêter . . . son stock d'histoires."

5. Mikkonen, Kai, *Narrative Paths: African Travel in Modern Fiction and Nonfiction* (Columbus: The Ohio State University Press, 2015), 4.

6. Matera, Marc and Kent, Susan Kingsley, *The Global 1930s: The International Decade* (New York: Routledge, 2017), 23.

7. Rhys, Jean, *Good Morning, Midnight* (New York: W. W. Norton, 1986), 91.

8. Leiris, Michel, *Phantom Africa*, trans. Edwards, Brent Hayes (York, PA: Seagull Books, 2017), 65. "comme une manière de confession." [Leiris, Michel, *Miroir de l'Afrique* (Paris: Gallimard, 1996), 85.]

9. Leiris, *Phantom*, 65. [R]épondant à un état d'esprit que j'estime avoir dépassé elles ont surtout pour moi valeur rétrospective de document quant à ce qu'un Européen de trente ans féru de ce qu'on n'avait pas encore appelé "négritude" et poussé à voyager dans ces contrées alors assez lointaines parce que cela signifiait pour lui, en même temps qu'une épreuve, une poésie vécue et un dépaysement, peut avoir ressenti quand il traversa d'ouest en est cette Afrique noire d'avant la dernière guerre en s'étonnant—bien naïvement—de ne pas échapper à lui-même quand il eût dû s'apercevoir que les raisons trop personnelles qui l'avaient décidé à s'arracher à ses proches empêchaient dès le principe qu'il en fût autrement. [Leiris, *Miroir*, 85.]

10. Cogez, Gérard, "Objet cherché, accord perdu: Michel Leiris et l'Afrique," *L'homme* 151 (1999), 237–255: 251, *my translation*. "S'attirer les bonnes grâces du genre féminin dans son ensemble, voilà peut-être par excellence le rêve africain de Michel Leiris crûment résumé."

11. Gide, André, *Travels in the Congo* (Berkeley: University of California Press, 1972), 10. "À vingt ans je n'aurais pas eu joie plus vive." [Gide, André, *Voyage au Congo: Carnet de route* (Paris: Gallimard, 1927), 17.]

12. Gide, *Travels*, 11. "Mon cœur ne bat pas moins fort qu'à vingt ans." [Gide, *Voyage*, 18.]

13. Mikkonen, *Narrative Paths*, 31.

14. Céline, *Journey to the End of the Night* (New York: New Directions, 1983), 97. "Une véritable réjouissance générale et morale s'annonçait à bord de l'*Admiral Bragueton*. "L'immonde" n'échapperait pas à son sort. C'était moi." [Céline, *Voyage au bout de la nuit* (Paris: Gallimard, 1952), 151.]

15. Waugh, Evelyn, *The Complete Stories of Evelyn Waugh* (Boston: Little, Brown & Company, 1999), 176.

16. Waugh, *Complete*, 183.

17. Céline, *Journey*, 122. "Je retrouvais chaque soir mon logis, sans doute inachevable, où le petit squelette de lit m'était dressé par le boy pervers. Il me tendait des pièges le boy, il était lascif comme un chat, il voulait entrer dans ma

famille. Cependant, j'étais hanté moi par d'autres et bien plus vivaces préoccupations et surtout par le projet de me réfugier quelque temps encore à l'hôpital, seul armistice à ma portée dans ce carnaval torride." [Céline, *Voyage*, 188.]

18. Céline, Louis-Ferdinand, *Cahier Céline 4: Lettres et premiers écrits d'Afrique 1916-1917* (Paris: Gallimard, 1978), 32, *my translation*. "Chaleur formidable Louis."

19. Céline, *Cahier Céline 4*, 33, *my translation*. "avons très chaud très mauvaise traversée t'embrasse bien."

20. Cooke, Roderick, "Bardamu's Triangular Trade: The Modern Slavery of *Voyage au bout de la nuit*," *The Modern Language Review* 11:4 (October, 2017), 882–898: 897.

21. Dinesen, Isak, *Out of Africa* and *Shadows on the Grass* (New York: Random House, 1961), 19–20.

22. Yiannopoulou, Effie, "Autistic Adventures: Love, Auto-Portraiture and White Women's Colonial Dis-ease," *European Journal of English Studies* 2:3 (1998), 324–342: 324–325.

23. Youngs, Tim, Review of *Women's Voices on Africa: A Century of Travel Writings* by Romero, Patricia W., *Africa* 63:2 (1993), 261–262: 261.

24. Smith, Sidonie, *Moving Lives: Twentieth-Century Women's Travel Writing* (Minneapolis: University of Minnesota Press, 2001), 27–28.

25. Kelley, Joyce, *Excursions into Modernism: Women Writers, Travel, and the Body* (New York: Routledge, 2016), 33.

26. Hemingway, Ernest, *The Short Stories* (New York: Simon and Schuster, 1995), 30.

27. Markham, Beryl, *West with the Night* (New York: North Point Press, 1983), 201.

28. Markham, *West*, 209.

29. Smith, Sidonie, "The Other Woman and the Racial Politics of Gender: Isak Dinesen and Beryl Markham in Kenya," in *De/Colonizing the Subject: The Politics of Gender in Women's Autobiography*, eds. Smith, Sidonie and Watson, Julia, (Minneapolis: University of Minnesota Press, 1992), 410–435: 411.

30. Markham, *West*, 11–12.

31. Markham, *West*. 186.

32. Markham, *West*, 186.

33. Dinesen, *Out*, 227.

34. Dinesen, *Out*, 229.

35. Dinesen, *Out*, 311.

36. Morand, Paul, *Paris-Tombouctou: Documentaire (notes d'un voyage africain)* (Paris: Flammarion, 1928), 46, *my translation*. "Où sont les coupoles rutilantes, les sacs de poudre d'or et d'ivoire des caravanes dont parlaient les livres?"

37. Leiris, *Miroir*, 66, *my translation*. "un document aussi objectif et sincère que possible"

38. Larson, Ruth, "Ethnography, Thievery, and Cultural Identity: A rereading of Michel Leiris's *L'Afrique fantôme*," *PMLA* 112:2 (1997), 229–242: 231.

39. Clarck-Taoua, Phyllis "In Search of New Skin: Michel Leiris's *L'Afrique fantôme*," *Cahiers d'études africaines* 42:167 (2002), 479–498: 489.

40. Clarck, "Search." 489.

41. Côté, Sébastien. "Michel Leiris et la fuite impossible: Ethnographie, autobiographie et l'altérité féminine dans *L'Afrique fantôme*," *MLN*, 20:4 (2005), 849–870: 868. "Car comment l'ethnologie peut-elle prétendre rendre compte objectivement d'une culture donnée lorsqu'une vie entière d'introspection n'a pas suffi à un seul homme pour se raconter?"

42. Clifford, James, "Negrophilia," in *A New History of French Literature*, ed. Hollier, Denis (Cambridge, MA: Harvard University Press, 1994), 901–908: 904.

43. Clifford, "Negrophilia," 901.

44. Clifford, "Negrophilia," 904.

45. Clifford, "Negrophilia," 904.

46. Leiris, Michel, *Miroir de l'Afrique* (Paris: Gallimard, 1996), 66, *my translation*. "Qu'y trouve-t-il? Peu d'aventures, des études qui le passionnent d'abord mais se révèlent bientôt trop inhumaines pour le satisfaire, une obsession érotique croissante, un vide sentimental de plus en plus grand. Malgré son dégoût des civilisés et de la vie des métropoles, vers la fin du voyage, il aspire au retour."

Chapter Five

1. Dinesen, Isak, *Out of Africa* and *Shadows on the Grass* (New York: Random House, 1961), 43.

2. Dinesen, *Out,* 47–48.

3. Dinesen, *Out,* 86.

4. Dinesen, *Out,* 348.

5. Dinesen, *Out,* 248–249.

6. These claims are curiously ironic given the forty-year controversy over *West with the Night*. According to the claims of several critics and friends of her ex-husband Raoul Schumacher, it was Schumacher, not Markham, who put her stories to paper. For the purposes of this book, I am gambling, in an informed manner, that Markham wrote *West with the Night*.

7. Markham, Beryl, *West with the Night* (New York: North Point, 1983), 293.

8. Markham, *West*, 3.

9. Markham, *West*, 8.

10. Markham, *West*, 8.

11. Céline, Louis-Ferdinand, *Cahier Céline 4: Lettres et premiers écrits d'Afrique 1916–1917* (Paris: Gallimard, 1978), 101, *my translation*. "Ce n'est pas de la littérature. Alors? C'est de la vie, la vie telle qu'elle se présente."

12. Céline, *Cahier Céline 4*, 101, *my translation*. "j'ai écrit comme je parle...et puis je suis du peuple, du vrai...J'ai fait toutes mes études secondaires et les deux premières années de mes études supérieures en étant livreur chez un épicier."

13. Qtd. in Thurman, Judith, *Isak Dinesen: The Life of a Storyteller* (New York: St. Martin's Press. 1982), 281.

14. Dinesen, *Out*, 235.

15. Dinesen, *Out*, 235.

16. Dinesen, *Out*, 382.

17. Dinesen, *Out*, 281.

18. Dinesen, *Out*, 29.

19. Dinesen, *Out*, 32.

20. Dinesen, *Out*, 166.

21. Memmi, Albert, *The Colonizer and the Colonized* (New York: Orion Press, 1965), 85.

22. Dinesen, *Out*, 19.

23. Gide, *Travels*, 80. "Il semble que les cerveaux de ces gens soient incapables d'établir un rapport de cause à effet, et ceci, j'ai pu le constater maintes fois dans la suite de ce voyage." [Gide, André, *Voyage au Congo: Carnet de route* (Paris: Gallimard, 1927), 334.]

24. Michael Taussig analyzes this practice in *Mimesis and Alterity: A Particular History of the Senses* (1993). For Taussig, the white man's fascination with the natives' assumed interest in the phonograph is one of the nineteenth century's longest-persisting topoi of non-European travel.

25. Waugh, Evelyn, *Remote People* (London: Duckworth, 1931), 49.

26. Waugh, Evelyn, *Black Mischief* (New York: Little, Brown and Company, 1960), 193.

27. Barnard, Rita, "Evelyn Waugh's *Black Mischief*," in *Modernism and Colonialism: British and Irish Literature 1899–1939*, ed. Begam, Richard and Moses, Michael Valdez (Durham, NC: Duke University Press, 2007), 162–182: 165.

28. Barnard, "Evelyn," 165.

29. Barnard, "Evelyn," 166.

30. Dinesen, *Out*, 236.

31. Leiris, *Phantom*, 89. "Au matin, départ avec le chef. Sur le point de sortir, étendant le drap qu'un habitant, la veille au soir, nous a prêté en guise de nappe, et que nous étions navré d'avoir légèrement taché de vin rouge tant il nous semblait blanc, je trouve au revers de la merde séchée." [Leiris, *Miroir*, 122.]

32. Dinesen, *Africa*, 138.

33. Londres, Albert, *Terre d'ébène: La traite des noirs* (Paris: Le Serpent à plumes, 1994), 207.

34. Memmi, *Colonizer*, 124.

35. Gide, André, *Travels in the Congo* (Berkeley: University of California Press, 1962), 357. "D'ailleurs ces gens de ville sont corrompus—je veux dire moins naïfs, et pourtant moins intéressant que ceux de la brousse." [Gide, André, *Le Retour du Tchad: Carnet de route* (Paris: Gallimard, 1928), 366.]

36. Gide, *Travels*, 372. "Ces deux tristes produits de grande ville (Yaoundé), voleurs, menteurs, hypocrites, justifieraient l'irritation de certains colons contre les noirs. Mais précisément ce ne sont pas des produits naturels du pays. C'est au contact de notre civilisation qu'ils se sont gâtés." [Gide, André, *Voyage au Congo & Le retour du Tchad* (Paris: Folio, 1981), 497.]

37. Gide, *Travels*, 95–96. ʿDe quelle sottise, le plus souvent, le blanc fait preuve, quand il s'indigne de la stupidité des noirs! Je ne les crois pourtant capables, que d'un très petit développement, le cerveau gourd et stagnant le plus souvent dans une nuit épaisse—mais combien de fois le blanc semble prendre à tâche de les y enfoncer!" [Gide, *Voyage*, 239–240.]

38. Gide, *Travels*, 295. "Je ne vois rien en lui que d'enfantin, de noble, de pur et d'honnête. Les blancs qui trouvent le moyen de faire de ces deux êtres-là des coquins sont de pires coquins eux-mêmes, ou de bien tristes maladroits." [Gide, *Retour*, 203.]

39. Gide, *Travels*, 241. "Les gens de ces peuplades primitives, je m'en persuade de plus en plus, n'ont pas notre façon de raisonner [. . .] Leurs actes échappent au contrôle de la logique dont, depuis notre plus tendre enfance, nous avons appris, et par les formes mêmes de notre langage, à ne pouvoir point nous passer." [Gide, *Retour*, 84–85.]

40. Gide, *Travels*, 295. "Mais partout et toujours c'est de la bêtise des nègres que l'on parle. [. . .] Et je ne veux point faire le noir plus intelligent qu'il n'est; mais sa bêtise, quand elle serait ne saurait être, comme celle de l'animal, que naturelle. Celle du blanc à son égard, et plus il lui est supérieur, a quelque chose de monstrueux." [Gide, *Retour*, 203–204.]

41. Gide, *Travels*, 294. "Adoum assurément n'est pas très différent de ses frères; aucun trait ne lui est bien particulier. À travers lui, je sens toute une humanité souffrant, une pauvre race opprimée, dont nous avons mal su comprendre la beauté, la valeur. . . que je voudrais pouvoir ne plus quitter. Et la mort d'un ami ne m'attristerait pas davantage, car je sais que je ne le reverrai jamais." [Gide, *Retour*, 200–201.]

42. Qtd. in Segal, Naomi, "Gide in Europe 1939," in *Cultural Encounters: European Travel Writing in the 1930s*, eds. Burdett, Charles and Duncan, Derek (New York: Berghahn Books, 2002), 143–158: 147. "Non, je n'ai plus grand désir de forniquer; du moins ce n'est plus un besoin comme au beau temps de ma jeunesse. Mais j'ai besoin de savoir que, si je voulais, je pourrais; comprenez-vous cela? Je veux dire qu'un pays ne me plaît pas que si de multiples occasions de fornication se présentent. Les plus beaux monuments du monde ne peuvent remplacer cela; pourquoi ne pas l'avouer franchement?" [Gide, André, qtd. in Lucey, Michael, *Gide's Bent: Sexuality, Politics, Writing* (Oxford: Oxford University Press, 1995), 195.]

43. Matera, Marc and Kent, Susan Kingsley, *The Global 1930s: The International Decade* (New York: Routledge, 2017), 23.

44. Leiris, *Phantom*, 457 "Quant à Griaule, il attend pour demain un trafiquant qui lui présentera une esclave à vendre, mère d'un petit enfant et enceinte. On effectuera la libération aussitôt que possible. L'idée anti-esclavagiste ne me plaît qu'à moitié. Le monde bourgeois s'indigne; mais je ne vois pas qu'il y ait tellement lieu d'être scandalisé qu'il existe encore des pays où se pratique couramment la traite des esclaves si l'on songe à la situation qu'ont dans nos sociétés, par exemple, les ouvriers. Éternelle hypocrisie. . . L'exposé de cette opinion m'attire la réprobation des membres de la Mission." [Leiris, *Miroir*, 561.]

45. Dinesen, *Out*, 251.

46. Céline, *Journey*, 121. "[E]n somme tout comme les pauvres de chez nous mais avec plus d'enfants encore et moins de linge sale et moins de vin rouge autour." [Céline, *Voyage au bout de la nuit* (Paris: Gallimard, 1952), 186.]

47. Self, Will, "Céline's Dark Journey," *The New York Times* (July 17, 2010), https://www.nytimes.com/2006/09/10/books/review/Self.t.html.

48. Both French original and English translation qtd. in Thomas, Merlin, *Louis-Ferdinand Céline* (London: New Directions, 1980), 160. "Quel est le véritable ami du peuple? Le fascisme."

49. Scullion, Rosemary, "Madness and Fascist Discourse in Céline's *Voyage au bout de la nuit*," *The French Review* 61:5 (1988), 715–723: 715.

50. Céline, *Journey*, 95. "C'est depuis ce moment que nous vîmes à fleur de peau venir s'étaler l'angoissante nature des blancs, provoquée, libérée, bien débraillée enfin, leur vraie nature, tout comme à la guerre." [Céline, *Voyage*, 149.]

51. Céline, *Voyage*, 149.

52. Céline, *Journey*, 95.

53. Waugh's occasional forays into right-wing writing were unfashionable and professionally embarrassing to him in his later years. When he compiled his 1946 collection of travel literature, *When the Going was Good*, he strategically left out the more fascist sections.

54. Waugh, Evelyn, "Evelyn Waugh on the Word 'Fascist,'" *The New Statesman*, (March 5, 1938), https://www.newstatesman.com/culture/2013/03/5-march-1938-evelyn-waugh-word-fascist.

55. The Chambre des députés was a parliamentary body in France in the nineteenth and twentieth centuries. In its second appearance (1875–1940) during the French Third Republic, it functioned as a legislative assembly of the French Parliament. Its members were elected by universal suffrage.

56. Londres, *Terre d'ébène*, 30, *my translation*.

57. Waugh, Evelyn, *Scoop* (Boston: Little, Brown and Company, 1965), 60.

58. Dinesen, *Africa*, 37.

59. Céline, *Journey*, 149–150. "[M]ais alors de ça, je pouvais dire qu'il m'en avait laissé. J'en ai vomi des boîtes." [Céline, *Voyage*, 224.]

60. Alcohol is an essential ingredient in most travel writing of this period. It is ironic that Thomas Cook, arguably the father of mass tourism with his famous Cook tours, was a teetotaler. His original tours began as an adjunct to the temperance movement. His first tour in 1841 carried 570 teetotalers to a temperance rally in Leicester.

61. Leiris, *Miroir*, 66, *my translation*. "Las de la vie qu'il menait à Paris, regardant le voyage comme une aventure poétique, une méthode de connaissance concrète, une épreuve, un moyen symbolique d'arrêter la vieillesse en parcourant l'espace pour nier le temps, l'auteur, qui s'intéresse à l'ethnographie en raison de la portée qu'il attribue à cette science quant à la clarification des rapports humains, prend part à une mission scientifique qui traverse l'Afrique."

62. Céline, *Journey*, 109. "Venue la nuit, la retape indigène battait son plein entre les petits nuages de moustiques besogneux et lestés de fièvre jaune. Un renfort d'éléments soudanais offrait au promeneur tout ce qu'ils avaient de bien sous les pagnes. Pour des prix très raisonnables, on pouvait s'envoyer une famille entière pendant une heure ou deux. J'aurais bien aimé vadrouiller de sexe en sexe, mais force me fut de me décider à rechercher un endroit où on me donnerait du boulot." [Céline, *Voyage*, 168.]

63. Greene, Jean, "Visions of Death and Dissolution," in *A New History of French Literature*, ed. Hollier Denis, 850–855: 852.

64. Céline, *Journey*, 76. "Après huit jours passés dans ce nouveau service, nous avions compris l'urgence d'avoir à changer de dégaine et, grâce à Brandledore [. . .] [u]n dru langage était devenu en effet le nôtre, et si salé que ces dames en rougissaient parfois, elles ne s'en plaignaient jamais cependant parce qu'il est bien entendu qu'un soldat est aussi brave qu'insouciant, et que plus qu'il est grossier et que plus il est brave." [Céline, *Voyage*, 120.]

65. Dinesen, *Africa*, 153.

66. Dinesen, *Africa*, 125.

67. Dinesen, Isak, *Letters from Africa 1914–1931*, ed. Lasson, Frans (Chicago: University of Chicago Press, 1978), 17.

68. Markham, *West*, 98.

69. Céline, *Journey*, 95. Nous voguions vers l'Afrique la vraie, la grande, celle des insondables forêts, des miasmes délétères, des solitudes inviolées, vers les grands tyrans nègres, vautrés aux croisements de fleuves qui n'en finissent plus [Céline, *Voyage*, 148.]

70. Céline, *Journey*, 95. "cette Afrique décortiquée des agences et des monuments, des chemins de fer et des nougats." [Céline, *Voyage*, 148.]

71. Céline, *Journey*, 95. "dans son jus, la vraie Afrique." [Céline, *Voyage*, 148.]

72. Putnam, Walter, "Raging Against the Night: Céline's African Episode," in *Discursive Geographies: Writing Space and Place in French/Géographie discursive: l'écriture de l'espace et du lieu en français*, ed. Garane, Jeanne (Amsterdam: Rodopi, 2005), 39–51: 47.

73. Dinesen, *Africa*, 75.

74. Dinesen, *Africa*, 75.

75. Markham, *West*, 276.

76. Hemingway, Ernest, *The Short Stories* (New York: Simon & Schuster, 1995), 56.

77. Céline, *Journey*, 139. "Mais d'abord existe-t-il encore des nègres à dessécher et pustuler dans cette étrave." [Céline, *Voyage*, 201.]

78. Céline, *Journey*, 140. "Ce que furent les dix jours de remontée de fleuve, je m'en souviendrai longtemps. . . Passés à surveiller les tourbillons limoneux, au creux de la pirogue, à choisir un passage furtif après l'autre entre les branchages énormes en dérive, souplement évités. Travail de forçats en rupture." [Céline, *Voyage*, 210.]

79. Céline, *Journey*, 140. "'[V]ous serez moins mal encore ici qu'à la guerre.'" [Céline, *Voyage*, 211.]

80. Waugh, *Remote People*, 240.

81. Qtd. in Dauphin, Jean-Pierre and Boudillet, Jacques, eds., *Album Céline* (Paris: Gallimard, 1977), 99, *my translation*. "L'auteur débute en pleine maturité après une expérience de vie extrêmement riche et diverse."

82. Qtd. in Thurman, *Isak Dinesen*, 385.

83. Markham, *West*, 247.

Chapter Six

1. Miller, Christopher L., *Blank Darkness: Africanist Discourse in French* (Chicago: University of Chicago Press, 1985), 246.

2. Greene, *Journey*, 20.

3. Greene, *Journey*, 19.

4. Greene, *Journey*, 19–20.

5. Hemingway, Ernest, *Green Hills of Africa* (New York: Scribner, 1963), 34.

6. Schweizer, Bernard, *Radicals on the Road: The Politics of English Travel Writing in the 1930s* (Charlottesville, VA: The University of Virginia Press, 2001), 64.

7. Fleming, Peter, "Long live Liberia," *The Spectator* (May 15, 1936), 890.

8. Hemingway, *Green*, n.p.

9. Hemingway, *Green*, n.p.

10. Greene, *Journey*, 250.

11. Greene, *Journey*, 19–20.

12. Greene, *Journey*, 249.

13. Greene, *Journey*, 102.

14. Greene, *Journey*, 167.

15. Greene, *Journey*, 248.

16. Brantlinger, Patrick, "Victorians and Africans: The Genealogy of the Myth of the Dark Continent," *Critical Inquiry* 12:1 (1985), 166–203, 193.

17. Reynolds, Michael, *The Young Hemingway* (Oxford: Basil Blackwell Ltd., 1986), 210.

18. Hemingway, *Green*, 193.

19. Greene, Graham, "Two Tall Travelers" in *Reflections* (New York: Reinhardt Books, 1990), 40–1: 41.

20. Greene, "Two," 41.

21. Youngs, Tim, *Travellers in Africa: British Travelogues 1850–1900* (Manchester: Manchester University Press, 1994), 3.

22. Hemingway, *Africa*, 142.

23. Greene, *Journey*, 20.

24. Greene, *Journey*, 38.

25. Greene, *Journey*, 21.

26. Greene, *Journey*, 20.

27. Greene, Graham, *Ways of Escape* (New York: Simon and Schuster, 1980), 48.

28. Greene, Graham, *The Lost Childhood and Other Essays* (New York: The Viking Press, 1952), 289.

29. Hemingway, *Green*, 70.

30. Hemingway, *Green*, 148.

31. Hemingway, *Green*, 148.

32. Hemingway, *Green*, 107.

33. Greene, *Journey*, 17.

34. Greene, *Journey*, 18.

35. Greene, *Journey*, 144.

36. Greene, *Journey*, 144.

37. Greene, *Childhood*, 17.

38. Greene, *Journey*, 178.

39. Greene, *Journey*, 192.

40. Greene, "Three Travellers," *The Spectator* (December 8, 1939), 838: 838.

41. Greene, *Journey*, 19.

42. Hemingway, *Green*, 73.

43. Hemingway, *Green*, 51.

44. Hemingway, *Green*, 283.

45. Hemingway, *Green*, 283.

46. Greene, Barbara, *Too Late to Turn Back* (London: Penguin, 1990), 43.

47. Greene, Barbara, *Too Late*, 43.

48. Greene, Barbara, *Too Late*, 48.

49. Greene, Graham, "Three Travellers," 838.

50. Fleming, Peter, "Long Live Liberia," *The Spectator* (May 15, 1936), 890.

51. Fleming, "Long," 890.

52. Mandel, Miriam B., "Configuring There as Here: Hemingway's Travels and the 'See America First' Movement," *The Hemingway Review* 19:1 (Fall 1999), 94–105: 95.

53. Meyers, Jeffrey, "Greene's Travel Books" in *Graham Greene: A Revaluation*, ed. Meyers, Jeffrey (New York: St. Martin's Press, 1990), 46–47: 46.

54. Hemingway, *Green*, 31.

55. Hemingway, *Green*, 31.

56. Strychacz, Thomas, "Trophy-Hunting as a Trope of Manhood in Ernest Hemingway's *Green Hills of Africa*," *The Hemingway Review* 13:1 (Fall 1993), 36–47: 40.

57. Hemingway, *Green*, 64.

58. Hemingway, *Green*, 3.

59. Hemingway, *Green*, 193.

60. Hemingway, *Green*, 193.

61. Hemingway, *Green*, 293.

62. Hemingway, *Green*, 240.

63. Hemingway, *Green*, 232.

64. Hemingway, *Green*, 240.

65. Greene, *Journey*, 51.

66. Greene, *Journey*, 119.

67. Greene, *Journey*, 119.

68. Greene, *Journey*, 119.

69. Greene, *Journey*, 66.

70. Memmi, Albert, *The Colonizer and the Colonized* (New York: Orion Press, 1965), 85.

71. Greene, *Journey*, 145.

72. Greene, *Journey*, 149.

73. Greene, *Journey*, 140.

74. Greene, *Journey*, 196.

75. Greene, *Journey*, 155.

76. Greene, *Journey*, 183.

77. Greene, *Journey*, 183.

78. Greene, *Journey*, 93.

79. Katz, Wendy, *Rider Haggard and the Fiction of Empire: A Critical Study of British Imperial Fiction* (Cambridge: Cambridge University Press, 1988), 32.

80. Pratt, Mary Louise, *Imperial Eyes: Travel Writing and Transculturation* (London: Routledge, 1992), 217.

81. Greene, *Journey*, 155.

82. Greene, *Journey*, 27.

83. Hemingway, *Green*, 12.

84. Hemingway, *Green*, 12.

85. Hemingway, *Green*, 25

86. Hemingway, *Green*, n.p.

87. De Voto, Bernard, "Review of *Green Hills of Africa* by Ernest Hemingway," in *Hemingway: The Critical Heritage*, ed. Meyers, Jeffrey (Boston: Routledge & Kegan Paul, 1982), 210–213: 211.

88. Greene, *Journey*, 115.

89. Greene, *Journey*, 100–101.

90. Greene, *Journey*, 20.

91. Greene, *Journey*, 36–37.

92. Greene, *Journey*, 37.

93. Greene, *Journey*, 162.

94. Hemingway, *Green*, 149.

95. Rancière, Jacques, *Short Voyages to the Land of the People*, trans. Swenson, James B. (Stanford: Stanford University Press, 2003), 2.

96. Hemingway, *Green*, n.p.

97. Hemingway, *Green*, 72.

98. Hemingway, *Green*, 285.

99. Hemingway, *Green*, 240, 55.

100. Esty, Jed, *A Shrinking Island: Modernism and National Culture in England* (Princeton: Princeton University Press, 2003), 8.

101. Hemingway, *Green*, 284.

102. Spilka, Mark, *Hemingway's Quarrel With Androgyny* (Lincoln: University of Nebraska Press, 1990), 230.

103. Hemingway, *Green*, 283–284.

104. Hemingway, *Green*, 285.

105. Hemingway, *Green*, 285.

106. Greene, *Journey*, 134.

107. Greene, *Journey*, 224.

108. Greene, *Journey*, 35.

109. Greene, *Journey*, 86.

110. Greene, *Journey*, 33.

111. Gikandi, Simon, "Race and the Modernist Aesthetic," in *Writing and Race*, ed. Youngs, Tim (Harlow: Addison Wesley Longman, 1997), 151.

112. Hemingway, *Green*, 287.

113. Greene, *Journey*, 51.

114. Hemingway, *Green*, 107.

115. Holland, Patrick and Huggan, Graham, "Varieties of Nostalgia in Contemporary Travel Writing," in *Perspectives on Travel Writing*, eds. Hooper, Glenn and Youngs, Tim (Burlington, VT: Ashgate, 2004), 139–52: 147.

116. Greene, *Journey*, 165.

117. Culler, Jonathan, *Framing the Sign*: *Criticism and its Institutions* (Norman: University of Oklahoma Press, 1988), 155.

118. Greene, *Journey*, 41.

119. Torgovnick, Marianna, *Primitive Passions*: *Men, Women, and the Quest for Ecstasy* (New York: Knopf, 1996), 5.

Terminus: Inward Travel Narratives of the War Years

1. Sartre, Jean-Paul, *War Diaries*: *Notebooks from a Phony War, 1939–1940* (London: Verso, 2011), 143.

2. Sartre, *War*, 219. "Il faut le dire; de deux choses l'une: ou bien le désir de l'authentique nous tourmente au sein de l'inauthenticité – et alors il est lui-même inauthentique tout entière mais qui s'ignore, qui ne s'est pas encore recensée. Il n'y a pas de place pour un tiers état." [Sartre, *Carnets de la drôle de guerre* (Paris: Gallimard, n.d.) e-book, 975.]

3. The term "subjunctive nostalgia" has been used differently by Gregory Mitchell to denote "a past that could have happened but didn't." *Tourist Attractions*: *Performing Race and Masculinity in Brazil's Sexual Economy* (Chicago: University of Chicago Press, 2015), 200.

4. Sartre, *War*, 55. "Depuis la mobilisation, il m'est souvent arrivé de regretter les villes et les paysages du monde que je connais et c'est quelquois amer. Mais ce soir, je regrette l'Argentine, le Sahara, toutes les parties du monde que je ne connais pas, toute la terre – et c'est beaucoup plus doux, résigné, sans espoir." [Sartre, *Carnets*, 520.]

5. Sartre, Jean-Paul, *Witness to My Life*: *The Letters of Jean-Paul Sartre to Simone de Beauvoir, 1926–1939*, ed. de Beauvoir, Simone (New York: Scribner, 1992),

267. "[C]omme c'est drôle de vivre avec des hommes." [Sartre, Jean-Paul, *Lettres au Castor 1926–1939* (Paris: Gallimard, n.d.) e-book, 757.]

6. Sartre, *Witness*, 267. "Je ne suis plus le même: mon caractère n'a pas changé mais bien mon être-dans-le-monde. C'est un être-pour-la-guerre." [Sartre, *Lettres au Castor*, 757.]

7. Sartre, *War*, 138. "Pourtant je suis resté plus de quinze ans sans me regarder vivre. Je ne m'intéressais pas du tout. J'étais curieux des idées et du monde et du cœur des autres. [. . .] Et puis l'orgueil m'en détournait; il me semblait qu'à mettre le nez sur de minimes bassesses on les grossissait, on leur conférait de la force. Il a fallu la guerre et puis le concours de plusieurs disciplines neuves [. . .] ainsi que la lecture de *L'âge d'homme*, pour m'inciter à dresser un portrait de moi-même en pied." [Sartre, *Carnets*, 761–762.]

8. Sartre, *War*, 138–139. "J'avais horreur des carnets intimes et je pensais que l'homme n'est pas fait pour se voir, qu'il doit toujours fixer son regard devant lui. Je n'ai pas changé. Simplement il me semble qu'on peut, à l'occasion de quelque grande circonstance, et quand on est en train de changer de vie, comme le serpent qui mue, regarder cette peau morte, cette image cassante de serpent qu'on laisse derrière soi, et faire le point. Après la guerre je ne tiendrai plus ce carnet ou bien si je le tiens, je n'y parlerai plus de moi. Je ne veux pas être hanté par moi-même jusqu'à la fin de mes jours." [Sartre, *Carnets*, 762–763.]

9. Sartre, *War*, 138–139. "Une fois lancé dans cette entreprise, je m'y acharne par esprit de système, goût de la totalité, je m'y donne tout entier par manie. [. . .] Mais je ne pense pas qu'il y ait avantage à s'épouiller toute sa vie. Loin de là." [Sartre, *Carnets*, 762.]

10. Qtd. in Sartre, *War*, viii.

11. Woolf, Virginia, *Moments of Being*, ed. Schulkind, Jeanne (New York: Harcourt Brace Jovanovich, 1985), 100.

12. Woolf, *Moments*, 107.

13. Woolf, *Moments*, 70.

14. Woolf, *Moments*, 89.

15. Woolf, *Moments*, 70.

16. Woolf, *Moments*, 72.

17. Stein, Gertrude, *Wars I Have Seen* (New York: Random House, 1945), 5.

18. Will, Barbara, *Unlikely Collaboration: Gertrude Stein, Bernard Fäy, and the Vichy Dilemma* (New York: Columbia University Press, 2013), xiii.

19. Qtd. in Will, *Unlikely*, 274.

20. Stein, *Wars*, 87.

21. Stein, *Wars*, 176.

22. Stein, *Wars*, 121.

23. Stein, *Wars*, 292.

BIBLIOGRAPHY

Baker, Carlos, *Ernest Hemingway: A Life Story* (New York: Scribner's, 1969).

Barnard, Rita, "Evelyn Waugh's *Black Mischief*," in *Modernism and Colonialism*: *British and Irish Literature 1899-1939*, eds. Begam, Richard and Moses, Michael Valdez (Durham, NC: Duke University Press, 2007), 162–182.

Bassnett, Susan, "Translation and Travel Writing," in *The Cambridge History of Travel Writing*, eds. Das, Nandini and Youngs, Tim, (Cambridge: Cambridge University Press, 2019), 550–564.

Baucom, Ian, "Mournful Histories: Narratives of Postimperial Melancholy," *MFS Modern Fiction Studies* 42:2 (1996), 259–288.

Baudelaire, Charles, *OEuvres complètes* (Paris: Bouquins, 2011).

———, *Out of Place: Englishness, Empire, and the Locations of Identity* (Princeton: Princeton University Press, 1999).

Begam, Richard and Moses, Michael Valdez, eds., *Modernism and Colonialism*: *British and Irish Literature 1839-1939* (Durham: Duke University Press, 2007).

Behdad, Ali, *Belated Travelers: Orientalism in the Age of Colonial Dissolution* (Durham: Duke University Press, 1994).

Booth, Howard J., "Making the Case for Cross-Cultural Exchange: Robert Byron's *The Road to Oxiana*," in *Cultural Encounters: European Travel Writing in the 1930s*, eds. Burdett, Charles and Duncan, Derek (New York: Berghahn Books, 2002), 159–172.

Boym, Svetlana, *The Future of Nostalgia* (New York: Basic Books, 2001).

Brand, Anthony, "'Far from Simple': The Published Photographs in *Death in the Afternoon*," in *A Companion to Hemingway's* Death in the Afternoon, ed. Mandel, Miriam B. (Rochester, NY: Camden House, 2004), 165–187.

Brantlinger, Patrick, "Victorians and Africans: The Genealogy of the Myth of the Dark Continent," *Critical Inquiry* 12:1 (1985), 166–203.

Burden, Robert, *Travel, Modernism and Modernity* (New York: Ashgate, 2016).

Burdett, Charles and Duncan, Derek, *Cultural Encounters: European Travel Writing in the 1930s* (New York: Berghahn Books, 2002).

Burton, Stacy, *Travel Narrative and the Ends of Modernity* (Cambridge: Cambridge University Press, 2014).

Byron, Robert, *The Road to Oxiana* (New York: Oxford University Press, 1966).

Casanova, Pascale, *The World Republic of Letters* (Cambridge: Harvard University Press, 2004).

Cazantre, Thomas, *Gide lecteur: La littérature au miroir de la lecture* (Paris: Kimé, 2003).

Céline, Louis-Ferdinand, *Album Céline*, eds. Dauphin, Jean Pierre and Boudillet, Jacques (Paris: Gallimard, 1952).

——, *Cahier Céline 4: Lettres et premiers écrits d'Afrique 1916–1917* (Paris: Gallimard, 1978).

——, *Journey to the End of the Night* (New York: New Directions, 1983).

——, *Voyage au bout de la nuit* (Paris: Gallimard, 1952).

Chevrillon, André, "Conrad," *Hommage à Joseph Conrad, La Nouvelle Revue française* 12:135 (December 1924), 62–65.

Cigoj-Leben, Breda, "Les idées d'André Gide sur l'art de traduction," *Bulletin des amis d'André Gide* 12:61 (December 1984), 31–46: 43.

Cioran, E. M., *Anathemas and Admirations* (New York: Skyhorse Publishing, 2012).

Clarck-Taoua, Phyllis "In Search of New Skin: Michel Leiris's L'Afrique Fantôme," *Cahiers d'études africaines* 42:167 (2002), 479–498.

Clifford, James, "Negrophilia," in *A New History of French Literature*, ed. Hollier, Denis (Cambridge, MA: Harvard University Press, 1994), 901–908.

Cogez, Gérard, "Object cherché, accord perdu: Michel Leiris et l'Afrique," *L'homme* 151 (1999), 237–255.

Collins, Steward, "Bull-Fights and Politics," in *Ernest Hemingway: The Critical Reception*, ed. Stephens, Robert O. (New York: Burt Franklin, 1977), 112–115.

Comley, Nancy R. and Scholes, Robert, *Hemingway's Genders* (New Haven, CT: Yale University Press, 1994).

Conrad, Joseph, *The Collected Letters of Joseph Conrad*, 9 vols., eds. Karl, Frederick, R., et al. (Cambridge: Cambridge University Press, 1983–2008).

——, *Conrad's Polish Background: Letters to and from Polish Friends*, ed. Nadjer, Zdzislaw (Oxford: Oxford University Press, 1964).

——, "Further Correspondence between Joseph Conrad and André Gide," eds. Vidan, Gabriejela and Vidan, Ivo, *Studia Romanica et Anglica Zagrabiensia* 29 (1970), 523–536.

——, *Heart of Darkness and The Secret Sharer* (New York: Signet, 2008).

——, *Last Essays*, eds. Stevens, Harold Ray and Stape, J. H. (Cambridge: Cambridge University Press, 2010).

——, *The Mirror of the Sea and a Personal Record* (Oxford: Oxford University Press, 1980).

——, "Thirteen Letters of André Gide to Joseph Conrad," ed. Vidan, Ivo, *Studia Romanica et Anglica Zagrabiensia* 24 (1967), 145–168.

——, *Typhon*, trans. Gide, André (Paris: Gallimard, 1923).

——, *Typhoon and Other Stories* (New York: Doubleday, 1921).

Cooke, Roderick, "Bardamu's Triangular Trade: The Modern Slavery of *Voyage au bout de la nuit*," *The Modern Language Review* 11:4 (October, 2017), 882–898.

Côté, Sébastien, "Michel Leiris et la fuite impossible: Ethnographie, autobiographie et l'altérité féminine dans *L'Afrique fantôme*," MLN, 20:4 (2005), 849–870.

Cowley, Malcolm, "A Farewell to Spain," in *Ernest Hemingway: The Critical Reception*, ed. Stephens, Robert O. (New York: Burt Franklin, 1977), 120–123.

Cronin, Michael, *Across the Lines: Travel Language and Translation* (Cork: Cork University Press, 2000).

Culler, Jonathan, *Framing the Sign: Criticism and its Institutions* (Norman: University of Oklahoma Press, 1938).

Curle, Richard, *Joseph Conrad: A Study* (London: K. Paul, Trench, Trüber & Co., 1914).

Das, Nandini and Youngs, Tim, eds., *The Cambridge History of Travel Writing* (Cambridge: Cambridge University Press, 2019).

David, Maurice, *L'homme et l'œuvre* (Paris: Éditions de *la Nouvelle revue critique*, 1929).

Davis, Thomas, *The Extinct Scene: Late Modernism and Everyday Life* (New York: Columbia University Press, 2016).

De Voto, Bernard, "Review of *Green Hills of Africa* by Ernest Hemingway," in *Hemingway: The Critical Heritage*, ed. Meyers, Jeffrey (Boston: Routledge & Kegan Paul, 1982), 210–213.

DeRosa, Aaron, "The End of Futurity: Proleptic Nostalgia and the War on Terror," *LIT: Literature Interpretation Theory* 25:2 (2014), 88–107.

DiBattista, Maria and Wittman, Emily O., eds., *Modernism and Autobiography* (Cambridge: Cambridge University Press, 2014).

Dinesen, Isak, *Letters from Africa 1914–1931*, ed. Lasson, Frans (Chicago: University of Chicago Press, 1978).

——, *Out of Africa* and *Shadows on the Grass* (New York: Random House, 1961).

Douglas, Ann, *Terrible Honesty: Mongrel Manhattan in the 1920s* (New York: Farrer, Straus, and Giroux, 1996).

Erdinast-Vulcan, Daphna, *The Strange Short Fiction of Joseph Conrad: Writing, Culture, and Subjectivity* (Oxford: Oxford University Press, 1999).

Esty, Jed, *A Shrinking Island: Modernism and National Culture in England* (Princeton: Princeton University Press, 2003).

Farley, David G., *Modernist Travel Writing: Intellectuals Abroad* (Columbus: University of Missouri Press, 2010).

Fleming, Peter, *Brazilian Adventure* (Evanston, IL: The Marlboro Press/Northwestern University Press, 1999).

——, "Long Live Liberia," *The Spectator* (May 15, 1936), 890.

Forsdick, Charles, "Sa(l)vaging Exoticism," New Approaches to 1930s Travel Literature in French," in *Cultural Encounters: European Travel Writing in the 1930s*, eds. Burdett, Charles and Duncan, Derek (New York: Berghahn Books, 2002), 29–45.

——, *Travel in Twentieth-Century French & Francophone Cultures: The Persistence of Diversity* (Oxford: Oxford University Press, 2005).

Francillon, Robert, "Conrad psychologue de l'imagination," *La Nouvelle Revue française* 12:135 (December 1924), 82–87.

Fussell, Paul, *Abroad: British Literary Traveling Between the Wars* (Oxford: Oxford University Press, 1982).

Garane, Jeanne, ed., *Discursive Geographies: Writing Space and Place in French/ Géographie discursive: l'écriture de l'espace et du lieu en français* (Amsterdam: Rodopi, 2005).

Gide, André, "Joseph Conrad," *La Nouvelle Revue française* 12:135 (December 1924), 17–20.

———, *Journal 1 1887–1925* (Paris: Gallimard, 1996).

———, *Journal 2 1926–1950* (Paris: Gallimard, 1997).

———, *The Journals of André Gide 1889–1949*, 6 vols., ed. and trans. O'Brien, Justin (Chicago: University of Illinois Press, 2000).

———, *Œuvres complètes d'André Gide* (Paris: Bibliothèque de la Pléiade, 2009).

———, *Travels in the Congo* (Berkeley: University of California Press, 1962).

———, *Voyage au Congo & Le retour du Tchad* (Paris: Folio, 1981).

Gikandi, Simon, *Maps of Englishness: Writing Identity in the Culture of Colonialism* (New York: Columbia University Press, 1996).

———, "Race and the Modernist Aesthetic," in *Writing and Race*, ed. Youngs, Tim (Harlow: Addison Wesley Longman, 1997), n.p., e-book.

GoGwilt, Chris, *The Passage of Literature: Genealogies of Modernism in Conrad, Rhys, and Pramoedya* (Oxford: Oxford University Press, 2010).

Gray, Jeffrey, *Mastery's End: Travel and Postwar American Poetry* (Athens, GA: University of Georgia Press, 2005).

Greenberg, Jonathan, "Travel Writing as Modernist Autobiography," in *Modernism and Autobiography*, eds. DiBattista, Maria and Wittman, Emily (Cambridge: Cambridge University Press, 2014), 69–83.

Greene, Barbara, *Too Late to Turn Back* (London: Penguin, 1990).

Greene, Graham, *The Lost Childhood and Other Essays* (New York: The Viking Press, 1952).

———, *Journey Without Maps* (New York: Penguin, 2006).

———, "Two Tall Travelers," in *Reflections* (New York: Reinhardt Books, 1990), 40–41.

———, "Three Travellers," *The Spectator* (December 8, 1939), 838.

———, *Ways of Escape* (New York: Simon and Schuster, 1980).

Greene, Jean, "Visions of Death and Dissolution," in *A New History of French Literature*, ed. Hollier Denis, 850–855.

Guillaume, Isabelle, "*La voie royale* et *Voyage au bout de la nuit*: Deux réécritures françaises de *Heart of Darkness*," *Cahiers de narratologie* 13 (2006), n.p., https://journals.openedition.org/narratologie/331.

Hand, Séan, *Michel Leiris: Writing the Self* (Cambridge: Cambridge University Press, 1991).

Hayot, Eric and Walkowitz, Rebecca, L., *A New Vocabulary for Global Modernism* (New York: Columbia University Press, 2016).

Heidegger, Martin, *Basic Writings* (New York: HarperCollins, 2008).

Hemingway, Ernest, *Death in the Afternoon* (New York: Charles Scribner's Sons, 1932).

——, *Green Hills of Africa* (Scribner: New York, 1963).

——, *For Whom the Bell Tolls* (New York: Scribner, 1995).

——, *Selected Letters 1917–1961,* ed. Baker, Carlos (New York: Charles Scribner's Sons, 1960).

——, *The Short Stories* (New York: Simon and Schuster, 1995).

——, *The Sun Also Rises* (New York: Charles Scribner's Sons, 1954).

Hervouet, Yves, *The French Face of Conrad* (Cambridge: Cambridge University Press, 1990).

Holland, Patrick and Huggan, Graham, *Tourists with Typewriters: Critical Reflections on Contemporary Travel Writing* (Ann Arbor: University of Michigan Press, 2000).

——, "Varieties of Nostalgia in Contemporary Travel Writing," in *Perspectives on Travel Writing*, eds. Hooper, Glenn and Youngs, Tim (Burlington, VT: Ashgate, 2004), 139–152.

Hollier, Denis, ed., *A New History of French Literature* (Cambridge: Harvard University Press, 1994).

Hooper, Glenn and Youngs, Tim, eds., *Perspectives on Travel Writing* (Burlington, VT: Ashgate, 2004).

Irmscher, Christoph, *Max Eastman: A Life* (New Haven: Yale University Press, 2017).

Islam, Syed Manzoorul, *The Ethics of Travel: From Marco Polo to Kafka* (Manchester: Manchester University Press, 1996).

Israel, Nico, *Spirals: The Whirled Image in Twentieth-Century Literature and Art* (New York: Columbia, 2015).

Jaloux, Edmond, "Joseph Conrad et le roman d'aventures anglais," *La Nouvelle Revue française* 12:135 (December 1924), 71–77.

Jean-Aubry, Gérard, *Joseph Conrad: Life and Letters*, 2 vols. (New York: Doubleday, 1927).

——, "Souvenirs," *La Nouvelle Revue française* 12:135 (December, 1924), 30–39.

Josephs, Allen, "*Death in the Afternoon*: A Reconsideration," *Hemingway Review* 2:1 (1982), 2–16.

Kaplan, Caren, *Questions of Travel: Postmodern Discourses of Displacement* (Durham, NC: Duke University Press, 1996).

Karl, Frederick R., "Conrad and Gide: A Relationship and a Correspondence," *Comparative Literature* 29:12 (1977), 148–171.

Katz, Wendy, *Rider Haggard and the Fiction of Empire: A Critical Study of British Imperial Fiction* (Cambridge: Cambridge University Press, 1988).

Kelley, Joyce, *Excursions into Modernism: Women Writers, Travel, and the Body* (New York: Routledge, 2015).

Kessel, Joseph, *Marchés d'esclaves* (Paris: Union Générale d'Éditions, 1984).

Kirschner, Paul, *Conrad: The Psychologist as Artist* (Ann Arbor: University of Michigan Press, 1968).

Korte, Barbara, *English Travel Writing: From Pilgrimages to Postcolonial Exploration* (New York: Palgrave, 2000).

Larbaud, Valery, "*Chance* par Joseph Conrad," *Nouvelle Revue française* 6:1 (1914), 527–529.

Larson, Ruth, "Ethnography, Thievery, and Cultural Identity: A Rereading of Michel Leiris's *L'Afrique fantôme*," *PMLA* 112:2 (1997), 229–242.

———, *Sous l'invocation de saint Jérôme* (Paris: Gallimard, 1946).

Lawrence, D. H., *The Letters of D. H. Lawrence*, Vol. 4 (Cambridge: Cambridge University Press, 2000).

———, *Mornings in Mexico* (Amsterdam: Fredonia Books, 2003).

Leander, Niels Buch, "The Colonial Metropolis and its Artistic Adventure: Conrad, Congo, and the *Nouvelle Revue française*," *Romanic Review* 99:1/2 (2008), 87–102.

———, *Mornings in Mexico* (Amsterdam: Fredonia Books, 2003).

Lefevere, André, *Translation, Rewriting and the Manipulation of Literary Fame* (New York: Routledge, 1992).

Leiris, Michel, *Miroir de l'Afrique* (Paris: Gallimard, 1996).

———, "Mort dans l'après-midi par Ernest Hemingway," *La Nouvelle Revue française* 47:309 (January, 1939), 1061–1063.

———, Michel Leiris to Olga and Pablo Picasso, May 20, 1932, *Archives Picasso*.

———, *Phantom Africa* (York, PA: Seagull Books, 2017).

Lejeune, Philippe, *Le pacte autobiographique* (Paris: Éditions du Seuil, 1975).

Lisle, Debbie, *The Global Politics of Contemporary Travel Writing* (Cambridge: Cambridge University Press, 2006).

Londres, Albert, *Terre d'ébène: La traite des noirs* (Paris: Le Serpent à plumes, 1994).

Lonsdale, Laura, *Multilingualism and Modernity: Barbarisms in Spanish and American Literature* (New York: Palgrave Macmillan, 2017).

Lucey, Michael, *Gide's Bent: Sexuality, Politics, Writing* (Oxford: Oxford University Press, 1995).

Mac Orlan, Pierre, "*La Folie-Almayer* et les aventuriers dans la littérature," *Nouvelle Revue française* 7:81 (June, 1920), 930–933.

Maher, Brigid, "Pseudotranslation," in *The Routledge Handbook of Literary Translation*, eds. Washbourne, Kelly, and Van Wyke, Ben (New York: Routledge, 2018), 382–393.

Mandel, Miriam, "Configuring There as Here: Hemingway's Travel and the 'See America First' Movement," *The Hemingway Review* 19:1 (Fall 1999), 94–105.

Manguso, Sarah, *Ongoingness: The End of a Diary* (Minneapolis: Greywolf, 2015).

Markham, Beryl, *West with the Night* (New York: North Point Press, 1983).

Matera, Marc and Kent, Susan Kingsley, *The Global 1930s: The International Decade* (New York: Routledge, 2017).

Maurois, André, "En marge des marées," *La Nouvelle Revue française* 12:135 (December 1924), 66–71.

May, Georges, "Valery Larbaud: Translator and Scholar," *Yale French Studies* 6 (1950): 83–90.

Memmi, Albert, *The Colonizer and the Colonized* (New York: Orion Press, 1965).

Meyers, Jeffrey, "Greene's Travel Books," in *Graham Greene: A Revaluation*, ed. Meyers, Jeffrey, (New York: St. Martin's Press, 1990), 46–47.

———, ed., *Hemingway: The Critical Heritage* (Boston: Routledge & Kegan Paul, 1982).

Mikkonen, Kai, *Narrative Paths: African Travel in Modern Fiction and Nonfiction* (Columbus: The Ohio State University Press, 2015).

Miller, Christopher L. *Blank Darkness: Africanist Discourse in French* (Chicago: University of Chicago Press, 1985).

Mitchell, Gregory, *Tourist Attractions: Performing Race and Masculinity in Brazil's Sexual Economy* (Chicago: University of Chicago Press, 2015).

Mongia, Padmini, "Between Men: Conrad in the Fiction of Two Contemporary Indian Writers," in *Conrad in the Twenty-First Century: Contemporary Approaches and Perspectives*, eds. Kaplan, Carola, Mallios, Peter Lancelot, and White, Andrea (London: Routledge, 2005), 85–100.

Monod, Sylvère, "Deux traductions du *Typhoon* de Conrad," *Bulletin des amis d'André Gide* 21:100 (October 1993): 577–592.

Morand, Paul, *Paris-Tombouctou: Notes d'un voyage africain* (Paris: Flammarion, 1928).

Nietzsche, Friedrich Wilhelm, *Beyond Good and Evil* (New York: Value Classic Reprints, 2018).

Orwell, George, *Down and Out in Paris and London* (New York: Shocken Books, 1961).

———, *The Road to Wigan Pier* (New York: Houghton Mifflin Harcourt, 1958).

Peat, Alexandra, *Travel and Modernist Literature: Sacred and Ethical Journeys* (New York: Routledge, 2011).

Perloff, Marjorie, *Poetry on & Off the Page: Essays for Emergent Occasions* (Chicago: The University of Chicago Press, 1998).

Pettinger, Alasdair and Youngs, Tim, eds. *The Routledge Research Companion to Travel Writing* (New York: Routledge, 2019).

Polezzi, Loredana, *Translating Travel: Contemporary Italian Travel Writing in English Tradition* (New York: Ashgate, 2001).

Porter, Dennis, *Haunted Journeys: Desire and Transgression in European Travel Writing* (Princeton: Princeton University Press, 1991).

Pratt, Mary Louise, *Imperial Eyes: Travel Writing and Transculturation* (London: Routledge, 1992).

Putnam, Walter, "De *Typhoon* à *Typhon*: Gide et sa traduction de Conrad," *Bulletin des amis d'André Gide* 24:89 (1991): 77–90.

———, *l'Aventure littéraire de Joseph Conrad et d'André Gide* (Saratoga: ANMA Libri, 1990).

——, "Raging Against the Night: Céline's African Episode," *Discursive Geographies: Writing Space and Place in French/Géographie discursive: L'écriture de l'espace et du lieu en français*, ed. Garane, Jean (Amsterdam: Rodopi, 2005), 39–51.

Rae, Patricia, "Double Sorrow: Proleptic Elegy and the End of Arcadianism in 1930s Britain," *Twentieth-Century Literature* 49:2, 246–275.

——, "'There'll be no more fishing this side of the grave': Radical Nostalgia in George Orwell's *Coming up for Air*," in *Modernism and Nostalgia: Bodies, Locations, Aesthetics,* ed. Clewell, Tammy (New York: Palgrave, 2013), 149–165.

Rancière, Jacques, *Short Voyages to the Land of the People*, trans. Swenson, James B. (Stanford: Stanford University Press, 2003).

Reynolds, Michael, "*The Sun* in its Time: Recovering the Historical Context," in *New Essays on* The Sun Also Rises, ed. Wagner-Martin, Linda (Cambridge: Cambridge University Press, 1987).

——, *The Young Hemingway* (Oxford: Basil Blackwell Ltd., 1986).

Rhys, Jean, *Good Morning, Midnight* (New York: W. W. Norton, 1986).

Rivière, Jacques, *The Ideal Reader: Selected Essays by Jacques Rivière* (New York: Meridian Books, 1960).

——, "Le roman d'aventure," *La Nouvelle Revue française* 10 (January–June 1913), 748–765, 914–932; (July–December 1913), 56–72.

Rogers, Gayle, *Incomparable Empires: Modernism and the Translation of American and Spanish Literature* (New York: Columbia University Press, 2016).

Romero, Patricia W., *Women's Voices on Africa: A Century of Travel Writing* (Princeton: Princeton University Press, 1992).

Rosaldo, Renato, *Culture and Truth: The Remaking of Social Analysis* (Boston: Beacon Press, 1989).

Said, Edward, *Freud and the Non-European* (London: Verso, 2004).

——, *Orientalism* (New York: Pantheon Books, 1978).

——, *Reflections on Exile and Other Essays* (Cambridge, MA: Harvard University Press, 2000).

Sartre, Jean-Paul, *Carnets de la drôle de guerre* (Paris: Gallimard, n.d.) e-book.

——, *Lettres au Castor 1926–1939* (Paris: Gallimard, n.d.) e-book.

——, *War Diaries: Notebooks from a Phony War, 1939–1940* (London: Verso, 2011).

——, *Witness to My Life: The Letters of Jean-Paul Sartre to Simone de Beauvoir 1926–1939*, ed. De Beauvoir, Simone (New York: Scribner, 1992).

Schweizer, Bernard, *Radicals on the Road: The Politics of English Travel Writing in the 1930s* (Charlottesville, VA: The University of Virginia Press, 2001).

Scullion, Rosemary, "Madness and Fascist Discourse in Céline's *Voyage au bout de la nuit*," *The French Review* 61:5 (1988), 715–723.

Self, Will, "Céline's Dark Journey," *The New York Times* (July 17, 2010) https://www.nytimes.com/2006/09/10/books/review/Self.t.html.

Sherry, Vincent, "T. S. Eliot, Late Empire, and Decadence," in *Modernism and Colonialism*, eds. Begam, Richard and Moses, Michael Valdez (Durham: Duke University Press, 2007), 111–135.

Smith, Sidonie, *Moving Lives: Twentieth-Century Women's Travel Writing* (Minneapolis: University of Minnesota Press, 2001).

———, "The Other Woman and the Racial Politics of Gender: Isak Dinesen and Beryl Markham in Kenya," in *De/Colonizing the Subject: The Politics of Gender in Women's Autobiography*, eds. Smith, Sidonie and Watson, Julia (Minneapolis: University of Minnesota Press, 1992), 410–435.

Spilka, Mark, *Hemingway's Quarrel with Androgyny* (Lincoln: University of Nebraska Press, 1990).

Spurr, David, *The Rhetoric of Empire: Colonial Discourse in Journalism, Travel Writing, and Imperial Administration* (Durham: Duke University Press, 1993).

Stape, J. H., "The Art of Fidelity: Conrad, Gide, and the Translation of *Victory*," *Journal of Modern Literature* 27:1 (1990), 155–165.

Stein, Gertrude, *Wars I Have Seen* (New York: Random House, 1945).

Starobinski, Jean, "The Idea of Nostalgia," *Diogenes* 54 (1966), 81–103.

Stephens, Robert O., *Ernest Hemingway: The Critical Reception* (New York: Burt Franklin, 1977).

Strychacz, Thomas, *Hemingway's Theaters of Masculinity* (Baton Rouge: Louisiana State University Press, 2003).

———, Trophy-Hunting as a Trope of Manhood in Ernest Hemingway's *Green Hills of Africa*," *The Hemingway Review* 13:1 (Fall 1993), 36–47.

Tadié, Jean-Yves, *Le Roman d'aventures* (Vendôme: Presses Universitaires de France, 1982).

Taussig, Michael, *Mimesis and Alterity: A Particular History of the Senses* (New York: Routledge, 1992).

Taylor-Batty, Juliette, *Multilingualism in Modernist Fiction* (New York: Palgrave, 2013).

Thomas, Merlin, *Louis-Ferdinand Céline* (London: New Directions, 1980).

Thompson, Carl, ed., *The Routledge Companion to Travel Writing* (New York: Taylor & Francis, 2015).

———, *Travel Literature* (New York: Routledge, 2011).

Thurman, Judith, *Isak Dinesen: The Life of a Storyteller* (New York: St. Martin's Press, 1982).

Thurston, Michael, "Genre, Gender and Truth in *Death in the Afternoon*," *Hemingway Review* 17:2 (1998), 47–63.

Torgovnick, Marianna, *Gone Primitive: Savage Intellects, Modern Lives* (Chicago: The University of Chicago Press, 1990).

———, *Primitive Passions: Men, Women, and the Quest for Ecstasy* (New York: Knopf, 1996).

Toury, Gideon, *Descriptive Translation Studies and Beyond: Revised Edition* (Amsterdam: John Benjamin's, 2012).

Valéry, Paul, "Sujet d'une conversation avec Conrad," *La Nouvelle Revue française* 135 (December 1924), 17–20.

Venuti, Lawrence, ed. *The Translation Studies Reader* (New York: Routledge, 2004).

———, *The Translator's Invisibility: A History of Translation* (New York: Routledge, 1995).

Warren, Calvin, ed., *Ontological Terror: Blackness, Nihilism, and Emancipation* (Durham and London: Duke University Press, 2018).

Waugh, Alec, *Hot Countries* (New York: Paragon House, 1989).

Waugh, Evelyn, *The Complete Stories of Evelyn Waugh* (Boston: Little, Brown & Company, 1999).

———, *Black Mischief* (New York: Little, Brown and Company, 1960).

———, "Evelyn Waugh on the Word 'Fascist,'" *The New Statesman* (March 3, 1938), https://www.newstatesman.com/culture/2013/03/5-march-1938-evelyn-waugh-word-fascist.

———, *Remote People* (London: Duckworth, 1931).

———, *Scoop* (Boston: Little, Brown and Company, 1965).

———, *Waugh in Abyssinia* (London: Methuen, 1984).

———, *Waugh Abroad: Collected Travel Writing* (New York: Alfred A. Knopf, 2003).

———, *When the Going was Good* (New York: Back Bay Books, 1985).

Weber, Robert, *Hemingway's Art of Non-Fiction* (Basingstoke, UK: Macmillan, 1989).

West, Russell, *Conrad and Gide: Translation, Transference and Intertextuality* (Amsterdam: Rodopi, 1996).

———, "Conrad, Gide and Dostoyevsky: Critical Intertextualities," *The Conradian* 20:100 (1995), 109–130.

———, "Gide traduit (par) Conrad," *Bulletin des amis d'André Gide* 21:100 (October 1993): 593–611.

Will, Barbara, *Unlikely Collaboration: Gertrude Stein, Bernard Fäy, and the Vichy Dilemma* (New York: Columbia University Press, 2013).

Williams, Ian, *Political and Cultural Perceptions of George Orwell: British and American Views* (New York: Palgrave, 2017).

Woolf, Virginia, *Moments of Being*, ed. Schulkind, Jeanne (New York: Harcourt Brace Jovanovich, 1985).

Yiannopoulou, Effie, "Autistic Adventures: Love, Auto-Portraiture and White Women's Colonial Dis-ease," *European Journal of English Studies* 2:3 (1998), 234–342.

Young, Philip, *Ernest Hemingway: A Reconsideration* (University Park: Pennsylvania State University Press, 1966).

Youngs, Tim and Das, Nandini, eds., *The Cambridge History of Travel Writing* (Cambridge: Cambridge University Press, 2019).

———, Review of *Women's Voices on Africa: A Century of Travel Writings* by Romero, Patricia W., *Africa* 63:2 (1993), 261–262.

———, *Travellers in Africa: British Travelogues 1850–1900* (Manchester: Manchester University Press, 1994).

———, Ed., *Writing and Race* (Harlow: Addison Wesley Longman, 1997).